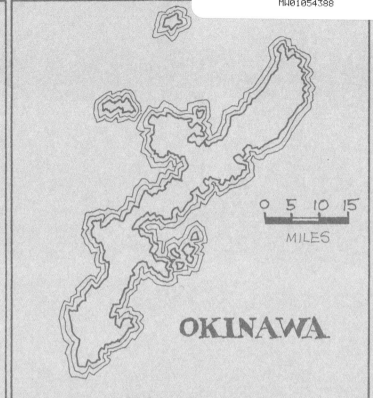

0   5   10 15
MILES

OKINAWA

C OCEAN

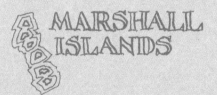 MARSHALL
ISLANDS

OKINAWA *Odyssey*

bright sky press

Box 416, Albany, Texas 76430

Text copyright © 2004 by Bob Green
Illustrations copyright © 2004 by Charles Shaw

10   9   8   7   6   5   4   3   2   1

Library of Congress Cataloging-in-Publication Data

Green, Bob, 1924–
    Okinawa odyssey : a Texas rancher's letters and recollections of the battle for Okinawa / Bob Green.
        p. cm.
    Includes bibliographical references and index.
    ISBN 1-931721-39-4 (alk. paper)
1. Green, Bob, 1924– 2. World War, 1939–1945—Campaigns—Japan—Okinawa Island.
3. United States. Army. Tank Battalion, 763rd. 4. World War, 1939–1945—Personal narratives, American. 5. United States. Army—Officers—Biography. I. Title.

D767.99.O45G74 2004
940.54'252294-dc22

                                                            2003069614

Author photo by Michael O'Brien

Book and cover design by Isabel Lasater Hernandez
Printed in USA

OKINAWA *Odyssey*

Bob Green

For Nancy

my typist and editor for life

and for the ones who did not make it back

Illustration by Charles Shaw

CONTENTS

PREFACE

This is a belated memoir concerning my participation in 1945 as a twenty-year-old second lieutenant during World War II in the invasion and battle to take the island of Okinawa from the Japanese. This island is only 350 miles south of the main home islands of Japan.

My son-in-law, Joe Hargrove, an attorney in Shreveport, Louisiana, has been appointed to a legal advisory board that meets quarterly in New Orleans. On one of these quarterly trips, he visited the Stephen Ambrose-sponsored museum of World War II's Pacific Theater and was favorably impressed. Knowing that I had served in that theater during WW II, he encouraged me to write down the account of my participation. To help me get started, he had the museum send me some instructions they had formulated. In them, they outlined what they thought was the best way for helping aged veterans, such as I, to successfully recall and write down the accounts of their wartime service. I found their instructions were helpful. They cautioned not to expect to be able to do this overnight, but that if you continued to think about it over a period of time, jotting down remembered items as they returned to memory in bits and pieces, gaps in the stories would fill in. I found that to be true. I even found myself waking up in the night to discover that my mind had been busy at work while I was sleeping and had dredged up things long suppressed or forgotten. Still, I found it was hard for me to get started.

More Americans were in the Armed Services in World War II than in any other war in the twentieth century. After Pearl Harbor, the United States quickly drew on the youth of the country to acquire an Army, Navy, Marine and Coast Guard force of over sixteen million citizen members. They were hastily trained by a cadre of regular service veterans that during the Depression years had shrunk to only a skeleton force. A little known fact is that out of this gigantic force of sixteen million, less than one million would actually participate in any significant, actual and prolonged combat. That means only one out of sixteen men who were in the various military services during World War II ever really participated in any armed conflict. The majority had served in the many support units necessary for maintenance of both overseas and continental based personnel. Others were in cadres who were involved in the housing, transporting and training of the steady inflow of new draftees at the large number of stateside bases. Still many soldiers served in the myriad other noncombatant roles that were considered necessary for the carrying on of the two-ocean war. But for the one in sixteen who actually did "see the elephant," their combat experiences would forever after haunt their memories. As one of the one in sixteen, I can attest to that.

It is my belief that the Pacific Theater's war against Japan, in which I participated, was in many ways a more brutal, uncivilized struggle than the European war with Germany. In our fight with the Japanese, there was no quarter given, or even expected to be given, by either side. At the time, our understanding of the Germans was much clearer and better than the conception we had of the Japanese. We had little if any knowledge of their Bushido warrior code, which we later discovered they really believed in and practiced.

George Feifer, author of *Tennozan*, which is a book about the Battle of Okinawa, says that bushido means "way of the warrior." It was originally developed during medieval times in Japan to guide the conduct of the Samurai warriors who served the early feudal lords. Like the code of chivalry espoused by European knights, it stressed self-discipline, unquestioned obedience, and loyalty. Surrender was considered to be deeply shameful, with suicide preferable. Hari-kari or Seppuki (ritual self-disembowelment) was regarded as a highly honorable act. This code was reinstated by Japanese military leaders in the 1920s and 1930s. Assembled school children, when asked what their dearest ambition was, were taught to shout fervently, "to die for the emperor." As a military recruit, a peasant boy was indoctrinated constantly with the idea that death in battle should not be regarded as just a possibility, but embraced more or less as a military duty. Self-sacrifice in the service of the emperor was regarded as sublime. A willingness to die for the emperor was held to be an essential part of "the Japanese fighting spirit." Nearly all Japanese soldiers of WW II preferred death to undergoing the eternal shame associated with surrendering, in which back home in Japan their names would be stricken from the village list and their manhood forever besmirched, disgracing their family name forever. On the other hand, if they met death in a kamikaze crash, or died in a wild "banzai" attack, or even killed themselves by holding an exploding grenade to their chest when all appeared lost, their spirits could go to the Yasukuni Shrine in Tokyo. There they could mingle with all the spirits of heroic warriors who had died fighting for Japan, and the emperors who gathered there. The Bushido Code also caused the Japanese to despise any enemy soldier who surrendered for allowing himself to be taken prisoner. They considered captives to be despicable cowards who deserved no consideration or pity. Consequently, their prisoners of war were horribly abused, which enraged the Americans, who could not fathom such barbarism.

I still remember well how I first reacted upon hearing of the Japanese sneak attack on Pearl Harbor. At that time, I fully believed without reservation that our Navy, Air Corps and Army were so superior to theirs that we would be able to clean their plow in short order. Alas, the many rude shocks soon to come!

We quickly were made aware that their Zero fighter planes were much superior to any we had at that time. Their naval torpedoes were also far superior to ours and remained so all during the war. Their skill at using the "Long Lances," as they had named their torpedoes, dealt us much misery. We soon discovered their Navy to be an excellent one, and even without the early advantage of radar, which we enjoyed, they were especially aggressive and skilled in night engagements. The expertise of their first-string Navy air personnel early in the war was as good, or even better, than ours in the practicing of carrier warfare. Their large army was filled with sturdy, tough, peasant boys who were well trained and eager to fight for, and even to die for, their emperor. Although much of their military equipment was certainly inferior to that of the Germans, and even much of ours, their diligence in using what they had with reckless abandon and even suicidal fervor made them a highly dangerous foe.

Most combat veterans of World War II whom I have ever talked to or read accounts of seem to be convinced that the battles they were involved in were, without a doubt, the fiercest ever fought anywhere, anytime. I'm sure I share some of that inclination in writing of my experiences. But you, the reader, must take into consideration that when someone is arduously trying to kill you twenty-four hours a day and is successful in killing many close around you, it becomes easy to believe that is surely the case. For dead is dead, and if it happens to you, the wherever or however or whenever it takes place doesn't matter, for being dead is as bad as it can ever get for you.

Like most veterans who have experienced the bloody horrors of real eye-to-eye combat, I have discussed it very little in my later life with anyone else. I found it better to just give God thanks for letting me live while so many others just as deserving had died and to get on with my life and try to forget how bad it had been. Even at this late date, I still find myself unable to discuss in public my personal memories of combat without becoming emotional. Much of it was such a searing experience, at least for me, that I later simply tried to forget the worst parts that happened, but found that to be impossible to do. At unexpected times, different stimuli to my senses would cause vivid memories to rush back. Such ordinary things as the look and smell of freshly turned earth around a noisy, working bulldozer, or the odor of fresh blood, or feeling the heat and seeing the flames and black smoke of a burning slush pit of oil that so resembled burning Napalm, or, most of all, the pungent smell of a decaying carcass would trigger bad memories.

So, over the long years, I attempted to just try to block them out when they did try to rise up and as the years passed, gradually I was pretty successful in doing this as I went about my life. I occasionally have discussed the war with friends who, like me, had been veterans of combat. We have shared with each other some war stories, but to talk with those who had never experienced it was always difficult. In trying to do that, I found there was little common ground to be covered and much room for misinterpretation. Unless you had been through it, it was almost impossible to conceive of the inhumanity you necessarily developed so that you, as a normal, decent human being, could continually do the horrible things to other human beings that the God of War demanded. So the really bad things I simply tried not to think about anymore, but endeavored, instead, to focus on remembering only the good times I had experienced in the service, and there were many of those.

As a kid of eighteen, I joined the Army with most of my closest friends. Since we had entered together in a large group, we brought along with us a built-in camaraderie or brotherhood from the very start. This feeling of camaraderie grew as time went on, since most of us stayed together as a true band of brothers during basic training and Officer's Candidate School. So, my memories of stateside service are good ones. Later, after I arrived overseas, I found the citizen soldiers I became associated with there to be a good solid cross-section of young American males.

I still have to smile when I think back to their somewhat irreverent attitude in how they regarded the pompous military high brass with all their imperious regulations. It seemed many of these regulations were centered on myriad "picky-picky" rules concerning busy work and spit and polish, while having absolutely nothing to do with being in combat, fighting the enemy. The citizen soldiers circumvented these despised tedious regulations as much as possible, or if not possible, only grudgingly accepted them. I also found these citizen soldiers, as a whole, to be humorous and fun loving, but also deeply patriotic, fiercely loyal to each other and both deadly serious and extremely skillful when actually engaged in fighting for their country. Their priorities were simple—to stay alive, to get the war over with as quickly as possible, and, with peace, to return to the people and places they loved and called home. They were all for getting back to civilian life after the war was won and letting the professional brass of the bureaucratic army do what they loved to do best. To the citizen soldier, this meant all the high brass could go back to shuffling paper and having constant inspections to let them be sure that the spit and polish and the busy work they seemed to revere so much was being adequately done by the yardbirds.

Had I known back then that I would someday try and write of my war experiences, I would have kept a diary. That is what most writers of wartime books did, carefully recording each night the exploits of the day. Well, I didn't do that, but my mother had carefully kept all my letters that I had written her during the battle for Okinawa. I ended up with these letters after her death years ago. When I wrote these letters, I was concerned about upsetting her, as she was a worrier, so I always tried to downplay how bad it really was during the fighting. But I have had the letters to refer to, and they have helped me immeasurably in my efforts to draw up memories from my fading memory bank of the details of long past events. Upon reading my letters today, I find myself appalled at their mawkishness and how they read like the writings of a callow youth. But then, of course, that is understandable for that is exactly what they were. A "callow youth" would have been an apt description of me at the time I wrote those letters.

Along with these letters to assist me in trying to write of long past events, I have also leaned heavily on the official publication of the Ninety-sixth Infantry Division called *The Deadeyes: The Story of the Ninety-sixth Division*. This publication is the complete and official account of that unit's actions during the war. The 763rd Tank Battalion I was with was attached to and worked with this division during the battle. I also found the official Department of the Army book titled *Okinawa: The Last Battle* to be of great assistance in helping me locate and coordinate where I was when writing certain letters with what was happening overall at that time on the island. This book contains many excellent maps showing the locations and movements of the units involved as the battle progressed.

My perspective during the battle was a narrow one, and my knowledge of what was actually taking place along the front lines away from my position was limited. Due to the deep impression that my personal participation in the invasion and battle for Okinawa made on me, over the years I have purchased and avidly read many books written about this event. At the back of this account, I have included a complete list of those books I have read concerning the battle. I'm quite sure they have had an influence on some of the personal perceptions I hold about what actually took place.

One of the books I read was written by a Japanese Colonel named Yahara. He was the third ranking Japanese officer on the island during the battle. He survived the war and wrote his memoirs seventeen years later. This book was published both in the U.S. and Japan. I found it to be fascinating reading as he presented the Japanese version of the battle. His descriptions regarding the details of the all but impregnable Shuri Line, designed mainly by him, answered many questions about the numerous difficulties the Americans had in overcoming this brilliantly conceived defensive layout.

Various other books concerning the battle of Okinawa presented still different viewpoints, which reflected the obvious allegiance of the writer to some branch of the service. I'm amazed at all the different slants, impressions, and attempts that often overly stress areas of importance in order to bolster the spin that various authors wished to convey in their writings. It seems that an inordinate number of books about the battle for Okinawa were written by Marine veterans and some of these give the impression that it was wholly the Marines who were responsible for taking the island of Okinawa. Some of the other accounts written by Marines do include the Army, but only just barely, in a secondary way. It seems for some reason that the Marines attracted more literary-minded personnel to their ranks to write of their exploits than did the Army. The Army always did think that the Marines over-did the aggrandizing horn blowing, and that they were always accompanied by an overabundance of photographers and correspondents, who were constantly hawking their accomplishments. However, the Marines felt it necessary to do this for the public to accept them as a separate military entity.

There is no doubt that the Marines were more successful in nurturing a much higher *esprit de corps* than was the Army. As Marines were mostly volunteers, that would be expected. But in the admittedly prejudiced opinion of an Army man who, none the less, was actually there, it always seemed to me that the 7th and 96th Army divisions were the units who did fully as much, or even more, than the vaunted Marine divisions did in the fighting on Okinawa. Still, they all did plenty. We always felt comfortable when Marines were emplaced adjacent to us, for we knew they would really fight, and we respected their aggressiveness.

Inter-service rivalry had always been around, but before the battle for Okinawa ended, there was enough ferocious fighting and high casualties among all segments of the Armed Services that the occasional taunting between different outfits had come to a stunned silence. The greatest American blood-letting of the Pacific War soon had every unit sharing with each other in the grief over the unprecedented numbers of fallen American youths. The average American fighting man struggling to stay alive in the mud on the battle line came to consider such adolescent behavior as trying to instigate inter-service rivalry to be odious. All such posturing was now looked upon disdainfully.

And in truth, such important events were taking place during this period of 120 days that, when combined with the high casualties America was taking on, frivolity ceased to exist. Several momentous happenings were crammed into this short time period. Early in the battle, the popular war correspondent, Ernie Pyle, was shot in the head and killed by a Japanese sniper. Then President Roosevelt died, and the hard-fought war against Germany ended in Europe while the fighting on Okinawa raged on. Also, during the later stages of the battle, the overall commanding officer of the Okinawan invading forces' Tenth Army, General Simon Bolivar Buckner, was killed by Japanese artillery. He became the highest ranking U.S. officer to die by enemy action in the Pacific Theater. Then, the Russians took Berlin, and Joe Stalin began to make plans to take over Western Europe and perhaps Asia, as well, while he still had his huge army intact. But Stalin's plans were stymied, or at least placed on hold, when a relatively unknown U.S. Vice-president from Missouri named Harry Truman took over as commander-in-chief of the U.S. and ordered the dropping of two newly and secretly developed atomic bombs on Japan.

Not only did this bring World War II to a quick and sudden end, but it also removed the necessity of U.S. forces having to invade the Japanese home islands. This, of course, held the greatest importance for us who would be participating in this invasion. But of even greater importance for world affairs was the fact that the U.S. at that time was the sole possessor of the A-Bomb. For a while, at least, that fact held a menacing club over Joe Stalin's head and delayed his plans for attempting the quick expansion of world Communism. So, it truly was a time period of epochal happenings that had far reaching influences for the future of the world.

My written contribution is certainly not going to contain any new information about the battle. I'm sure my account of various aspects of the battle will differ from how others who were there saw it happen, but I have written this account as accurately as my memory allowed, fully aware that the recollections of other men are not infallible. It might convey to a latter-day reader the sense of some of the everyday travails of combat that were encountered by a twenty-year-old, ranch-raised Texan. How, with the naiveté of the young, he had to quickly learn to cope with the really serious side of life. This learning experience took place while he was desperately trying to stay alive and yet hold on to the feeling that he really might be participating in something of epic, world-shaping proportions.

—Bob Green
Green Ranch
Albany, Texas

Chapter 1

HOME RANCH TO
NEW MEXICO MILITARY INSTITUTE

"Mine is a rugged land but good for raising sons—and I
myself, I know no sweeter sight on earth than a man's own
native country."

The Odyssey

In the older countries of Europe, it wouldn't be unusual for someone to be born, live out his life, and be buried in the same place, but in our more mobile American society that is rarely done. I will soon be an example of one of the few who have done that in this country, for I was born in 1924 on this cattle ranch near Albany, Texas, where I still live today with Nancy, my wife of over fifty-four years. With the exceptions of going off to schools and my service in the army during World War II, my whole life, which is now approaching eighty years, has been spent in this one place, the Green Home Ranch. Nancy and I raised our three children here on the ranch, but they have long since grown up and moved away to raise their own children in other places.

Long ago, when I was growing up on this ranch, I had two older brothers and a sister. We grew up far out in the country with the great out-of-doors as our playground. There were guns behind every door in the house and hunting game for the table was commonplace. We also grew up in friendly association with the somewhat tough, rough-hewn men who worked on the ranch and participated with them in the never-ending ranch work. This outdoor work often started before dawn and lasted until dark in all kinds of weather. We children soon learned that if we were allowed to participate in the work, which we dearly loved to do, there could be no complaining about our creature comfort. Later, these things made army service easier for me, as I found the army stateside training, in most cases, not as arduous as the work of the ranch.

The story of how the Green branch of my family got to Texas and to that ranch where I was born is that sometime in the 1830s two brothers, James and Thomas Green, came from Tennessee. It is recorded in the Bounty and Warrants Book in the state archives at Austin that they were awarded land in Lampasas County for "services rendered" to the Republic of Texas. We have no knowledge today as to what the "services rendered" were or what later became of James Green. We do know that Thomas Green and his son Ezekiel left the Lampasas area and joined early settlers in moving up the Trinity, Colorado, and Brazos Rivers as the Anglo frontier advanced. Their wanderings can be traced by the abstracts of land they pre-empted and then later sold. There is an Ezekiel Green survey up the Trinity in Limestone County and a Thomas Green survey near Whitney close to the Brazos. Finally they settled down for good in Hill County, where today old Thomas and Ezekiel Green's graves may be found, side by side in a little country cemetery named Woodbury, just west of Hillsboro. Thomas died in 1858 at age eighty, while Ezekiel died in 1868 at age forty-six.

When Ezekiel Green came to Hill County in the 1840s, he was a widower with a small son, Thomas Henry. He soon remarried and had two more children. Thomas Henry, only child of his first marriage, grew up in Hill County and with the onset of the Civil War, at age sixteen, joined the 19th Texas Cavalry of the CSA, a Hill County Regiment. In deference to his age, he was given the job of securing horses for the Confederate Army instead of going to combat. I looked him up in the State Archives at Austin where they have card files on nearly everyone who served in the Confederate Army from Texas. Along with the person's name, the card contains the record of whatever equipment he had brought into the army upon enlisting. On my grandfather's card it reads "very little." I'll bet that was the truth.

At the end of the Civil War, Thomas Henry Green returned to Hill County where he soon married a local fifteen-year-old girl named Mary Catherine Frazier. Her family called her "Kitty." Thomas Henry entered the business of raising and trading horses, about which he had gained experience in the army. He and Kitty soon had a strapping baby boy, my father, born in 1868. They named their son William Henry. Kitty never recovered from a difficult childbirth and died about seven or eight months after my father was born. She was only eighteen years old. My grandfather, Thomas Henry, took his baby boy over to Kitty's mother who was still having babies, and she nursed my father along with her most recent one. Later little William Henry was passed around among the female relatives while Thomas Henry, of necessity, traveled and tended to his far-flung horse business that had now expanded to running herds of mares, colts and stallions on the vast open ranges of West Texas.

Ezekiel Green died in 1868 and his widow, now along in years and known to all as "Granny Green," took little Henry to live with her. The old lady, a staunch Cumberland Presbyterian, while not true blood kin, was none the less always remembered by my father as the one who taught him at an early age that "the Lord helps those who help themselves." This work ethic was so firmly implanted in little Henry that it dominated his later life.

When Henry reached adolescence, his father was financially able to send him to Trinity College, located at nearby Tehuacana, Texas. It was a highly regarded Presbyterian school that is still going strong today, now located in San Antonio. Henry was evidently a good student, and the curriculum taught, including Latin and Greek, was far advanced for the times. He graduated with highest honors, being valedictorian of his class of 1885. We still have his diploma, beautifully hand-lettered in Latin on a real sheepskin. My dad always credited this school with much of his later business success.

Now at age eighteen and a college graduate, he found out that things were not booming in Hillsboro in 1885. The only job he could get was in a furniture store that belonged to someone in the family. He didn't like the job and was very restive. Meanwhile, Thomas Henry's open range horse business was having trouble. One of the areas where Thomas Henry had a free-ranging horse herd was on vacant Peters Colony lands along Hubbard Creek in eastern Shackelford and western Stephens counties, east of Albany. It turned out that the free open range where his herds had flourished wasn't really free after all. The land belonged to someone and was now being sold off. Texas Emmigration and Land Company (formerly the old Peters Colony Land Company) controlled options on vast acreage of Texas real estate, including the area on Hubbard Creek where Thomas Henry was running one of his herds of horses. This land company had recently reorganized and opened an office in the new town of Graham, Texas. Under its new management, directed by Colonel E. S. Graham, the raw land was aggressively being sold off to incoming people, many from the defeated Southern states, who were seeking a fresh start in a new country.

Henry's father received word that the open range in Stephens and Shackelford counties, where his band of horses ran, was being squeezed out in the TE&L Company sell-off. Previously, Thomas Henry had made a deal with a man named J. J. Witty, who lived in a dugout east of Albany, to keep tabs on that band of horses. There were probably eighty to one hundred horses in the herd that was running on about eight thousand acres of still unsold TE&L

surveys along Hubbard Creek. All carried the THG brand of Thomas Henry Green. Much of the surrounding land had been recently sold and was rapidly being fenced with the new-fangled barbed wire. Witty wrote to Thomas Henry that he thought it would be only a short time before the Hubbard Creek pasture land would be unavailable for the herd of horses, and that they probably should be moved or disposed of soon. While mulling over Witty's report, my grandfather came up with the idea that maybe this would be a good place to break the new, restless eighteen-year-old college graduate into the business world. So, he decided to send his son Henry, my dad, to Albany to sell the horses and return with the money to Hill County.

Thomas Henry Green, my paternal grandfather, joined the Confederate Army at age 16. After returning home from the Civil War, he ran horses on the open range of Northwest Texas, in Palo Pinto, Stephens, and Shackelford Counties. He lived in Hill County at Peoria, west of Hillsboro and is buried there.

The Texas Central Railroad had built from Waco to Albany in 1881. Albany was the end of the line, so that made it easy to get there from Hill County. Soon, my dad got off the train there with his saddle and bedroll. He rented a horse from the livery stable and rode it out to J. J. Witty's dugout. They made plans for Witty and some other cowboys to help round up the horse herd and sell them. Dad always said it was an exciting gathering as the horses were pretty wild, but they got it done. While gathering the horses, Dad became greatly impressed with the Hubbard Creek bottomland where they were running. It was a unique lay of land where Hubbard Creek had divided. Instead of having one main channel, it had made two for about three or four miles before coming back together into one channel again. The island made between the two forks of the creek was called Hitson Island, after the Hitson family who were the earliest open range cattlemen of the area. The bottom land of the island had great big pecan trees and wonderful grass. My dad became enthralled with the land and made an epic decision. Instead of returning to Hill County with the money he had received for the horses, he borrowed an old wagon from J. J. Witty and set up a camp in a large grove of huge pecan trees at the head of the island.

He had sold off the mares and stallions but kept some of the colts. He said all the horses were in fine condition from running on such good pasture. They were just as sleek as seals and mud fat. The creeks, fed by springs, ran pure, crystal-clear water all the time. It was a beautiful piece of ground, and he now made inquiries and was told it was owned by the TE&L Company, which was run by Colonel Graham from an office in Graham, a new town named for him

about thirty miles away. Dad decided to go see if he could make a deal to lease this land. He rode horseback to meet with Colonel Graham and found him to be a stern man. When the colonel heard that this big old kid wanted to lease the Hubbard Creek land, he said, "Young man, you're wasting your time and mine. We just sell land, not lease it." Having said that, Colonel Graham turned away in dismissal, but my dad spoke up. "Well, Colonel Graham, if it were me, and I owned that land, I would rather have a good tenant leasing it who would take care of it rather than have it being ruined by those itinerate bands of sheep that are grazing it off now, for nothing."

Mary Catherine Frazier Green, nicknamed "Kitty," married Thomas Henry Green at age 15. At age 18, she gave birth to William Henry Green and died soon after from childbirth complications. She is my paternal grandmother and is buried beside Thomas Henry Green in Peoria Cemetery in Hill County.

When Colonel Graham heard that, he wheeled around and said, "Are there any sheep on that land?" My dad assured him there were many. The colonel unrolled a map, and my dad showed him where the bands of sheep were located. (Today, there are still remains of dugouts on this ranch where those old sheepmen stayed while grazing their flocks.) Colonel Graham tugged on his beard and said, "Well, I think you have a point there, Son. I'm going to lease you that land if you will promise to keep those sheep off it. But understand, I still want to eventually sell it." So my dad came trotting back to his wagon camp with a signed-up lease in his saddle bag. Next day, he wrote a long letter to his dad down in Hill County telling him what he had done.

Several days later, old J. J. Witty came riding up with a telegram that had come to the Albany depot, addressed to Henry Green c/o J. J. Witty. It read

My father, William Henry Green, was born in 1868. He was a graduate of Trinity University, class of 1885. At age eighteen, he was sent to Albany to sell his dad's horses, which had been running on Hubbard Creek pasture. He sold the horses, but leased land instead of returning home to Hill County with his father's money.

something like this: "Meet the train in Albany on Tuesday at 10:30 A.M." It was so terse that it kind of worried my father. When he met the train and his father got off, he always said that he was the maddest man he had ever seen. They rented a buckboard and started for the lease with his dad giving him hell all the way because he had spent the horse money. "I had made plans for that money," his dad said angrily. "It wasn't your money; it was mine!"

Dad kept saying, "Now just wait; just wait till you see it." And they traveled the rest of the way in silence. Finally Dad stopped the buckboard and started pointing. "Now here's where the lease starts," he said. Dad always said he drove them across the running creek two or three times at different crossings to be sure his father saw all that pretty

water. His father got noticeably quieter the more they drove around. Finishing up with their survey, they came to the wagon camp under the huge pecan trees. While Henry cooked supper on an open fire in a Dutch oven, his father sat on the tongue of the wagon and watched him. Dad said it was good news to his ears when his father finally spoke. "Well, Son, I'll have to admit, you've got yourself a real nice ranch. But you don't have any money or any credit, so how are you going to stock it?"

My dad always said, "I was ready for him. I told him, well, if you'll go on my note and let me borrow money on your credit for stock, if I can't make this work in a year or so I'll come back to Hill County and go back to work in the furniture store."

I always liked the way my dad finished this story. He said his father got up off the wagon tongue and reaching down in his pocket, pulled out two twenty dollar gold pieces. He said, "This is all the money I've got with me and I'm going to give you one of them, but don't you spend it unless you really have to. If things don't work out for you here, use it to come on back home."

Henry never did have to spend the coin he got from his father that night at the wagon camp. We still have that twenty dollar gold piece, and the fact that we do is a good indication of the kind of guy Dad was, for he never did believe in frivolous spending. One of his stock statements was, "Nothing is a bargain if you don't really need it."

That first winter, Henry lived in the old wagon he had borrowed from J. J. Witty. It was his ranch headquarters. He built a round pen of post oak logs and, by himself, broke thirty head of young gelding horses. One day, he drove them into Albany to try and sell them. In telling about it he said, "I was always kind of lucky. As I was driving that bunch of horses down the main street of Albany, this old boy came out of a café picking his teeth and stood there on the boardwalk watching them as I went by. He hollered at me, 'Hey! Are those horses for sale?' I said they were and he said, 'Where you taking them?' And I said, 'Out to the railroad corrals.' 'Well, I want to come out and talk to you about them,' he said and he did. His name was Liggertwood, and he had just been hired as manager of the Matador Land and Cattle Company. They needed horses and bought all thirty of my horses for thirty dollars each. So now I had nine hundred dollars and thought I was rich." I guess in that day, nine hundred dollars would have gone a long way, especially the way Dad was living.

For the next few years, he kept living out of that wagon until during one unusually bad winter when he got pneumonia. One bitter cold, sleeting day a neighbor named Uncle Jack Jones came by and looked in the wagon. There was Dad, sick in his bed roll, running a high fever. Jones said, "Henry, I'm not going to leave you here by yourself. You're bad sick and I'm going to take you home with me." So he took Dad to his place which was just up the creek a few miles where he had a nice house for the times. They put Dad to bed in a sleeping loft, and Mrs. Jones nursed him and got him well. Years later, after Mr. and Mrs. Jones had died, Dad bought their little place and added it on to his ranch. It had a big dugout on it where the Joneses had first lived before building their house.

After that experience of illness, Dad decided maybe he had better quit living in that old wagon and build himself a house. He was having success in a new kind of horse business. He had acquired some big Percheron mares and by breeding them with mammoth Jacks, had raised some excellent mules. Mules

My father's box house on Hubbard Creek.

were a good commodity then. All the farmers needed them, and the army did, too, so there was a good market for them. He now traded a bunch of mules and horses to a lumberman in East Texas in exchange for a big load of lumber. He said the lumber was 1" x 12" boxing boards, eighteen feet long, cut from virgin East Texas timber and was really fine. It came to Albany on the train, and he hauled it down to his camp and sawed the long boards in two, right in the middle. That is why the walls of the old ranch house he built are nine feet high. He didn't lose anything but the sawdust!

The two-room house he built was not right where his wagon camp site was, but on a nearby high rise of ground. This ground was covered with chips of flint, mussel shell, arrowheads, and burnt rocks that clearly showed Indians had camped there many times in the past. That made Dad think the site might be safe from flooding which later proved to be the case. As the years passed, every now and then Hubbard Creek would go on a high-lonesome rise, with the water many times getting very close to the house, but it never did quite reach it. That little box house did fine as long as he was a bachelor, and it sure did beat living out of a wagon.

As the years passed, Dad developed into a sagacious businessman. He had learned how to buy steer calves cheap from farmers and small ranchers who lived to the southeast of him and grow them out on his ranch. He would take a neighboring teenager along with him to help as he made a big circuit through that area, buying calves. Years later, when this same teenager was an old man, he told me how it had been to go along on these jaunts.

"Every now and then," he said, "your dad would come riding up on his big horse to our house and say to my father—'Mr. Lawrence, I sure could use Albert to help me for a few days. Can he go with me?' And my father would say—'Why he sure can, Henry. Albert! Go saddle your horse and go with Mr. Green!' So I'd get my horse and off we'd ride, and I wouldn't have any idea where we were going or when we would be back or what we were aiming to do. I'd just follow him, and we'd go off down toward Cisco and Eastland and De Leon, and he would dicker and buy steer calves from those people who lived down that way. At night, if we couldn't pen them in somebody's corral, we would just hold the calves he had bought in the fenced lane with your dad sleeping in the road on one end of them and me on the other to keep them in a bunch. They were pretty gentle little old calves being raised on those small places. Come morning, we would just push 'em on down the road and keep making our circle, and after a while, we'd get back to his ranch, sometimes with two or three hundred head of steers he had bought."

Dipping cattle at the Green Ranch, 1917, in the Tick Eradication Program.

Years later, when this "kid" had grown up, he worked for my father, managing one of his ranches for many years. As long as he lived, he always called my father "Mr. Henry."

Before the turn of the century in the Albany, Texas, area, there weren't many six-foot-four, barrel-chested young men who had spent a winter alone breaking thirty head of bronc horses. There sure weren't many men of that description who also had a good, solid college degree. Dad's expertise at judging and knowing cattle and his prowess on horseback led to his becoming very popular with the mostly illiterate, hard-twisted local cowboys of the area, and he was asked to help them with their major roundups and cattle workings. He enjoyed doing this, and it gained him the friendship and respect of that stratum of the cattle business, which he retained all his life. Conversely, his college degree and intellect stood him in good stead with the bankers and, later on, with those in the higher echelons of the livestock trade at far-off, big, central cattle markets. He profited greatly from such a wide circle of acquaintances spread across a broad spectrum of the livestock trade, and through the years, his ranching business prospered.

When drouth periodically came to the Texas ranges, Dad avoided the disaster that many ranchers experienced when they ran out of grass and water and had to sell off their cattle for whatever they would bring on the glutted local markets. Dad's Midwest contacts enabled him to ship many trainloads of cattle he bought in the drouthed-out areas to the stockyard markets in far off Kansas City and Chicago. Often, he went along on the same train as his cattle in order to keep an eye on them. In good weather, he rode on top of the cattle cars and watched the country go by during the day, while sleeping in the caboose at night. With no wife or family waiting for him at home, he was free to come and go as he pleased, and he played the game of cow trading to the hilt.

But events were already in motion that would bring his wife, my mother, to him one day. My mother's family was named Robertson. They had come from Virginia to Missouri where they were living when the Civil War started. They were southern sympathizers living in an area dominated by Yankees who harassed the womenfolk continuously, as all the grown men were away in the Confederate Army. After their houses were burned down, the men got word of it and returned to take care of their families. It was a turbulent time for Southerners in their area, and the Robertsons decided it would be best for them to leave Missouri. My grandmother, Molly, was five years old when two large families who were close friends, the Robertsons and the Donnells, left Missouri for Texas. They traveled along together for protection. When they reached Texas, they settled on the Clear Fork of the Brazos River north of where Breckenridge is today. Being millers by trade, they knew how to build dams and mills that were used to grind corn and other grains. They labored to put in a mill at Eliasville, only to see their dam wash out three times, but they persevered and the last mill and dam they built is still there today. My grandmother grew up and married a man named Thomas Weaver, a school teacher who taught at a country school called "Snake Den." One day, at age thirty-one, he got a severe headache which steadily worsened. Not knowing what else to call it, people said it was "brain fever." It was most likely a cerebral hemorrhage. They told how they would pour cold well-water on rags to put on his head to try and relieve the pain, but he died after four or five days, leaving my grandmother with two little girls, ages two and four, and eight months pregnant with my mother. They were hard up and facing destitution with no provider.

One of my grandmother's brothers, Jack Robertson, had a mill and general store in the village of Crystal Falls, up-river from Eliasville, and he came to the rescue. Near his home, he built a small house for his sister Molly, the new widow, where she lived for nine years with her three little girls. Mother always described the Jack Robertsons as busy, prosperous people who always considered them to be poor relations, more or less.

Through the years, the Robertsons and Donnells had intermarried and remained close friends. They also remained unreconstructed Confederates. I can remember as a small child seeing Uncle Jack lying in his coffin, dressed in his gray Civil War uniform. He had left firm instructions that he wished to be buried in his rebel uniform. None of the older Robertsons or Donnells ever did stop hating the Yankees or verbally fighting the Civil War until they died.

A man named George Ritchey, who had also come to Texas from Missouri, had a ranch on Hubbard Creek, just east of my dad's place. His wife had died, leaving him with six children, all still at home, so Ritchey needed help. He heard about a widow living down the creek at Crystal Falls, so he went down, liked what he found, and immediately started courting my

G.W. Ritchey's ranch house was just east of my dad's ranch. Dad, being a bachelor, was a steady visitor at the dinner table. My mother, Willie Weaver (seen here in the white dress, bottom right), came to live here when she was nine years old and, consequently, met my dad.

grandmother. Soon they were married. It might not have been a marriage made in heaven, but it was a union that helped them both, so they were happy about the situation. Molly now moved up Hubbard Creek to Mr. Ritchey's ranch house with her three girls. That made nine children, and then Molly and Ritchey soon had three more so it was a house *full*.

Ritchey's place was more like a Missouri stock farm than a West Texas ranch. He had sheep, hogs, registered Durham cattle, split rail fences, beehives, a big orchard, a garden, and a blacksmith shop, as well as a large smoke house. Ritchey was a master at butchering, curing, and smoking meat, and my grandmother was a fine cook, so the meals at their house were always good. It didn't take my dad, living by himself across the creek to the west, very long to discover that fact and he soon became a regular guest at meal time. He was always welcomed and enjoyed coming to visit at the rollicking houseful of people whenever he got lonesome or wanted a good meal.

Dad was eighteen or nineteen years older than my mother so he thought of her then as just a little girl, if he thought of her at all, but in her memoirs, written when she was in her eighties and long after Dad was gone, she states that she had picked him out then as the man she was going to marry. That she later did so says a great, good deal about my mother. She usually did what she set out to do.

One of the things she was later determined to do was to get a good education that would prepare her to make her own way in life and avoid ever finding herself dependent, as her poor mother had been, on the charity of relatives. She was a good student and obtained a scholarship from the state to attend college in return for teaching at a country school. In 1906, she graduated from North Texas Normal College, now the University of North Texas at Denton.

Her first teaching job after college was in the Texas Panhandle at a large ranch west of Amarillo. Mr. Ritchey drove her from his ranch to Albany in a wagon to catch the train to Stamford. In Stamford she would change to a railroad that went to Wichita Falls. There she would catch the Ft. Worth and Denver to Amarillo. At the Albany depot that day, a noisy group of young women from some of the more socially prominent families around town were getting on the same train to ride west, just ten miles or so, where the train would stop and let them off. There they would be met by friends who would take them to a nearby ranch where they would have a big party. They were all dolled up in fancy dresses and big stylish hats, and they carried parasols. They had picnic baskets loaded with delicacies and champagne. Everything was very festive indeed.

I can imagine how my mother eyed those frivolous-acting young women that day in the Albany depot, as she sat there in her plain gingham dress waiting to go to her teaching job. Of course, none who were there that day knew what the future held in store for them. They sure never dreamed that the country girl sitting there in the homemade dress would one day marry a man—old hard-working Dad—who would have to loan several of those fancy ladies' husbands large sums of money and hold mortgages on their ranches to support their high-spending lifestyles.

While my mother was teaching at the ranch school in the Panhandle, occasionally she would accompany groups on Sunday picnics to a place called Willow Water Hole. It was a very pretty spot on a creek with large willow and cottonwood trees around a rock hole of clear water fed by a big flowing spring, and it was just a nice place to have a picnic. Many years later, my father bought the ranch where Willow Water Hole was located. It is where my brother Tom lives today. After Dad owned the place, when we would occasionally go up to visit Tom, Mother, now up in years, would want to drive over and see Willow Water Hole again. We would take her, and I always enjoyed watching her as she sat and looked at it, reminiscing. Even today, it is still a very pretty place.

My mother, Willie Weaver, in 1906, the year she graduated from the North Texas Normal College, now known as the University of North Texas at Denton.

Mother left the Panhandle teaching job and taught school in Houston for a while. Then she was hired as principal of the Breckenridge school system, which let her move back and be near her family at the Ritchey Ranch. One day, while she was visiting the Ritchey Ranch to see her mother, Dad came by, still availing himself of a good, free meal. He hadn't seen Mother in a long time and probably still remembered her as a little girl, but she had grown up into a pretty woman. Years later, my mother wrote in her memoirs, "I knew the way he looked at me that day we were going to be more than just friends." That proved to be true, for after a pleasant courtship he asked her to marry him, and she said yes, of course, as that had been her plan all along.

My dad was fifty years old and my mother was thirty-four when they married in 1917. They both wanted a family, so because of their ages and being somewhat late in getting started, they hurriedly had four children in six and one half years—Bill, Tom, Mary Anna and me. I was the youngest.

They added on to my father's little house and continued to do so as the kids came along, sprawling it out in all directions. Growing up there I remember how it was such a comfortable old house—lots of porches and fireplaces, built not to impress but to shelter, a typical old West Texas ranch house of the day.

My dad had always been pretty progressive. He had driven one of the first automobiles in the area, and now he wanted his ranch house to give his family some of the modern conveniences town houses enjoyed. Most houses far out in the country like his didn't have indoor plumbing or running water, but depended on an underground cistern that caught water off the roof, if and when it rained. That was all the water they had, unless they hauled some from the creek in a barrel. Dad, with the help of another man, hand dug a ditch and put in a steel one-inch pipeline running from a wind mill at the creek to a storage tank on a tower near the house, and we had the luxury of an indoor bathroom and running water in the house.

Next, he ran a single wire on white porcelain insulators that were nailed on the top of fence posts and extended some twenty-three miles to Albany. This afforded us a hand-cranked telephone of sorts. Next, electric lights were provided for the house by his bringing home a green generator with "Delco" on the side. The generator put out thirty-two volts for light bulbs, which replaced the coal oil lamps we formerly had used. The "Delco," as we always called it, could light up about five bulbs in the house at night. If you turned on six, all of them would dim and were liable to go out, so we would go through the house turning out lights before we turned others on. Someone had to go outside at night and turn the Delco off when we went to bed.

We kids had a good time growing up, as we all had our own horses and there were always lots of dogs and other pets, many times domesticated from various wild animals found on the ranch. I have many fond memories of those early days and it was a very happy childhood.

I recall one time when there was a white Christmas. My dad got up on a ladder (he would have been pretty old at the time to be doing this) and with a long pole, reached up and made what looked like sleigh and reindeer tracks in the snow on the roof near the chimney. Then he rang a couple of little bells he used on his horses to help him find them in the brush. The next morning—Christmas morning—we kids got almost hysterical when we went outside to investigate what the ringing bells had meant during the night and saw the tracks in the snow on our roof. It was pretty hard to convince me later on that there wasn't a Santa Claus, as I had seen and heard the proof that there was with my own eyes and ears.

Dad was always bringing surprises home when he returned from a trip. One time it was a big windup Victrola, an Edison Diamond Needle phonograph with many World War I camp songs sung by George M. Cohan. The machine really did have a little diamond for a needle. It's still in the old ranch house and still works.

Another time the surprise was a tiny Shetland pony standing sedately on the floor of the back seat of his car. We named the little steed "Teeny-Weeny." He would grow up and later buck me off, breaking my arm.

In hot weather, when we would be riding while Dad drove the car near the creek, we would holler, "let's go swimming!" He would grin and pull over and park, and we would all go skinny-dipping. We little ones would ride on his back while he swam like he was a big old whale.

Once in a while on winter nights, when he was in his big chair in front of the fire place, we would crawl up on him and get him to sing us old cowboy songs, like "Sam Bass" and "The Texas Rangers." Both were songs that had many verses he had sung to calm the cattle when riding night guard around a herd.

So, when we were growing up, Dad had been a lot of fun, although he was older for a father, and I remember that time as being a wonderful up-bringing. Both Mother and Dad tried hard to be good parents, and they really were. I think maybe they tried so hard because they both had been deprived of a parent while they grew up.

Then came the Depression of the 1930s, and it began to look like they might lose everything they had worked so hard for all those years. As the Depression worsened, Dad became very depressed and morose. I never heard him sing again after the Depression started. As it turned out, although it was a painful period of loss, his solidly based business weathered the storm pretty well, while many of his old rancher friends didn't, which caused him grief.

Through the years, Dad had consistently increased his land holdings. Besides the "Home" ranch on Hubbard Creek, which he had steadily enlarged, in 1909 he had bought the Rockwell Ranch southwest of Albany. After World War I, he had bought the Poindexter Ranch southeast of Albany and in 1930, in a big trade with a man named Dick Moberley, he had acquired the Moberley Ranch, south of Albany, that lay contiguous with the east side of his Rockwell Ranch. These two places, joined together, became known as the South Green Ranch. Included in this trade with Dick Moberley was also a house in Albany which was now used by our family for us children to attend school. We weren't ever very happy living in town. The ranch was where we wanted to be and where we would go at every opportunity.

Dad was fifty-eight years old when I was born. As I got old enough to associate with him, he seemed a giant to my childish eyes. I was impressed by the respect shown him by the tough, working cowboys who were usually so archly critical of someone in a managerial position, especially if he couldn't ride a horse very well or recognize one cow from another. But Dad could certainly do both these things—even better than they could—and they knew it.

Aerial view of the old Green Ranch headquarters, prior to WW II and before Hubbard Creek Lake was built. The house was moved out of the proposed lake bed and relocated to another area on the ranch in 1958–1959.

He was a leader who always led by personal example, directing all cow work from the back of a horse and was, at least to me, quite impressive in action.

His ideas about handling cattle were ahead of the times. Many of the bigger ranches of the area had non-resident owners who issued broad instructions from their offices far away in the city and depended on a foreman to see that their wishes were carried out. In many cases, the ranch hands were prone to chase the company cattle wildly, for fun and recreation, even roping them in playful contests for sport. Training their horses by harassing and abusing the stock was considered a perk. This was a common practice of times past, which was accepted as routine behavior by both ranch owners and their hands and still goes on to some extent today. There was none of that on my father's ranches. He believed in, and insisted on, handling his cattle with the least amount of violence possible—the "Nester Way," he called it. If his way were too tame and unsporting for the more high-spirited, rope-happy cowboys, well, he could, and did, do without their services. His hands were usually older, calmer men with a great understanding of animal behavior. Dad believed in out-witting cattle, not overpowering them. "I'd rather have a live one in the pasture, than a dead one in the corral!" he would say when refusing to let a rebellious animal be roped, choked down and dragged into submission. When a nervous, wild acting animal began to cause trouble on a round-up, an attempt was made to get it mixed in with some calmer, gentler cattle when possible. If this couldn't be done, they were allowed to just drop out and be gathered up in the next round-up by carefully mixing them in early on with a bunch of gentle ones. It usually worked.

In Dad's heyday, physical toughness was so common and necessary to the men involved in the early days of ranching that it was simply taken for granted.

I well remember how creature comforts meant nothing to my father. Getting tired, hot, thirsty, cold, dirty, wet or hungry was just ignored by him—if not by those of us accompanying him and carrying out his orders—until the work at hand was completed. Arising well before daylight and working until dark was the rule of his range, and he pursued this rugged regime all of his life as he followed his old Granny Green's advice—"the Lord helps those who help themselves." With a strong belief in such a work-ethic credo, he put together a ranching empire starting from scratch.

Dad was killed in a car wreck in 1950 on his way to the Panhandle to sell a big string of steers. He was eighty-two years old. All four of us children had wanted to be nothing but ranchers, so after his death, we still operated all the ranches together for several years in a company called "The Green Land and Cattle Company." When, much to our stunned surprise, plans were made by Abilene and three other towns to build Hubbard Creek Lake, which would take a big chunk out of the Home Ranch, we were forced to reassess the family business.

We were all now married with children of our own, so we decided with so many involved it was time to divide up the company holdings. My sister, Mary Anna, took the Poindexter Ranch. Tom, who had moved to the Panhandle ranch after his service in the army during World War II, wanted to remain on that place, so he did. Bill and I remained partners with

My eldest brother Bill Green with his cutting horse, Cowboy. Circa 1939 or 1940.

what was left of the Home Ranch and with the South Green Ranch as our share. Bill and I then bought a ranch in the Panhandle north of Tom's place across the Canadian River; Mary Anna bought a ranch in Motley County near Matador, and Bill and I swapped out with Tom on some land he still had an interest in down here in the Albany area.

So, the legacy that began back in 1885 with a big kid getting off the train in Albany with nothing but a saddle and a bed roll had evolved into a sizeable ranching operation that now was spread out over six counties in Texas.

In the years just before World War II, as my dad aged, Bill, being the oldest child, became the one he really began to depend on the most to help him manage his far-flung ranching enterprise. In 1936, Bill had gone to New Mexico Military Institute (NMMI) to attend school, and the next year Tom went also. Without the two older boys and with war threatening, help to run the ranches became critical for Dad. At last, he wanted Bill to forget school and come on back and help him with the business, so Bill did. It was a shame because he was really making a great record at the school and was slated to have been one of the top officers in the cadet corps had he returned for his last year. But Dad was desperate, so Bill left school and returned to help run the ranches. All during the war years, Bill and Dad, almost by themselves, ran the ranches and kept things together for the rest of us.

My brother Tom Green mounted on the Stonewall County paint, Old Stoney. Circa 1939 or 1940.

Tom went on to graduate from NMMI Junior College and then from Texas Tech with a degree in animal husbandry. He then moved to the Panhandle ranch just before Pearl Harbor, but when the country entered the war, he immediately went into the service. He was with some of the first American troops to go to Europe, arriving in England in 1942. With his college degree, he was offered a commission but he refused, saying," I just don't want to always be having to tell somebody else what to do all the time." He ended up his long military

My brother Tom in England as a Master Sergeant. The Buick car we enjoyed was his.

service as a Master Sergeant, the highest ranking a non-commissioned officer could obtain.

When I had reached school age, I started my elementary schooling in Albany and then, when it was time for me to enter junior high, I followed in the footsteps of my two older brothers by attending school at NMMI at Roswell, New Mexico, in 1939. Along with being an excellent high school and junior college, there was also a Cavalry R.O.T.C. affiliated program at this school. When I first attended NMMI in the fall of 1939, I was just thirteen years old and had never been away from home very much. Boy! You talk about a weaner calf! I was really homesick. Also, the hazing of new cadets by old cadets was pretty rough. After being there only a short while, I got sick, probably because it had, for me, become a traumatic experience. I was like a calf that had come down with shipping fever when hauled away from home. They put me in the little school hospital, and I was the only patient there. While the lone patient, I was attended to by the two school nurses whom the cadets, who always gave everything and everybody a new title, had named "Sunshine" and "Moonbeam." I remember Moonbeam kind of "mothered"

Mary Anna Green Musselman—my sister. She was quite a rider and is seen here mounted on Chico, the horse she rode as sponsor at the Stamford Cowboy Reunion Rodeo in approximately 1938. She died in 1973 at age 51 and is buried in Green Ranch Cemetery.

me until I soon recovered, but old Sunshine didn't coddle me at all. She was a pretty tough old bird.

A cadre of regular army personnel was assigned at NMMI to afford instructions for mounted cavalry drill and tactics and to care for the big stable full of horses owned by the army. All these horses bore the U S brand signifying that fact. Back then, the motto of the school was, "Every boy rides," and in truth, they did, or at least, tried to. Two full troops of cadets at a time were put on horseback once a week for "mounted drill." This inclusion of regularly riding horses was greatly appealing to ranch-raised boys like me, who had grown up riding horses, as had many other boys from New Mexico, Arizona and Texas ranches who attended this school. That was not the case for many of the poor city boys who had a miserable time learning to ride at mounted drill. I still well remember the instructors screaming at them—"Cadet Arbuckle! (Or whatever the name), Control that horse! Control that horse!" as out-of-control horses with frantic riders, or mounts that had already dumped their riders on the ground, would go flying off in all directions across the sagebrush desert.

During mounted drill, we ranch-raised boys were insufferably smug at the

problems being encountered by the usually so in-control city-slicker cadets as they tried to learn how to ride. Because they were usually so elitist and condescending toward us country bumpkins, we sadistically enjoyed their dilemmas. We not only found the mounted drill they struggled with to be a piece of cake, we often were given the option of riding "remounts" or

Photograph courtesy NMMI
The slogan of the Cavalry ROTC program at NMMI was "Every boy rides." They could mount two complete troops for mounted drill.

young, untrained horses during the mounted drill period. We basked in the glory of doing that, as "remount riding" was a position that was considered to be one of somewhat higher repute among our peers, as well as a chance for much freedom to ride where we pleased during the mounted drill period.

The school had secured easements from ranchers for us to ride across their ranches northwest of Roswell while mounted drill was being conducted. I often found it dramatic to be riding in formation in a long column, winding along westward across the sagebrush desert toward the blue cone in the distance of Capitan Mountain. It was easy for me to imagine that we were on the way to fight the Comanche or Apache Indians as the old cavalry arm signals were used, and the shouted commands floated through the air to be repeated and passed along back down the line. These were followed by the leader at the head of the column bellowing a long, drawn out "HO" that was meant to implement whatever had been signaled and ordered. By the end of the year, the drills had the formations looking pretty snappy as most boys had learned to ride, and many of the old horses knew how to do the drills and formations better than the riders.

All formations and activities were heralded by bugle calls. I liked hearing those old calls. Sometimes, due to weather, drill would be cancelled. First, the bugle would blow for drill, and if the weather was doubtful, like maybe beginning to drizzle a little, we would all wait anxiously to see if the call for drill would be followed by the bugle call for "Recall," which meant drill was canceled. If, indeed, Recall was sounded, a great cheer would be sent up by all. My favorite bugle call was "Tattoo." I think it is prettier than Taps, and I may want it played at my funeral.

In looking back, I remember it as being the school that had the best instructors of any I ever attended. I think maybe part of the reason for that was the fact that during the Great Depression good teaching jobs were hard to come by; therefore, many great teachers found themselves jobless. NMMI was able to draw from a large pool of excellent, but unemployed teachers, thereby creating a first rate faculty. For example, Paul Horgan, who later received a Pulitzer Prize for writing, was our librarian.

Our Dean of English was named Maurice Garland Fulton. We called him "Old Baggy Butt," but not to his face! He had been teaching at Colgate, but due to his asthma the doctors recommended that he seek a drier climate, so he came

to New Mexico. He wrote all kinds of English textbooks, but what appealed to me was that he was the acknowledged, foremost authority on Billy the Kid. Sometimes on weekends, he would take several of us with him while he interviewed old people who lived up the Hondo Valley about the Lincoln County War. Some of these old characters who had participated in this war and really knew Billy the Kid were still

Photograph courtesy NMMI
Aerial view of New Mexico Military Institute campus, at Roswell, NM, as it looked in 1939 when I started high school there.

alive then. I remember we visited an old man named Coe who showed us his hand that had three fingers missing. They were shot off by Buckshot Roberts at what was called "the Battle at Blazers' Mill." I thoroughly enjoyed these outings.

The commandant of the school was named Colonel H. P. Saunders. There was sure no doubt about his being in charge. I was just as scared of him as I would have been of a grizzly bear. Handling all six hundred boys in that school was kind of like a rancher trying to handle a herd of frisky yearling bulls, but Colonel Saunders had us pretty much under control. We learned to hold him

in the greatest respect, and along with fearing his displeasure, we were surprised, as time went by, to find ourselves wanting to please him. Long after leaving the school, I found myself measuring other men's characters by how they stacked up with that of Colonel Saunders. I have met few men who, in my estimation, reached his caliber in exhibiting the traits of a complete gentleman, while also possessing such a strong underlying core of firm resolve and steely strength. He was quite a man.

Photograph courtesy NMMI
This picture is from the NMMI album of mounted drill.

This military school was full of rules, of course. I was not naturally a neat person, and the rigorous personal and room inspections we endured once a week were very painful for me. The personal inspection was Saturday morning. While we were formed up at attention, Colonel Saunders and staff would come down the ranks, slowly passing by, scrutinizing each cadet for any out of order or unclean article of uniform. Shoes had to be shined to a mirror gloss, as did all brass buttons and insignia, hair recently cut and clean shave noted, and occasionally a rifle would be inspected for cleanliness. Next came room inspection with everything required to be neat, clean, and in its ascribed place. I never did enjoy either one of these inspections and often received demerits for some infraction.

Cadets had to have a written permit to leave the campus for any reason. One fall, I discovered that the school encouraged students to pursue manly hobbies such as hunting, and that in season you could get a permit to go duck hunting early on Saturday mornings and legally miss both inspections. At that instant, I became an avid duck hunter. A taxi from the school downtown cost a dime. We got a dollar and a half weekly allowance. For one dollar, a taxi would take two hunters several miles down the nearby Pecos River, and let them out where they could spend the day hunting ducks as they walked back four or five miles upstream until they reached a bridge over the river. There the taxi driver would pick them up late in the afternoon and return them to the school. This round trip of the taxi was included in the dollar fee, which the two hunters would split. It was good hunting, for there were lots of ducks, and it was nice to be free out in the countryside, and especially nice to miss both inspections.

Surprisingly, I found those duck hunts to come in handy for Spanish class. I had this old maid Spanish teacher named Miss Decker. We all called her "Ma" Decker. I discovered she had a big bunch of cats at her house, so one day, in a flash of brilliant inspiration, I asked her if she would want some ducks for her cats to eat. She became simply ecstatic at the idea. "Oh my, *Señor Verde! Sí! Sí! Les gustan mis gatos los patos!*" So after every duck hunt, I would put a bunch of dead ducks on the floor of her old car in the parking lot. That became a big help in raising my grade in Spanish.

On one duck hunt, this old boy and I were making our way stealthily up the Pecos River, trying to periodically sneak up within shotgun range of ducks we spotted in the river. We still had about two or three miles to go to get to the

bridge where the taxi was going to pick us up when a fierce "blue norther" blasted in, complete with driven snow. We quit hunting and walked rapidly to the bridge to take shelter under one end of it while we waited for the taxi to come for us. We were about an hour early so while we waited we cleaned the ducks we had killed. We talked about how the Indians, upon killing a buffalo, would sometimes

Photograph courtesy NMMI
This picture is from the NMMI album and shows Colonel Saunders at his desk.

remove the hot, bloody liver, sprinkle gall on it from the gall bladder, and eat it raw while it was still hot. My hunting companion, a funny old kid, said "What do you suppose this raw duck gizzard would taste like?"—holding up a large, iridescent, mottled red disc he had just removed from a mallard duck's belly. "Well, I don't know but I don't think it would be very good," I replied.

He kept staring at it in his hand and said, "It looks to me like it would kind of be like those Indians eating a raw buffalo liver, and they thought that was good, and I sure am awfully hungry." And with that, he suddenly took that thing and bit into it like it was a Delicious apple. I'll swear to you, every hair on his head stood straight up, and he began to gag and spit and vigorously rub his mouth. It must have been really bad. He quickly went to the water's edge and began to rinse out his mouth with salty Pecos River water and continued to choke and gag until the taxi finally drove up through the snow to rescue us.

Some funny pranks took place at the school, which was not surprising with six hundred high-spirited youths who were chafing under the strict military discipline. One famous incident there took place early during study hall. Study hall lasted two hours and began soon after supper with all cadets required to be in their rooms, seated at their desks, looking at a book, busily writing or otherwise exhibiting fervent studious activity for the benefit of the tactical officers. These officers strolled along the stoops and looked in the windows at the occupants to ensure that the proper demeanor was being maintained for the pursuit of higher learning. Everything was always deathly quiet during study-hall, with the only noise being the footsteps of the patrolling officers.

One memorable night, study hall had begun and all was quiet when all at once, from out of an ornamental bush near the sally port, a large sky rocket came blasting forth and arched across the quadrangle. Instead of rising up and bursting high into the clear New Mexico sky in a flamboyant display, it went in a low trajectory across the quadrangle and smashed through a basement window into the laundry room. It was there, deep in the basement of Lea Hall, amidst the piled high bags of dirty clothes, that the head of the rocket fulfilled its mission and exploded, setting many of the bags of laundry afire.

All the ostensibly deep study being conducted in study hall came to an immediate halt as a dense cloud of greasy-looking white smoke began pouring out of the smashed window. Rooms emptied as everyone rushed out on to the stoops to be sure they missed nothing of this unprecedented interruption. The patrolling tactical officers were as agog as anyone, frozen in place and staring unbelievably as the column of smoke got larger and larger. Then, to a cheering, screaming welcome from the whole watching cadet corps, a red fire truck came through the sally port into the quadrangle, siren blaring, and rushed over to Lea Hall were they soon had the fire under control.

It was years later at a class reunion, long after the war, that the culprit who had done the deed confessed. He told how the night before he had secretly placed the sky rocket in the bush in the wee hours after lights-out. He had attached a long Pall Mall cigarette to the fuse to make a slow time fuse that allowed him to light it surreptitiously the next evening just before the bugle blew for study hall. The long fuse had given him plenty of time after he lit it to saunter slowly up to his room and get seated at his desk before the rocket launched. He apologized for not having set the rocket in the bush at the proper angle to make it soar and burst correctly, and he hoped none of us had lost any clothing in the fire. We were quick to congratulate him on a feat well done, even though at the time Colonel Saunders hadn't been amused about it.

But the care-free school days were coming to an end. One Sunday afternoon in 1941, our touch football game was interrupted by the news of a Japanese air strike without warning on the U.S. Navy base at Pearl Harbor. We were incensed no end and wanted retaliation. There were many military brats, especially navy, well represented in the student body, and our country's military was respected and admired by us. We were extremely patriotic. "My country, right or wrong"—that kind of thing. When the U.S. entered into World War II we were eager and ready to go. We eventually had our wish fulfilled—in spades.

Photograph courtesy NMMI
Commandant Colonel H. P. Saunders conducting an inspection. It was a very strict school, mainly due to Col. Saunders, who was very demanding, but also highly respected.

Private James R. Green, #18059563, U.S. Army at Ft. Riley, KS. Basic training in the cavalry branch.

Chapter 2

FORT RILEY
TO PEARL HARBOR

"No less dear than a brother, the brother-in-arms who shares our inmost thoughts."

The Odyssey

In 1943, my entire NMMI class was called to active army service. Most of us were just eighteen years old. We had enlisted in the fall of 1942, but were allowed to finish the school year, and in the spring of 1943 we were formally taken into the army at Fort Bliss, located at El Paso, Texas.

We went through the initiation suffered by all new enlistees—short haircuts, multiple shots. After three weeks at Fort Bliss, we traveled by train to Fort Riley, Kansas, near Junction City. At Fort Riley, there was the old regular cavalry post up on a hill with ancient stone stables and barracks that had been used by General Custer and his Seventh Cavalry during the Indian Wars. We were sent instead to a big sprawling layout of newly built wooden barracks and stables constructed on the flat below the old post near the Republican River. This newly built part of the post was called the Republican Flat and was the Cavalry Replacement Training Center, or CRTC, for the U.S. Army. There, soldiers were trained to go into the cavalry branch of service, which at that time still used horses along with jeeps and scout cars. All this training of cavalry tactics was old hat to us, as we had gone through four years of that at NMMI, and we were good at it.

About half way through basic training, which lasted seventeen weeks, the army finally decided, much to the distress of the older officers at Fort Riley, that the horse was obsolete for modern warfare. Accordingly, the horse cavalry was dropped from the service immediately. Everyone then switched over from horses to what was termed mechanized cavalry, where we used jeeps and M-8 scout cars instead of horses to practice and be trained in cavalry tactics. These tactics still mainly involved scouting and reconnaissance of enemy forces to obtain information concerning their location, strength, and equipment, just as the horse cavalry had done for a hundred years.

At the end of this basic training period, we went on maneuvers, going from Clay City, Kansas, to Emporia, Kansas, about one hundred miles away, as if we were advancing into enemy territory. Emporia was a nice little town. Some of us were put on guard duty around the courthouse. I was on a corner, standing there with my rifle at parade rest when I heard a whistle to get my attention. I turned around, and an old boy had come out of a grocery store with his apron on. He threw me a great big apple. I put my gun down to catch it!

Three friends and Acting Corporals at age eighteen, Basic Training, Ft. Riley, Kansas. Left to right: Robert Dillman, Bob Green (center), and B.G. Cummins.

When we were finishing up our maneuvers, two jeep loads of us were assigned to guard a crossroad out in the boondocks. There was a big farmhouse on one corner, and we were there all night. Early the next morning, about daylight, this old gal comes out of the farmhouse and says, "You boys come on in the kitchen, and I'll fix you some breakfast." Someone said, "We can't leave this crossroad we're guarding." She answered, "Oh, just leave some boys there on guard, and the rest of you come on in." That seemed like a good idea, so half of us went in and she fixed us the biggest breakfast you ever saw. Then we went back and let the other guys go in and eat. During the war, people were always doing things like that for servicemen.

Because of our military proficiency, upon completion of basic training at Fort Riley, most of my class was again sent en masse to Fort Knox, Kentucky, near Louisville. The Armored School was located there, so soldiers could be trained to use and operate all kinds of tanks, which unlike the obsolete horse had now become one of the foremost weapons of the modern war being waged around the world. This was really much more serious training than the Fort Riley basic training had been.

Fort Knox was another big sprawling prewar post with 70,000–80,000 men stationed there, some to train and some to be trained as tankers. Within this post there was a special school that was used specifically to instruct and train future tank officers like us. It was called Armored Officers Candidate School or AOCS.

Former NMMI cadets in front of their barracks at Ft. Knox O.C.S., 1944. Left to right: Leslie Porter (deceased), B.G. Cummins (retired colonel, deceasedl), Bob Green (rancher), and Sam King (lives in a nursing home, now).

The first three or four weeks there were unbelievable. They tried to either kill us or run us off, and they did it deliberately to see how we would react under adverse conditions and under stress. Finally, they let us leave the post and gave us weekend passes to go to nearby Louisville. I had my brother Tom's car. When he had gone overseas he left his car in Wilmington, North Carolina. He sent me the garage check for the car and in the letter said, "If you want my car, go get it." Boy, I wanted it, so before I entered the army I rode the train over and brought it back to the ranch. After discovering that personal cars were allowed on base at Fort Knox, I got Tom's car from home and took it up there. It was a funny old car, a Buick. It had a tear-drop back. It didn't have a back seat, just a big space extending into the trunk compartment. We swiped a mattress out of a barracks and put it back there. Sometimes there would be ten or twelve guys crammed in that old car.

When we were finally allowed to go to Louisville, which was just twenty miles, we reacted like Coca-Cola does when the bottle is shaken up and suddenly opened. It was to be a big, big time for us. The towns we had visited near Fort Riley had been small ones and rather countrified, but *Louisville!* Now there was a real city! The Fort Knox scuttlebutt from members of the permanent cadre who served as our OCS instructors proclaimed the city was full of good looking girls who worked at Seagram's big distillery. Rumor had it that they were very friendly, lonesome, and seeking to have a good time on weekends. Our adolescent ears pricked up, and our minds reeled at such thoughts. We were advised by these old hands of what they considered the right way of doing the town.

They informed a rapt audience that Louisville had three big downtown hotels, and the proper way of doing the town was to visit these three hotels in sequence. They termed this as "running the obstacle course." That was done by visiting one hotel bar, ordering drinks and sitting for a while, seeing what action might develop. In the unlikely event that nothing transpired, we were to go on down the street to the bar of the second hotel. Then, if incredibly, there

was still no action, and we were still able, we should stagger on farther down the street to the third hotel. They sagely suggested to us neophytes that we go first to the Brown Hotel bar, which was considered to be the highest class one in town and where the top of the line girls would probably eagerly be awaiting our arrival. But, if there was a disappointing wait with no

Tom Green's Buick, which I went to Wilmington, NC to get after he shipped overseas. I took it back to Ft. Knox and kept it until I shipped overseas, too.

damsels appearing, we were to shift locations farther on down the street to the bar in the Kentucky Hotel. They considered the Kentucky Hotel to be middle class, but OK, and lastly, if we still hadn't succeeded in obtaining feminine companionship for the evening, we should make our way down the teeming sidewalks full of noisy soldiers to the old Seelbach Hotel, which was the rowdy one. They explained it had a big beer hall down in the basement where, as the evening passed, an explosive ambience usually kept building up until, invariably, something would trigger a spontaneous and violent, mass reaction.

Our eyes widened as we heard them describe how pandemonium would always follow, sweeping across the basement and through the crowd, accompanied by thrown beer bottles, chairs, and the like in what they told us could accurately only be called a riot. They solemnly averred that when that happened, those still sober enough to have their wits about them should immediately make a hasty exit out of the basement to avoid the inevitable appearance of the Military Police riot squad. Misbehaving soldiers were loaded up in their paddy wagons and hauled away to the Fort Knox Post Stockade. We were warned that if we took that ride in the paddy wagon, it would be the immediate termination of our career at OCS. All sorts of visions filled our imaginations. Some were erotic, but all were exciting as we awaited the day of our first weekend pass, which would allow us to leave the base.

At last, the day arrived. Right after lunch on a Saturday, we stood in line in the orderly room to obtain our meager monthly wages and receive our passes. Then, as many of the NMMI group as could, squeezed into Tom's old Buick, and we headed for the bright lights of Louisville. We all went in to the Brown Hotel bar to properly start the evening.

None of us were drinkers. We had drunk beer at Fort Riley in the PX's, but the state of Kansas was dry then for hard liquor. While growing up, I never saw any alcoholic beverage in our home, as my folks didn't drink at all, but we thought it was the thing for soldiers to do, so we got a menu of all the drinks. We started at the top of the menu, intending to work our way down. There was a whole row of us bellied up to the bar, trying hard to look as if we did this sort of thing all the time, but we didn't get very far down the list until some began to drop out. By the time we got down to the Zombies, we were pretty well finished off. I still remember that Zombie, but barely. It had five different colors of rum, or something, layered in the tall glass. With no success in finding girls, we left for the Kentucky Hotel bar, which was also a washout. Then we staggered on down to the old Seelbach beer-hall basement where, sure enough, a fight started, and we made a hasty exit in fear of the riot squad. We had managed to get only one room at the Kentucky Hotel for the weekend, so the evening of debauchery we had daydreamed about ended with about twenty of us sleeping on the floor, in the bath tub, and everywhere else.

Our advisors hadn't been entirely off the mark. During the war, it did occasionally get pretty wild on weekends in big towns like Louisville, when 80,000 soldiers would suddenly descend on the place looking for a good time. However, most soldiers in towns on weekend passes would usually just eat and drink, or maybe go to movies, dance halls or various honky-tonks. Sunday mornings would find many attending churches, as they had been raised in church-going families.

At the end of our weekend pass, we returned to Fort Knox, somewhat sadder and wiser, but feeling much more experienced. On the drive back, one known blowhard tried to convince everyone that he had experienced grand and glorious romantic success in being picked up and ravished by a visiting Hollywood starlet, but no one believed him. And now it was back to the old grind.

Officer Candidate School was truly tough. There was no fooling around, there. We had been sent to the school for another seventeen weeks of extremely intense training in the use of tanks, as well as being instructed on how to be a commissioned officer in the U.S. Army. There were about thirty-six of us from the NMMI class still together, and we had all been assigned to what they called OCS Class #66, which would consist of about 175 soldiers or "candidates." In this class, we were joined by boys from other military schools such as Culver, Kemper, the Citadel, Texas A&M, and also the University of Arkansas, as well as Army personnel selected for officer training from out of the ranks.

We found both the physical and mental training at OCS to be far more demanding than the Fort Riley basic training had been. Classroom courses were as rigorous as any we had ever attended, while the arduous training in the field was conducted in all kinds of weather. A great emphasis was placed on map reading. That course was held to be the hardest and was the most dreaded course of the school. It really was the downfall of many.

Fortunately, I had a natural affinity for map reading, but woe to those who didn't. Night assignments were the most complicated. We had to take turns being the leader of groups that attempted to navigate through the dark Kentucky hills following a prescribed course using only a prismatic compass, a map, and a few given coordinates. Within a few days following these harrowing problems, empty beds would appear in the barracks, indicating those who had failed in the task and been sent packing to God knows where.

Considerable time was spent on the Cedar Creek gunnery range, and that was my favorite part of the whole school program. This gunnery range was far out in the country on the big military reservation, and the landscape was surreal looking from all the deep ruts in the ground made by the tanks in wet weather. It was easy to imagine that the deep tracks winding about had been made by huge prehistoric animals. As the tank tracks were often filled with water, they rendered the terrain completely impassable for jeeps and other wheeled vehicles, but not the tracked weasels (a small track vehicle) and half-tracks. While at Cedar Creek, we lived in the Field of Tents, and it was a relief being away from the constant tension always present from the strict regimen in the barracks and classrooms. I found it to be really kind of fun—learning how to drive the tanks, firing the tank cannon at moving targets, practicing anti-aircraft defense by firing .50 caliber machine guns both at towed aerial targets and radio-controlled flying drones.

There was also an excellent, but noisy course in the use of demolitions. A shouted "fire in the hole!" was now added to our vocabulary and proudly used in all kinds of situations to warn others that immediate caution might be called for. However, its use was mainly to show that we now knew what it meant.

I still fondly recall an interesting thing that happened one day as we were returning to our red-brick barracks on the post proper after a stint spent on the Cedar Creek range. The whole class had been divided up into groups of ten or twelve, each group being assigned to ride in the open back of one of a long line of half-tracks. It had been a long ride in cold, drizzling rain and we were huddled over in misery, trying to stay warm. Just before reaching the main gate of Fort Knox proper, the convoy of half-tracks had to travel down the public highway for several miles. All of us riding in our half-track were suddenly roused from our lethargy by the insistent, loud honking of an automobile horn. Looking over the metal side, we beheld a rattling, old civilian car being driven dangerously close to our half-track by a big black-haired girl who was constantly turning her head back and forth in order to gauge her distance so she didn't run into our half-track. But what really caught our attention was a blowsy-looking blonde girl, perilously leaning halfway out of the front passenger side window of the car, loudly yelling and wildly waving her hands to attract our attention. We quickly noticed one of her hands was holding the neck of a brown bottle that could contain nothing but whiskey, and it was obvious she was offering this bottle to us. It only took an instant for her proffered gift to be accepted by a quick thinking—and acting—candidate who leaned far out over the side and retrieved it. With the successful transfer of the bottle, the black-haired driver really gunned it, which caused a black cloud of greasy smoke to shoot out of the exhaust pipe. As they roared on off down the highway, the blonde, still hanging dangerously out of the window, was vigorously throwing us kisses with both hands as we all waved and screamed our appreciation until they were out of sight. The soldier who had successfully taken the bottle from the girl now uncorked it, took a healthy slug and then passed it on to eager hands. It barely made it around the group before it was drained and discarded over the side. Had an empty whiskey bottle been found in the back of our half-track, we undoubtedly would all have been kicked out of OCS.

By the end of that seventeen-week training course, only about one hundred candidates remained in our OCS class due to the attrition from the very strict and grueling regimen. Every week some washed out for various reasons and were assigned to other places, many to the infantry which seemed always to need replacements. Those of us who lasted and successfully completed the course were now to be commissioned as second lieutenants in the U.S. Army. This was done at a ceremony much like a college graduation. I still recall with pleasure the last formation we had as OCS candidates.

We had formed up in front of our three-storied, red-brick barracks just as we had been doing for seventeen weeks, but this morning was to be different. As we stood in rigid formation, the big Fort Knox band, drums thumping and rattling, came marching up the street and, wheeling around in front of our formation, suddenly burst out with a rousing rendition of the "Col. Bogey March." Then it was off down the street with us marching along behind in proud formation. We marched to and entered a large auditorium where we were seated. After a speech by a general who congratulated us, we advanced up on the stage when our names were called out, and we shook the general's hand as we received our commission, which looked much like a diploma. Many boys had parents or girlfriends present who pinned the gold bars of the second lieutenant on their proud soldiers. Some even had their wives present. We who had no one took turns pinning them on each other. As we left the auditorium, a group of non-commissioned officers who had been our instructors in OCS were busy saluting us as we left the building. This was an old army custom whereby a newly commissioned officer had to give the first enlisted man who saluted him a dollar.

After this graduation, we strolled leisurely back to our barracks, enjoying our new status as officers. There, we found printed orders to new posts, and the NMMI group was scattered to the four winds. Six of us were sent to Camp Bowie near Brownwood, Texas, to take part in the final maneuvers of the 13th Armored Division, which was stationed there before it embarked overseas to Europe. We were primarily sent there in case any second lieutenant of the 13th Armored Division needed to be replaced before the division left for Europe. After two months, it turned out I was not needed as a replacement officer in that division, and as they left for Europe, I received orders to return to Fort Knox. There, I was assigned to be in a training company to instruct sullen inductees. I found it to be a very boring job. Most of the other officers in the training company were much older, married men, many with children, and they were desperate to avoid going overseas and, therefore, tickled to death to be doing such work. I found I didn't fit in with them too well and become pretty restless.

Fortunately, at Christmas time, I received a three-day pass. My sister, Mary Anna, with whom I had always enjoyed a very close relationship was living in Bay City, Michigan, with her husband, John Musselman, and their little son, Johnny, who was just beginning to walk. John was now a lieutenant in the Navy and was paymaster at the Bay City shipyard for the Naval personnel stationed there. Most of the older officers I was with now at Fort Knox were involved with their families for the Christmas holidays, and rather than just hanging around the post for Christmas, I decided to use the three-day pass to drive up to Michigan in Tom's old car to spend Christmas with my sister's family. That way I could at least be with some family members, even though it would be a long drive straight north from Fort Knox across Indiana and most of Michigan. Since I didn't get to leave until the training day was completed late in the afternoon, I had to travel all night through swirling snow, but arrived safely in Bay City at dawn on Christmas Day. For two days we had a

Three new shave-tail Second Lieutenants at Green Ranch. After completing OCS at Ft. Knox, KY, we were assigned to the 13th Armored Division at Camp Bowie, near Brownwood, TX. We went to the ranch at every opportunity. Left to right: Second Lieutenants Porter, Green, and King.

delightful time playing on toboggans with little Johnny. We transplanted Texans frolicked like otters in the deep snow, even if it was twenty degrees below zero.

With the typical poor planning of a nineteen year old, and because I was having such a good time, I overstayed my visit. The deadline I had set for leaving Bay City in order to get back to Fort Know in time for Reveille had long since passed. Finally, hours behind schedule, I loaded up in the car and started back south about sundown. I faced another all night drive, and the radio was giving out ominous weather warnings about a bad storm, even a blizzard, that was moving in off the Great Lakes. I soon discovered this weather forecast was all too accurate, for I hadn't gone very far when I encountered heavy snow that grew worse and worse. I had never seen anything like this blizzard! My progress slowed to the crawl of the snow plow, which I followed for mile after mile.

After several hours, I stopped in a small town and bought chains to put on the car. The local teenagers had created quite an ice skating rink on a vacant lot. They had flooded it with water, and it was now frozen solid. This rink was complete with colored lights strung across on wires and a booming nickelodeon that was under a small shed. The couples skated beautifully, and the swirling snow bothered them not at all. To a kid from the arid Southwest, it was an engrossing spectacle I had never seen before, and I tarried longer than I should have. At last, I forced myself to drive away and leave the pretty girls, colored lights, and juke box music. I knew I was never going to make Reveille at Fort Knox on time, so while driving I started considering what my older, grouchy company commander might consider a likely excuse for my being late. Blaming this blizzard seemed to me the most likely avenue to pursue, and the storm really was intensifying as I drove along. I marveled in innocent ignorance as it worsened, blithely oblivious to the very real danger of being stranded. There were no interstate highways then, just narrow roads with many abrupt turns. About three o'clock in the morning, somewhere in southern Michigan, the road turned, but the car and I did not.

We ended up far out in a snow-covered field, the snow piling up completely onto the hood of the car. It looked bad! It was bad! I had trouble getting the door open, but finally did and foundered back down the ruts the car had made to where the road had turned without us. I started trudging down the road the way I should have gone. Previous snowplows had banked the snow up on either side, so it was easy to follow the road, although the fresh snow was getting pretty deep. I had no idea where I was going. I remembered the countryside had been pretty thickly settled, so with the optimism of the youthful I felt something would turn up on down road, and on I walked.

It was, nevertheless, with great relief that before long I saw the bulk of a large farmhouse looming up by the side of the road and heard dogs barking. Turning in, I carried on a very friendly conversation with two large, shaggy dogs, and stepping up on the porch, I began to pound loudly on the front door. Today, anyone beating on a front door at such an hour would run the risk of being thought to be a drunken villain, but in that more law-abiding age, I really felt no fear of being shot as a brigand. Before long, lights appeared inside the house, and soon the front door opened. I beheld a room full of people in night clothes. It seemed the whole family was curious about who in the world was roaming around in the snowy night at this ungodly hour. The farmer and his wife had a very large family, and they were all up and peering avidly at me. I told them my plight, and the farmer rubbed a big hand over his head as he digested my tale of woe. At last, he told me to come on in and go thaw out in the kitchen while he and his eldest son got their tractor out of the barn and got my car back on the road. In those war-time days, nearly every family had someone in the service, and helping out servicemen was *de rigueur*.

The mother, a large, plain-looking woman in her robe and with her hair down for the night, led me back to the kitchen where she stoked up the coal-fired cook stove and started warming up leftover food from their Christmas dinner. Her efficient movements around the big, cast iron stove were so natural and easy that I wondered if she even knew she was doing them. Although my eating hadn't been mentioned, it evidently was taken for granted that I would do so, for before long a smoking plate of turkey and dressing was placed before me. I didn't argue or act like I wasn't hungry; I just started eating.

The mother started questioning me as to where I was from, and I told her I was from Texas and was raised on a cattle ranch. She smiled at hearing this, and the kids began to draw in closer around the table. They stared at the brass tank insignia on my lapels and blurted out questions. "What was it like riding in a tank?" "Did I really live on a ranch in Texas?" "Did I know a boy at Fort Knox named Kleber?" I answered their questions between bites, warming up in every way in this nice old farm kitchen.

Before I finished my third mountain of hot, gravy-covered dressing, lights flashed around outside, and the farmer and his young helper entered, stomping the snow off their boots and pulling off their heavy coats. They reported they had my car out of the field and on the road again just outside, and that it appeared to be alright. They had left it running so it would be warm for me. They said it was not snowing nearly as hard now, and it looked as if the worst of the storm might have passed. I slowly got up from the table, hating to leave this comfortable, plain kitchen, so full of warmth, good smells, and friendly humanity, to return to the cold, dark stormy night.

"Now you be careful, son," the mother said to me as she handed me a brown paper sack heavy with turkey sandwiches in the unlikely event that I might get hungry again soon. "We're losing enough of our boys in this war without losing any in a snow bank."

"Good luck to you, fellow," said the farmer, shaking my hand with his big, rough, callused one. "The roads will be better after you get to the Lansing cutoff.

The plows run all night down that way. Just try and drive like we have to up here, instead of like you do on your Texas plains."

I grinned at his gentle reproof and ended my profuse thanks by saying "I sure didn't have any idea that Yankees could be this nice!"

He looked at me sharply at this remark and then he said, "We are all one breed now, son. One and the same." I nodded in agreement and then turned and trudged out to the car. Putting it in gear, I drove out of their yard and their lives forever, but down through the years I have never forgotten their genuine kindness. The aura of that old farm kitchen and it inhabitants has retained its glow in my memory. I hope through the years that fate has dealt as kindly with them as they did with me on that snowy night.

When I finally drove in to Fort Knox, being late from my three-day pass was no longer an issue, as I had received orders to report to Fort Ord near Monterrey, California. I knew this meant going overseas to the Pacific Theater to fight the Japanese, which was all right with me.

I got to go home for two weeks-delay enroute—and when I left the ranch to go to California, my brother Bill and my dad drove me to Fort Worth, where I got on a plane for California at Meacham Field. In those days you had to have a priority to get on a plane. I was going overseas, so I had top priority, which surprised me. I bumped a full colonel and was he upset that he didn't get to go to California on the plane because this kid got his seat! That morning when I left the ranch, my poor mother wouldn't even get out of bed and tell me goodbye. She looked at me and then turned her face to the wall. She thought that was the last time she would ever see me.

When I flew to California, it was the first time since I entered the Army that I wasn't with anyone from NMMI, but there were two guys I knew from my OCS class—Jones and Lewis—from the University of Arkansas, so I hooked up with them. Friends came and went quickly as the Army moved you around.

At Fort Ord, there was yet another physical with multiple shots, this time for exotic diseases such as bubonic plague, yellow fever and cholera besides the usual ones for typhoid, tetanus, and smallpox. New clothes, boots, a new M-1 Carbine, along with a new duffel bag were issued, and in a few days I joined a group of new second lieutenants boarding a train and left Fort Ord with orders to report to Fort Lewis near Seattle, Washington.

We knew this was a port of embarkation for the Pacific Theater. Upon arrival, I found myself to be one of thirty new second lieutenants assigned to board a brand new Navy Destroyer Escort, or DE, that would go in convoy with eight other DEs to Pearl Harbor, Hawaii. Our new DE had just been made nearby at a Bellingham, Washington, shipyard and many of its crew members were just as new to ocean voyaging as we were. Our DE accommodations were crowded, with all of us in one compartment below deck. The narrow bunks were three high and, luckily, had a safety net you hooked up upon retiring so you would not fall out as the ship maneuvered. We found out later on that this net was essential.

The nine DEs left the Fort Lewis vicinity and headed out single file across Puget Sound and through the Juan De Fuca Strait toward the Pacific Ocean. We passed by Port Angelus and then cleared the entrance to Puget Sound where our convoy turned north. After a couple of days we were traveling in zigzag formation up toward the Aleutian Islands. The sea had now become very rough, and as a DE is not a very big ship, it did dip and dive and turn and twist. All we Army personnel got terribly seasick as did many of the new sailors.

South of Dutch Harbor, Alaska, a U.S. submarine appeared and joined up with the convoy of DEs. For several days the DEs practiced anti-submarine maneuvers with this American sub. This involved lots of zipping and turning around at high speeds by the DEs, which didn't help those of us suffering from seasickness one bit. Late in the evenings the sub surfaced and there was a long period of blinking messages sent back and forth between the DEs and the submarine. I guess they were rehashing the day's activities and planning for the next day, but we passengers were too sick to care what they were doing. I guess I got seasickness out of my system on this trip, for I never suffered from it again on the many other wartime trips at sea—not even during a couple of typhoons!

After about ten or eleven days the submarine disappeared. The sea had become much calmer and our seasickness had subsided. Then one day someone shouted "Land Ho!" We rushed out on deck and saw we were sailing past a large, pretty, green island. It turned out to be Molokai, the Hawaiian Island famous for having a leper colony. Soon other islands appeared in the distance, and before long the nine DEs curved around Diamond Head on Oahu and proceeded into Pearl Harbor single file, passing through the anti-submarine net which was pulled open for us by a tugboat.

We were big-eyed and solemn as we docked amid the wreckage and damage done by the Japanese attack of less than a year and a half before. It was sobering; for the first time, the war was more than a newspaper article or newsreel. The half-sunk ships, burned out buildings, and scars that Japanese bullets had made on the streets and sidewalks were true testimony that there really was a war.

Now we left the vomit-smelling quarters of the DE with little regret and loaded into the back of one of several army 6X6 trucks that were awaiting us on the dock. Soon we were driven out of the Pearl Harbor base, which was a very busy place with all kinds of ships coming or going or at anchor, and all kinds of air activity taking place at Hickam Field.

Before going overseas to the fighting, I found time to take a break on the lawn of this hotel located on the North Shore of Oahu, HI.

As we traveled north from Pearl Harbor in the open back of the truck, we looked with great interest at the passing countryside. The weather was nice, the fields of pineapples were something new, and everything was green and pretty. After about an hour's drive along winding roads and through several small towns, we arrived at a large military post called Schofield Barracks. This was an old pre-war post containing many brick barracks with stoops around quadrangles that reminded me of NMMI. But instead of the big, buff-colored brick barracks with red tiled roofs, which, like Pearl Harbor, still showed much damage that had been done during that infamous Japanese attack, we were assigned to billet in some small wooden barracks that had a sign reading "Transient Officers." Our little single-story board and batten barracks reminded me of the small oilfield pumpers' shacks at home we called "shotgun" houses. There were about a dozen or so of these buildings, with one used as a mess hall and one used as an "Officer's Club," where beer and liquor were available. Liquor cost fifteen cents a shot, and beer ten cents a bottle. There was a centrally located latrine and shower house, spartan but clean.

We soon discovered the sign that said "Transient Officers" referred to people like us, on the way out as replacements to where actual fighting was going on, as well as to people coming back from the far-off front. These returning veterans could be instantly identified by the lemon yellow color of their skin, due to the prolonged taking of Atabrine pills to prevent malaria. We didn't know it at the time, but in a few months our skin would be as yellow as theirs.

Most of the veteran personnel returning from the war zone appeared lean, leathery and very tired, but very, very happy to be eastern bound transient and not western bound, as we new arrivals were. It became apparent that the method of travel depended on your priority. Officers just returning to the states for some reason such as reassignment or maybe advanced training might be placed aboard a slow moving ship. With some surprise, we discovered that second lieutenants like us, slated to replace some poor wounded, injured, or dead soul in a line outfit that was actually fighting the Japanese, had the highest priority. They were flown out to the west on the first available transport plane, many of which were constantly shuttling from Pearl Harbor to the far-off battle front and back.

We discovered that these planes were four-engine models called C-54s and, at that time, they were considered to be very large, holding about forty to fifty people who sat in canvas seats. There were no frills to these planes. Everything was very sparse, requiring passengers to share their space with important cargo, such as blood plasma, or wooden crates of hand grenades or mortar shells that might be temporarily in short supply. On their return trip, they mostly brought back the badly wounded. Unlike today's jets, a C-54 had to land periodically for refueling in order to fly across the vast Pacific Ocean west of Hawaii.

We soon received orders and were trucked back to Pearl Harbor and Hickam Field on Ford Island, where about forty of us boarded a C-54, and off we went, westward. After several hours of flight, we landed on Johnson Island for our first fuel stop. Johnson Island was a tiny dot, just big enough for a landing strip, several large, steel fuel-storage tanks, and some tin Quonset huts where personnel lived. It looked like a poor place to be stationed. The old boys assigned there had just about lost their minds from the solitude of the place, and it was pitiful how they wanted to talk to someone like us, just out from the states. After refueling, we were off again. There were green army blankets available, and many of us rolled up in them on the floor and slept as the C-54 droned on westward through the night. At that age, I could sleep anywhere, anytime.

By dawn's early light we landed on Kwajalein, a small atoll in the Marshall Islands. The U.S. Marines had taken it a few months before. Evidence of the fierce fight to take the island was everywhere. All the palm trees were just blackened stubs, craters from bombs and naval shells pocketed the whole area, and Jap concrete bunkers were blasted open and blackened by flame-throwers.

It was a sobering sight. After refueling, we were on our way to Guam, in the Marianas Islands, which our forces had recaptured shortly after Kwajalein. A final refueling stop at Guam, and we took off on the last leg of our journey westward from Pearl Harbor to Tacloban, on the island of Leyte in the Philippines, where a shooting war was actually taking place right then.

Chapter 3

THE PHILIPPINES
AND SHERMAN TANKS

*"Many cities of men he saw and learned their minds,
many pains he suffered, heartsick on the open sea."*

The Odyssey

Leyte, Philippine Island near Tacloban
8 March 1945

Dear Mother,

Well, had a very nice trip…. It's pretty hot here, hotter than it was on Oahu but we have a nice sea breeze blowing thru the tent so do pretty well. Jones didn't come with me so I'm all alone now, much to my displeasure. I have already been assigned and am in a crack tank outfit that has had plenty of experience. I felt like a trainee all over again. Most of these guys have been overseas longer than I've been in the army, but I wouldn't trade places with anybody now—though I'll probably be singing a different tune later on….

All the natives here seem to be a pretty happy bunch. They live in the littlest houses I ever saw, and everybody from grandma to baby have some kind of G.I. clothing on. I've seen several water buffaloes, and everything is about what you would expect the place to be like. From the air the jungles look just like a big lawn, they are so dense. A woman tried to sell me a chicken about the size of a canary yesterday, but I wasn't quite set up well enough to fry a chicken at the time. They make a good profit doing laundry for the G.I.'s, though some are offended if you try to pay them.

There is a major in my outfit from Stephenville so we hit it off very well. Hope everyone is OK. I am fine.

Lots of love,
Bob

Leyte—near Tacloban
14 March 1945

Dear Mother,

This is the wettest country I ever saw. It rains all the time, and the tent leaks like a shower bath. It just slows the rain down a little but never stops it. I sleep in a poncho every night.

We have two monkeys here who get into everything. They are a lot of fun, but cause lots of trouble too. They eat everything including tooth paste, soap, cigars, and erasers.

The roads around here are like ours were Christmas, only a little worse. They lay coconut tree logs down and cover them with dirt over the worse places.

The natives use everything we throw away. They use the wing tanks for gasoline from airplanes to make boats out of and the whole jungle looks like a junk yard as they build houses with barrels, packing cases and what not.

Haven't had any mail yet but it should catch up pretty soon. Haven't seen Jones yet, but he is here. They put him in the Infantry which is a pretty rough deal over here.

Send me something to eat. There is no place we can get it over here. Hard candy would be good or anything like that. This is about the first place I've been where I couldn't eat when I got ready.

The ocean practically got in our tent last night. It usually is about fifty yards away but it got to about ten yards last night.

Saw Irving Berlin the other night in a USO show, and it was pretty good.

I haven't had much to do since I've been here, as they are just letting me get acquainted with the way they do things here in contrast to the way they do them in the states, and there is a world of difference.

I hadn't realized just how far I was from home until I saw a map of the world. Even Tokyo is closer than where I am, and Tokyo used to seem just about the fartherest away you could get, but all in all there is a little difference being here or in the middle of the Kentucky hills—you're still away from home.

Well, had better stop.

Lots of love,

Bob

After another long, boring period of flight, someone said, "Look down there." Hastily looking out the window, we saw we were no longer flying over water, but over a solid mass of greenery that from the air looked exactly like a lush, green lawn, but in reality was the solid-appearing tops of the trees of a dense, tropical forest. Soon we circled around and landed on a steel-mesh landing mat that our Seabees had placed over the (formerly) Japanese airstrips at Tacloban, Leyte, Philippine Island. When the door of the plane opened, the hot, muggy, smelly air of Asia rushed in. The odor was somewhat like a sewer, and the sun was very bright and hot.

After thirty-three flying hours from Pearl Harbor, we were stiff, dog-tired, and somewhat apprehensive as we gathered our new duffel bags, new musette bags and new carbines, then jerkily disembarked from the plane. The whole area was a mess. There were many wrecked Japanese planes and a few badly damaged American navy planes that had been pushed off away from the runway by Seabee bulldozers. A wrecked Japanese tank and several Japanese trucks in disrepair had also been shoved out of the way to make room for the many American fuel trucks, jeeps and anti-aircraft gun positions. Many American navy planes of various kinds were being rearmed and refueled. It was a very busy place.

Filipinos of all sexes and ages were everywhere, as were water buffaloes and mangy looking dogs. The town of Tacloban could be seen a short distance away. Other than a few masonry buildings, it consisted mainly of fragile-looking shacks and didn't look very prosperous. All the roads were unpaved, deeply rutted and muddy. Some of the worst mud holes were covered with logs and steel landing mat sections, and many had water buffalo and pigs lying in the mire.

After a roll call on the air strip by an officious staff sergeant carrying a clipboard, we were directed to climb with our gear into the back of a couple of army 6X6 trucks. Then off we went down a terrible road that led south out of Tacloban, following the coast. The tents of various rear echelon army support outfits were pitched all up and down both sides of the road, along with sprawling big supply dumps, fuel dumps, field hospitals and the like. There were identifying arrows and signs of all these different units placed along the road we were traveling, which was evidently the main drag of Leyte Island. Traffic was heavy. Anti-aircraft guns were prominent and manned.

The always present army rumors, spreading thick and fast, were passed along by the truck driver, who told us about the fighting that was still going on down at the south end of Leyte, where we were headed. According to the truck driver, there were air raids every night. Japanese paratroopers had recently leaped and descended from a formation of thirty-eight Betty bombers and had come down near a small airstrip we were presently passing. Although most of the Japanese paratroopers had been killed, there still were some lurking in the jungle, "over there right now." Everyone eyed the thick jungle with misgivings. We greenhorns were really being filled up with the BS by the veteran who had only preceded us by a month or so on Leyte. Regardless, it was none the less exciting to hear and think that we might actually be subject to a Jap air raid at nightfall.

We now entered a tremendous grove of very tall coconut trees aligned in straight rows that stretched clear out of sight in every direction. The all-knowing truck driver said it was French owned, or had been. The trees were full of coconuts, and I saw several monkeys scampering about.

At last we arrived at a group of tents with a sign and arrow saying "Replacement Depot," and there we stopped. The tail gates were lowered, and we thirty new second lieutenants, tired, disheveled and wondering what lay in store for us next, unloaded with our gear. We entered a large squad tent that sported a sign that said, "Headquarters." Inside were several desks, people typing, file cabinets, a large array of radio equipment, and all the amenities of the rear echelon staffed by soldiers. These non-combatant soldiers were much scorned and maligned, or really, perhaps in truth, envied by the front line soldiers actually shooting and being shot at, killing and being killed just down the road.

Another roll call from a massive, heavyset, old master sergeant, who then proceeded to read off several names and said, "You are now assigned to 96th Infantry Division, please stand over here." He then read off another bunch of names and announced that they were now assigned to the 7th Infantry Division and directed them to stand together in another area. This group included David Paul Jones, the University of Arkansas football star and my friend from my OCS class. After these two assignments were sorted off, there were only two of us left—Jack Lewis, also from the University of Arkansas and my OCS class, and me. The master sergeant then said, "Lieutenants Green and Lewis are assigned to Twentieth Armored Group." The two large groups immediately and vigorously started objecting that there must be a mistake. They weren't infantry trained, but had had various other training in a variety of branches other than the infantry, such as, in Jones' case, armored, another in running a quartermaster laundry, and so on. While they were loudly arguing their case and protesting being assigned to the infantry, a tall, lank corporal approached Lewis and me and said he had been sent to pick up whoever was assigned to Twentieth Armored Group. He had a jeep outside.

While Lewis and I received our new written orders to place in our 201 file, the corporal loaded up our gear. We waved a farewell to a distraught-looking David Jones as we left the tent full of unhappy second lieutenants still loudly complaining to the stone faced, imperturbable master sergeant. We climbed into the jeep, and the corporal drove rapidly on south down the road through the towering coconut trees.

Lewis and I now exchanged incredulous remarks about what had just happened to all the others in the group we had been traveling with—how they had all been assigned to become infantry officers and how lucky we were to avoid that fate. The driver laconically offered his view that the line infantry outfits were always short of second lieutenant platoon leaders because even though during combat all American troops were dressed alike, the Jap snipers were well trained in picking officers out by observing their actions and shooting them first. Anytime a watching Jap sniper saw an American soldier looking through binoculars or pointing or obviously directing another soldier, he was very likely to be considered an officer and shot. So line platoon leaders' life expectancy was not good, and due to this rapid turnover, replacements were always needed. Later on, in the battle for Okinawa, I found that to be very true.

We drove on down the road and passed through a little coastal town named Tanuan. Here there were signs of a fierce bombardment. Our driver was a good tour guide and informed us that from Tanuan on down the coast south six or seven miles at a town named Dulag was where the 96th and 7th Infantry Divisions had come ashore when Leyte was invaded by our forces.

The navy had bombarded all up and down these beaches before our troops had landed. This was also the area where General Douglas MacArthur had waded ashore and declared, "I have returned." The driver now pointed to a high hill he called "Catmon Hill" that was just inland and said the 96th Division had had a hell of a time taking it as the Japs were dug in all over it. We looked at it with respect. Now he told us that the fighting was about over on Leyte. What fighting was still going on was being done by heavily armed American patrols assisted by Filipino guerrilla fighters. These guerrillas harbored a fierce hatred for the Japanese, and with good reason, for the Japanese had abused the Filipinos something terrible. The guerrillas were very eager to help and really provided valuable assistance in this mopping-up, as they had complete knowledge of the terrain where the Japanese were now trying to hide out. This clean-up was going on several miles west and north of our present position.

We turned off the main road at a sign saying "20th Armored Group," with an arrow pointing the way off into the trees. Soon we came to a clearing with several tents and the driver stopped before one and said, "Here we are." It didn't look like much, a few jeeps and trucks but no tanks in sight. In fact, there was no ordinance of any kind to be seen. There were some dug slit trenches between the tents, but no anti-aircraft guns or machine gun emplacements.

Lewis and I entered the tent that had "Headquarters" printed on a sign in front of it. We handed our orders to a first lieutenant seated at a desk who scanned them. Then he informed us that 20th Armored Group was just a clearing house, so to speak, that took care of all official correspondence for over a dozen tank battalions known as "bastard" tank battalions that were in the Pacific Theater. Unlike Europe where tank battalions belonged to whole armored divisions and were used en masse in sweeping panzer-like operations that might swiftly cover miles, the Pacific style of tank fighting was to use tanks as mobile pill boxes in close support of infantry. As a rule, a tank battalion was attached to an infantry division and as it turned out, both Lewis and I had been assigned by 20th Armored Group to the 763rd Tank Battalion, and it was attached to the 96th Infantry Division.

The officer now informed us that we were to spend the night here at 20th Armored Group and transportation to the 763rd Tank Battalion would be furnished the next morning. He said that there was usually a nightly air raid or two, but most of the time the actual bombing would take place at Tacloban or on the concentration of navy ships off shore in Leyte Gulf. At any rate, we were welcome to use any of the slit trenches between the tents if, by chance, bombs were dropped nearby. We listened to him bleary-eyed, so tired we really didn't care about the possibility of being blown up and only wanted to go to bed. It had been a long trip from Hawaii.

Once in a tent, on canvas cots with a mosquito net, deep sleep came quickly. I only dimly remember awakening far in the night to what sounded like thunder and then realizing it was anti-aircraft gunfire. Distant explosions were heard as well as the whistling sounds made by anti-aircraft shell fragments falling down out of the sky, like steel rain plopping on the ground around our tent.

I thought the far away sound of an aircraft flying high overhead actually did have a different engine sound from ours, or at least it seemed to me that it did, but maybe that was just my imagination. "Washing machine Charlie" was the name the old Leyte hands called this Japanese plane the next morning at breakfast as we ate our powdered eggs. They said he was a nightly visitor, coming from one of the still Japanese-occupied islands a short flying distance to the west, but they didn't seem to be too concerned about him.

Since the battle for Leyte Island was about finished, elements of the 763rd Tank Battalion were returning to a bivouac on the coast to prepare for the next sortie against the Japanese. Lewis and I were driven the next morning to this bivouac, which was nearby and right on the beach. We reported in to a friendly first lieutenant named Murphy, who was acting as adjutant. He greeted us warmly, shook our hands and gave us our new orders.

Lewis was now assigned to C Company, and I was assigned to A Company. We carefully placed the orders in our 201 File. A 201 File was like an abstract for land, only instead of tracing and connecting all the previous transactions that led to the present ownership, your personal 201 File contained copies of all the army orders that had been issued to you. Filed chronologically, these previous army orders that had attached or assigned you to different units during your service was the history of where you had been in the army.

Lieutenant Murphy then gave us a rundown on the history of the 763rd Tank Battalion. It had taken a very active role in the battle for Leyte as they assisted the 96th Infantry. The 763rd had started out as the 193rd Tank Battalion, a Colorado National Guard Unit, before the war. Immediately after the attack on Pearl Harbor, a frantic War Department called up all National Guard units to active duty. They were fearful the Japanese might attempt to invade the Hawaiian Islands. So they rushed some National Guard units there as quickly as possible, one of these being the Colorado National Guard 193rd Tank Battalion. This unit was greatly under-manned, and since there was no Japanese invasion, a new full strength medium tank battalion was formed on Oahu around the nucleus of the old 193rd National Guard Unit in March

1942. The reformed unit was given the name of 763rd Tank Battalion. Original members of the old National Guard unit had been overseas, away from homes and families from these earliest days of the war. Those that survived had put in nearly four years overseas when the war ended and were understandably among the first soldiers allowed to return to the states.

Lieutenant Murphy handed us a large paperback book that had "Top Secret" in big red letters on the cover above the title, "Operation Iceberg." It was as big as a Sears and Roebuck Catalog, He told us to study it because it told what we and the 763rd Tank Battalion were going to be doing in the very near future. Then, for the first time in my life, I heard about an island only 350 miles south of the Japanese home islands. Okinawa.

Following proper army protocol for newly assigned officers, we reported in to the commanding officer of the tank battalion, Lt. Col. Harmon Edmondson. He was a tall, somewhat taciturn man who seemed preoccupied. He gave us a perfunctory welcome and then dismissed us. The much friendlier Lieutenant Murphy took us in tow and explained that orders for Operation Iceberg had already been received, and a crash program was in effect to get the battalion ready to load up and leave in less than a month. Hence the colonel's preoccupation.

Lewis now left to join C Company, while I was assigned to help Lieutenant Murphy do whatever he was doing. It turned out that was a pretty simple job, as he was an easy-going kind of guy. We were engaged in packing up all the office equipment and official correspondence in big, trunk-like containers to take aboard ship for the upcoming Operation Iceberg. While we worked, he told me all about how he had been shot in the head while leading a platoon of tanks when they first came ashore on Leyte. In order to see better, he stuck his head up out of his tank. He was shot in the face just to one side of his right nostril by a sniper. The bullet had gone completely through his head, beneath his brain, but had missed all the essential parts of his cranium.

He proudly showed me the steel helmet he had been wearing when he was shot. The medics had saved it for him. After the bullet passed through his head, it failed to penetrate the backside of his helmet where it was now still embedded solidly. He had just returned to duty from a hospital and no longer acted as a platoon leader but as the adjutant for A Company. I was to assist him until further notice. I was glad of that, for I enjoyed working with him.

I found it was kind of reassuring to be around snorting, roaring Sherman tanks again, and they were everywhere. The model of the Sherman tanks used by the 763rd on Leyte was the M4A3. Lewis and I had trained in this model at Fort Knox, so we were very familiar with it. Until 1940, the U.S. Army's development had been woefully behind that of European countries, particularly Germany and Russia. The swift defeat of France by Hitler's swift moving Panzers prodded the U.S. military into recognizing they needed to quickly modernize their armored force to keep pace with President Roosevelt's plans for the country to come to the aid of England.

With the nation's excellent automobile, farm equipment and locomotive factories, along with a vigorous steel industry, plans were quickly made for turning out a newly designed series of tanks for our armored force. This operation was soon highly successful in producing a great quantity of tanks, but we never really did catch up, design-wise, with the quality of tanks produced by both Germany and Russia. Our tankers who fought in Europe were always forced to compete with the far superior German Panther and Tiger tanks that had much thicker armor and were armed with better cannons, such as their high velocity 75s and 88s, which had far more range and power of penetration.

But the Shermans could be mass produced, and over 49,234 were produced by the U.S. during World War II. This was a greater number of tanks than was produced by both Germany and England combined during that war. Shermans were relatively small and light to facilitate overseas shipments. They were also faster, much more mechanically dependable, and easier to repair than their competitors. The complete air supremacy we enjoyed over the Germans late in the war let our air force help out our tankers in their battles with the superior German armor. The U.S. P-47s and British Typhoon fighter planes equipped with rockets and cannons were efficient antitank weapons and dealt the Panzers much misery.

The first M4 Sherman rolled off the production line in February 1942, with the tank engines being a major problem. The M4A1 models were powered by Wright-Continental Whirlwind radial aircraft engines. As these motors were in great demand at the time for aircraft, diesel engines were tried in the new tanks. They were soon discontinued when the Quartermaster Corps complained about the logistic problem of handling and transporting two different types of fuel.

Next, four Chrysler engines were mated together, but this was never too satisfactory, and, finally, the Ford 500 Horse power GAA V-8 engine was developed and used in the M4A3 model. This was a good tank engine and was what the 763rd Tank Battalion was equipped with. These M4A3 medium tanks weighed thirty tons, had armor plate from one-and-a-half to three inches thick, and a crew of five men.

The driver was located in the left front hull, the assistant driver/bow machine gunner, called the bog, sat in the right front hull, and there were three men in the fighting compartment basket suspended in the turret. The tank commander stood in the right rear of the turret, the gunner sat immediately in front of him, and the loader sat on the left side of the turret.

There were five entrances or hatches in the tank model we had. The driver and bog each had a hatch in front of the turret, there were two hatches on top of the turret and an escape hatch was in the floor just behind the bog's seat. There was also a very small hatch, called a pistol port, in the left side of the turret near the loader's seat. We used it mainly to eject empty, brass cannon shells to get them off the floor and out of the way.

The turret could be traversed, or turned, 360 degrees by the gunner or the tank commander, who each had a traversing lever. The gunner also had manual control wheels, one for elevation and one for making the fine traversing adjustments he used when aiming the guns. The turret was turned by an electric/hydraulic motor, and it did so relatively quickly. It was far speedier traversing than either German or Russian tanks, many of their turrets having to be cranked around by hand.

The tanks of the 763rd were armed with the M-3 75mm cannon. This cannon had a relatively low velocity, but since Japan had no armored force to speak of at that time, there were no tank duels in the Pacific as there were in Europe. The model M-3 75mm gun we had was considered to be better for infantry support against enemy emplacements than some of the higher velocity anti-tank weapons used in the European Theater.

Our tanks also had two .30 caliber air cooled Browning Machine guns, one in a ball mount in front of the bog and another mounted coaxially in the turret with the cannon. Coaxially meant that the machine gun and cannon were mounted side by side and were aligned in the same plane. Up to a range of about 500 to 600 yards, when properly sighted in, bullets firing from the machine gun and a round fired from the cannon would hit right in the same place. Every fifth round fired from the machine gun was called a "tracer" and left a bright red streak through the air. That allowed you to visually adjust where the bullets were striking. The bullets from the coaxial machine gun could be "walked" onto a target by watching and making adjustment to the gun according to where the tracers were striking. When they were hitting right where you wanted them to, then the cannon could be fired and its round would explode right there in exactly the same spot. It was very accurate.

There was also a .50 caliber machine gun mounted on the turret top behind the tank commander's hatch. This gun was mainly for anti-aircraft defense, but, if used, the gunner was exposed from the waist up when manning it. As this would have been deadly to the gunner because of Japanese snipers, most of the time the .50 caliber machine gun was left off the top to avoid having it battered by Japanese machine gun fire.

Around 100 rounds of cannon ammunition were stowed, along with metal cans of belted machine gun ammunition, in every nook and cranny of the insides of the tank. Ten or twelve rounds for the cannon were placed vertically in what was called a "ready rack," which curved around the inside back wall of the fighting compartment cage just behind the breech of the cannon. This "ready rack" was kept full because the rounds were easily available for the loader when rapid fire was called for. Other cannon rounds were stored in the "sponsons," as the two interior sides of the hull were called. The greatest number of cannon rounds were located underneath the floor of the turret cage. A section of the steel flooring could be lifted up and the turret revolved so as to recover all of them when needed.

We carried three types of cannon ammunition. These three types of shells had their noses painted different colors for quick identification. Armor piercing or AP had the nose painted black. High explosives or HE noses were yellow, while white phosphorous or "Willie Pete" noses were painted blue. The white phosphorous shells were mainly used for smoke screens. All this stored ammunition became a deadly fire danger that led to the Shermans having a bad reputation for blowing up if struck by anti-tank gunfire.

There was a small gasoline-powered generator in the left sponson that was called, for some reason I never understood, a "Little Joe." This generator was started and used to keep the batteries fully charged up when the tank stayed in one position for a long time with the engine turned off to conserve fuel. As tanks got only about a mile and a half to the gallon of gas, fuel consumption had to be taken into serious consideration. Every hatch except the escape hatch in the floor had a periscope through which you could look outside when the tank was "buttoned up." These periscopes could be swiveled 360 degrees to try and see about, but even so, when buttoned up, vision was limited and poor at best. Some of the very latest models, of which we had very few, had a ring of bullet proof glass segments in a complete circle just below the tank commander's hatch, and that was a big improvement in allowing safe outside vision when buttoned up. These particular tanks were highly sought after.

All five crew members wore leather helmets that contained earphones and throat mikes. The tank commander could talk to crew members on an intercom system, or, by flicking a switch, to other tanks. As the tank platoon leader did most of the talking, he used a larger, hand-held microphone which transmitted more clearly than did the throat mikes. The large radio was in the upper rear part of the turret, and by pushing buttons the tank platoon leader could talk or listen in to various other units connected into his radio "net."

Communication by radio between tanks was constant and of extreme importance when we were trying to engage the dug-in enemy. A platoon leader was almost constantly on the radio to the tanks in his command, getting them located where he wanted them so they could afford mutual protection for each other and particularly for the flame-throwing tanks when they moved up front to saturate with napalm some strong point of the dug-in Japanese.

Radio talking procedure was supposed to follow strict rules but in the heat of battle, it soon deteriorated with exchanges between tanks becoming short, obscene messages, such as "Green, this is Dial [tank commander of another tank] look out for that blankity-blank Jap behind that blankity-blank rock wall to your f-----g left." Or, "Oh, Goddamnit to hell, George just hit a Goddamn, mother f-----g mine!"

One day an official message came down through channels from the higher-ups for us to try and clean up our radio procedure. They could tune in our channel and listen in on our transmissions from headquarters behind the lines. But no one in the tanks at the front paid it any attention. Our attitude was if they wanted the communication between the tanks cleaned up, they could come up to the front, get in the blankity-blank things themselves and see how long it took them to forget to talk nicely to each other.

The radio call-signs prefix for our tanks to use on Okinawa were selected from the names of animals in the movies. A Company's call sign prefix was Flicka. Other companies call signs were Lassie, Rin-Tin-Tin, Cheeta, Silver, etc. The tanks also had large white numbers painted on the sides of the turret for identification. My first tank had the number "20," and its radio call sign was Flicka Two Zero. Before great losses of tanks to the enemy, a platoon normally would have five tanks, so the platoon leader's call sign was Flicka Two Zero and the other four tanks in the platoon consecutively numbered Flicka Two-One, Flicka Two-Two, and so on, but heavy losses soon ruined this neat method. The maintenance crews tried to repaint numbers to make the replacement tank's number fit.

At the beginning of the battle, some tanks had names painted on them whose first letter was the same as the company they belonged to, such as an A Company tank having "Alley Brat" or some such name starting with "A" painted on it. The flame-throwing tanks of the 713th tank battalion that worked with us had radio call signs that instantly identified them, such as "Zippo One-Six" or "Ronson Two-Two," or "Vulcan One-Three." As the battle increased in intensity and tank losses mounted, such things as cute names were very soon forgotten. Nevertheless, the phonetic alphabet remained strictly in use. Able for A, then Baker, Charlie, Dog , Easy, Fox, George, and so forth on through the whole alphabet to Zebra for Z.

Tanks were noisy, rough riding, and uncomfortable, but usually those inside them were much safer in comparison to our infantrymen on the outside who were exposed to every piece or shard of flying metal or bullet that came by. Casualties among armored personnel in the Pacific Theater were nothing as high as those suffered by the infantry. There were excellent battalion maintenance and armorers who kept the tanks and guns in good condition. Far back behind the lines, there was backup maintenance division that handled the more serious problems. They were equipped with big tank recovery vehicles and many of the knocked out tanks were repaired and returned to service

1. Driver's seat
2. Steering tillers
3. Gear shift lever
4. .30 caliber machine gun ammunition
5. Hull gunner's seat
6. Commander blade sights
7. Sighting periscope
8. Periscope
9. Turret gunner's seat
10. Commander's seat
11. Radio operator/loader's seat
12. Radio
13. Fuel tank
14. Auxiliary generator

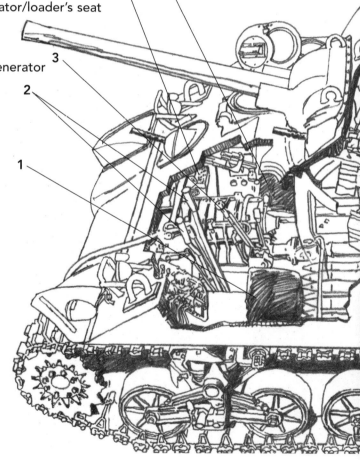

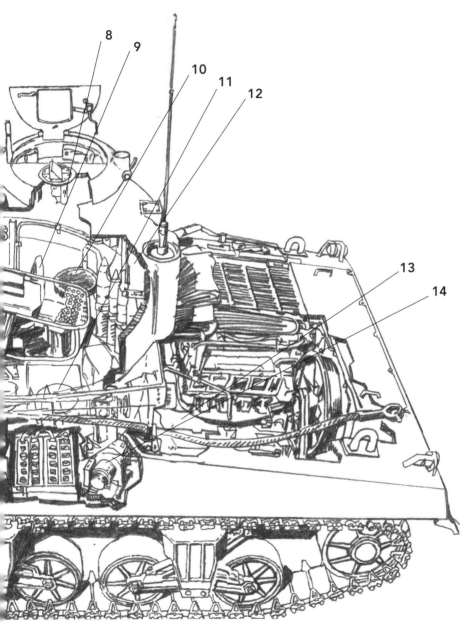

Illustration by Charles Shaw

Interior view of a Sherman tank.

Upper deck of a loaded LST. Tanks were confined to the lower deck, not shown here.

Chapter 4

SUZY-Q AND LSTs

"The ship sped on her way through the watches of the night from dark till dawn."

The Odyssey

One afternoon when I finished work with Lieutenant Murphy, I was taking a walk down the beach and came upon a group of Filipino boys grouped around a small, dark, round object sticking up out of the sand. As the waves came in, they would wash over and completely cover the object, and the boys would leap around and scream with laughter. My curiosity aroused, I walked over to the group to see what was so funny. I discovered they had buried a very small monkey up to its chin in the wet sand and were delightedly watching the waves wash back and forth over the sad little face.

As I had always been an animal lover, this situation made me very uncomfortable. Before I knew it, I had made the native youths understand that I wanted to trade for the little, embedded monkey. In the end, I walked back to camp with a sneezing little ape about the size of a can of beer, but minus my olive-drab fatigue jacket, the ransom I had paid to free her. I had no idea at the time how attached I would become to this little creature. For almost two years, she became my inseparable companion.

Back at camp, a helpful supply sergeant assisted me in making a small harness for her that had to be fastened with brads as her little fingers could untie, unfasten or undo anything. A length of cotton rope attached to the harness allowed me to tie her to the nearest banana tree, plenty of which were everywhere. When hungry, she simply helped herself to a banana. It soon came out, however, that what she really preferred to eat was a big helping of reconstituted powdered eggs—something the army seemed to have laid in a huge supply of for the boys overseas. Everyone hated powdered eggs, maybe even worse than Spam. She was possibly the only one on Leyte, or maybe the whole Pacific Theater, that thought they were good, and she thrived on a diet of them.

She grew rapidly, although her particular species of monkey, even when mature, never did get very big. A big old, A Company maintenance sergeant who came from a farm was also an animal lover and quickly became enamored of the little monkey and she of him. She was funny. Some people she liked and some she wouldn't have a thing to do with. I still wonder what her criterion for judging people consisted of, but whatever it was, it really was pretty good. She liked this old boy, though, and he offered to keep her with him in his maintenance half-track if it ever became necessary. Some of his fun-loving friends now declared that the little monkey's facial characteristics were the spitting image of the girl's picture this old sergeant had pasted up inside his half-track. Across the bottom of the picture was scrawled the words, "Much love from Suzy-Q." Immediatedly they started calling the little monkey "Suzy-Q," and she learned very quickly to recognize her name.

The old sergeant took it all good naturedly and began to call her Susy himself. Later, on board the LST and then on Okinawa when I was engaged in combat, I took him up on his offer to take care of her when it was impossible for me to do so. But the immediate problem for me was how to get her on board the LST when we loaded, and rumor had that happening very soon.

I was worried about a communiqué I had seen in the office from the navy. It said, in no uncertain terms, that absolutely no pets were to be brought aboard the LSTs. I discussed this dilemma with a somewhat laid-back medical officer in the outfit, and he suggested giving the little monkey a small shot from a morphine styrette to knock her out. Then I could simply put her in my musette bag—a small canvas bag with a shoulder strap officers could carry things in— and take her aboard.

A morphine styrette was a small, toothpaste-like tube containing morphine, which could be injected by a needle attached to the end of the tube. The needle was covered with a protecting cap. They were used to sedate the wounded by removing the cap, jabbing the needle in an arm or leg and squeezing. Every tank carried a supply, as did the medics. I asked the doctor if he would help me sedate the monkey when the time came and he said he would.

Over the next few weeks, with the exception of a few combat patrols still mopping up the remnants of Japanese on Leyte, all the other U.S. Army units on the island were busy as ants—packing, crating up, and palleting all kinds of their equipment in preparation for Operation Iceberg. Now the word was that the LSTs we were to ride on were going to come right up on the beach just down the road from our camp to load up the 763rd Tank Battalion.

This time, at least, the rumor was true, for sure enough one day we were surprised to see several large LSTs had pulled up on the shore near our camp. Now, feverish loading began, and a snappy looking ensign with a bull horn came out onto the ramp of the LST we were getting ready to board. "Attention!" he roared over the bullhorn. "Absolutely no pets of any kind will be brought on board!" He repeated this loud order several times to a disinterested looking bunch of army people lined up in vehicles on the beach in preparation to load.

I looked up my medical friend, and we got ready to prepare my monkey for boarding. "How much does she weigh?" he asked.

"Oh, I don't know. Not much," I replied.

"Well, we will just play this by ear and give her just a little bit," he said. I held the monkey while he jabbed her and administered the morphine.
"How long before it takes effect?" I asked.

"Oh, not very long. She's pretty tiny," he answered. We watched her closely. Soon she began grinding her teeth, and her eyes crossed. "I believe it's starting to work," he said, and I agreed and opened up my musette bag, put her down into it, closed the flap, and put the carrying strap over my shoulder.

I was walking across the beach toward the ramp of the LST when I heard a sharp whistle and looked back. The medical officer was pointing urgently at the musette bag, and I glanced down and saw that the little monkey was holding up the flap with one arm and peering out at the world. I quickly pulled the flap down and returned to the doctor. This time he gave her quite a jolt. "That would sedate a full grown man," he muttered. "I hope it doesn't kill her." It didn't kill her but it never did put her completely out either. But she did quit holding up the flap and just sat inside the bag grinding her teeth like crazy.

I was one of the later ones to board, and before long the LST raised up the ramp, closed the two big front doors, and backed off the beach. The 763rd Tank Battalion had now completely loaded up on several LSTs, which now one at a time, backed off the beach into deep water and wallowed out into Leyte Gulf to join a huge convoy of ships.

I was assigned to a tiny, strangely shaped compartment at the front of the ship near the big, front doors. It was just big enough for one narrow bunk and a little space to stand up in at one end. There was an oval opening in the steel wall into this cubicle, but no door. I discovered that the old time officers of the 763rd were assigned to much nicer staterooms that had double bunks, a lavatory, small desk and a closet, but those quarters were not for newly arrived replacement second lieutenants. Later on, after serving my apprenticeship, I did get to stay in those better quarters several times as we toured the Pacific *a la* LST.

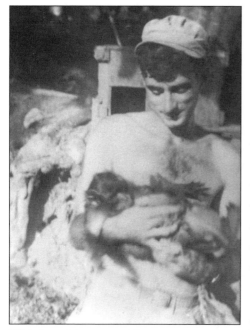

This is Suzy-Q in my arms. She was my companion for nearly two years, until she was killed by a truck in Manila.

Although LSTs had quarters with bunks in narrow spaces along each side of the tank deck for the enlisted men, if the weather was good the enlisted men slept anywhere and everywhere. I looked up the animal-loving maintenance sergeant who was in his half-track up on the upper deck. He gladly took the still slightly sedated little monkey, which I fished out of the musette bag, and handed to him. "I'll take good care of her," he promised. "We'll stay right here in this old half-track. I've got a good bed made up in the back."

The next morning, dawn found us far out at sea. It also found aboard our LST, dogs barking, goats baaing, roosters crowing, parrots squawking and a sizable troop of monkeys frolicking about the densely packed upper deck. So, dream on, navy! The 763rd wasn't about to leave their little friends behind. It seemed no one had taken very seriously the young ensigns admonition about no pets being brought aboard. The captain of the LST was wise enough to see that a hard-line approach with this heavily armed, tough looking bunch might start a worse war with them than with the Japanese. After all, it was going to be a short trip anyway, so nothing further was done concerning the stowaway pets which were a source of enjoyment for so many.

LSTs were unique ships. They had a system of ballast tanks that could be filled or emptied with seawater to raise or lower different parts of the vessel. When coming in to land on a beach, rear ballast tanks were filled to lower the stern and make the front ride higher. This usually allowed the ship's front end to actually reach the shore and let troops and equipment disembark quickly onto land. The LST also had two big cat-head winches on either side of the stern deck. When coming in close to a shore, before landing, two anchors could be dropped into the sea. These were attached to cables that the cat-head winches on the stern would later wind up, and by doing so, pull against the embedded anchors out behind and help get the loaded vessel back off the beach into deep water. When possible, loaded LSTs tried to pull off a beach at high tide which would also help in getting them out to deep water.

There were also two large smoke generators on the stern that could be used to create dense clouds of smoke for a smoke screen. These smoke generators were soon to be used often on Okinawa by the many LSTs lined up like cars in a parking lot on Hagushi beaches. Collectively, the beached LSTs could produce quite a cloud of smoke for hiding from Japanese planes. The LST had two huge front doors that, when closed, formed the prow of the vessel. Upon reaching a beach, the doors were opened and a ramp lowered down, much like a drawbridge, onto the sand.

Tanks, because of their weight, were carried in the lowest deck, called the tank deck. They were driven in one at a time, up the ramp and into the tank deck, where they were turned around so as to be facing forward for unloading, and then crammed together so close you could barely walk between them. They were secured to the deck by chains and fasteners to prevent any movement during rough seas. They were full of gas and ammunition, ready to charge out of the ship and engage the enemy. After the tanks were loaded in the bottom hole, another longer ramp was lowered from the top deck. It was cleated and at a slant that was slight enough so that loaded trucks, half-tracks and jeeps, many pulling loaded trailers, were able to climb up to the open, top deck and be positioned and secured there for the trip.

When fully loaded, the LST was literally jammed to the rails with men and equipment. This loading might appear harum-scarum, but it wasn't. Each vehicle was numbered and assigned a place by the loading officer who had used a blue-print-like plan of the LST decks, as well as scale-sized cardboard templates of the various vehicles. These templates were positioned onto the blueprint to fit closely to each other and avoid wasted space. Each vehicle was then given a number to be chalked on the side. When the process was completed, all vehicles and equipment to be loaded were lined up on the beach according to their large chalked-on number that allowed them to load in the proper sequence according to how the loading officer had figured it out. It was American ingenuity at work, and it really functioned very well. After Okinawa, I was a loading officer myself in the Philippine Islands, and somewhere still have the LST blueprint and templates I used and brought back home when I returned from overseas.

After feverish loading, we were off to Okinawa, joining up with a huge convoy of ships. Everywhere you looked there were ships. Of course I didn't have any idea at the time of the enormity of Operation Iceberg. One of the largest armadas in history was assembled for the invasion. 182,000 American troops—75,000 more than landed on D-Day in Normandy—embarked for the invasion. There were more than forty aircraft carriers, eighteen battleships, two hundred destroyers, and hundreds of transports, minesweepers, gunboats, landing ships and crafts, along with a multitude of repair and supply vessels. Task Force 51, the advance navy strike force, had 1,213 ships alone. Before Okinawa was declared secured, over 548,000 U.S. servicemen were involved in Operation Iceberg.

The 1,350-mile trip from Leyte to Okinawa took eight days for our LST, which was an average of only one hundred seventy miles a day, or only between seven and eight miles an hour for the heavily loaded ship.

Along with the other army officers on board, I got to eat in the wardroom with the navy officers. After meals, we could stay in the wardroom all day if we wanted to, which many did. A rather large room with tables and chairs for eating, and sofas and lounge chairs for relaxation, it was strictly officer country. Coffee was constantly available due to the presence of a large Silex coffee urn along with a big stack of clean coffee cups. A tattered selection of magazines, along with an assortment of the small-size editions of paperback books, specially printed for the Armed Services, were stacked about. I must confess I pocketed several of these books and kept them with me for many later re-readings. My favorite, which I still have, is titled *We Pointed Them North* by Teddy Blue and is about trail driving cattle and cowboys, which I liked to read because it reminded me of my ranch home in Texas.

Except at meal times, dominos and poker games were always being played on the tables in the wardroom, as were bridge and other card games such as acey-ducey, pinochle, black jack and the like. Mess boys served all the meals in the officers' mess. They were all Filipinos. The food was excellent and eaten off china plates with silverware.

The army enlisted men slept in those long narrow bunk spaces and ate with the seamen in a mess near the stern, adjacent to the galley. Fully loaded, an LST was one crowded ship. Many army men preferred to sleep topside if the weather was pleasant, mainly due to a strong belief that if the ship were suddenly sunk, you would have a better chance of surviving on the open deck than if you were below. There were many large, rectangular life rafts that were loosely retained in brackets that would allow them to simply float free if the ship went down. The sight of them was somewhat reassuring. Also, every man on the ship was issued some kind of life preserver that had to be kept up with.

General Quarters, or GQ, was the call to battle stations for all navy personnel aboard. GQ alarms were given by the blast of a bugle call, ringing bells, loud buzzers, and a strident voice calling out loudly over the sound system, "GQ! GQ!" This took place every sunrise and sunset. The navy reasoning had it that sunrise and sunset were supposed to be the most likely times for a submarine or air craft attack. When a GQ alert came over the loud speakers, the navy crewmen of the LST all simply raced to their battle stations in different parts of the ship. Some of them manned the anti-aircraft guns while quickly donning life jackets and steel helmets.

Our LST was armed with several twin 40mm Bofors automatic cannons mounted in round gun tubs in various places about the ship, as well as a bunch of 20mm machine guns mounted all along the sides of the upper deck. These guns were mainly for defense against aircraft. When all the guns were firing, they could put up a pretty good screen of bullets, as there were maybe six or seven twin Bofors and perhaps as many as twenty 20mm guns, all automatic and capable of sustained fire.

Since the kamikazes had first appeared at Leyte, the navy was very apprehensive of these suicide planes and with good reason, as was discovered at Okinawa. They were often deadly for us. GQ calls didn't concern us army personnel very much. We were just along for the ride and tried to stay out of the way of the racing, scurrying sailors as they hurried to their battle stations. Also, during a GQ alert, all watertight doors were slammed shut and dogged down, so movement throughout the vessel was limited until recall from GQ was given, usually in only ten or fifteen minutes. No one got very alarmed at these routine GQ calls, but an unexpected GQ, now that was something else, and usually meant real trouble was brewing from air attack or submarine.

At night the ship would be completely blacked out with heavy black curtains covering all outside doors and openings. Smoking was allowed only at certain times and places. During daylight, specified hours for smoking on the upper deck were made known by a droning voice that repeated over and over on the ubiquitous sound system, "Now hear this! The smoking lamp is lit on all outside weather decks."

Another much repeated daily order over the sound system, which I always got a kick out of hearing, was the one that came periodically and imperiously demanded, "Now hear this! Sweepers, man your brooms! Clean sweep fore and aft! Clean all scuppers and passageways—clean all such and such," and on and on it would go with lengthy detailed instructions to the bored looking sailors on how to tidy up the ship.

Most sea-going LSTs, such as we were on, were a little longer than a football field and about fifty feet wide. They were powered by two 900-horse power diesel engines and capable of making eight or nine knots when fully loaded, which we most definitely were.

A normal LST crew was usually eight to twelve officers and two-hundred-ten to -twenty seamen, but this would vary with different circumstances. Often there were extra special-duty officers on board going somewhere on assignment. Sometimes, there might be another much smaller complete tank-carrying ship loaded onto the upper deck of an LST. These smaller ships were called LCTs (Landing Craft Tank) and could carry five tanks for short distances. They only had a crew of one or two officers and eight or ten seamen. They could be placed only on the open top deck of an LST by the large crane in the Pearl Harbor Navy Base or in large shipyards in the U.S. Upon arrival in the war-zone islands, where they were mainly used for inter-island transport, they were unloaded by the LST flooding its ballast tanks on one side to cause it to list over far enough to allow the LCT to slide off the greased, large timbers it rested on and into the water with a mighty splash. I was amazed the first time I witnessed this dumping-off of an LCT from an LST upper deck, but after seeing it done several times I realized it was a fairly common practice. I still wonder who had the nerve to try it the first time.

The atmosphere on an LST, combat-loaded and headed for an invasion of enemy-held territory where coming to grips with the enemy was a certainty, was somewhat heady and exciting, especially for novices on their first invasion, like I was. The feeling was somewhat like I remembered it had been on a bus carrying our football team to the big game. Older veterans of previous campaigns were full of advice and admonitions about fighting the Japanese. They always had a rapt audience around them.

So there was tension in the air among the fighting men crowded on board as the LST plowed along. Many older men could be seen off to themselves, leaning on the rail and looking reflectively eastward toward homes and families thousands of miles away. The younger ones, trying hard to look fiercely eager, sharpened bayonets and bowie knives or cleaned weapons, and secretly worried about what it was going to be like, killing an enemy before he killed you.

The navy personnel, both crewmen and officers of the LST, tried to be accommodating to the army personnel they were transporting to battle, knowing many of them soon would face death or injury at the hands of our nation's enemy. I still remember with pleasure this respect shown by the naval personnel toward us. It was a nice feeling of solidarity and shared patriotism that I have never forgotten. Just a short time before, practically all of us, army and navy alike, had been mere civilians living in all parts of the United States. Now we were all involved together as citizen soldiers or sailors in an incredibly complex and dangerous operation clear on the other side of the world against an implacable enemy. It was almost unbelievable.

As we sailed farther northward and got nearer to Japan, at night we began to occasionally be able to pick up the faint radio broadcasts of Tokyo Rose on the wardroom radio. The last few nights aboard, as we neared Okinawa, she came in very loud and clear. She played good, current American big band music, but it was somewhat disconcerting to hear her chide, "You boys going to Okinawa are sure going to be sor-r-ry!" She might have been right about that for many of us, as it turned out.

Photograph courtesy U.S. Coast Guard

This is how Corporal Stone, my radioman, and I climbed down a cargo net to board the control boat going to Hagushi Beach on L-Day. Luckily, there was no Japanese opposition to the landing.

Chapter 5

HAGUSHI BEACH AND THE TOMB-CAMP

"That night we rested, and nursed our anger—for Jove was hatching mischief against us."

The Odyssey

[Hagushi Beach—near Kadena Okinawa]
5 April 1945

Dear Mother,

I've just had dinner. Roast pig. We chased him for about 2 hours this morning and it looked doubtful as to which would give out first, the pig or us. I killed and butchered him, as I was the only one who had even seen it done. I would say it was rather a crude job but eatable.

We got here Easter Sunday early. I stood on the bridge at dawn watching big V's of our planes go in and blast the beach while battleships lay right offshore and threw broadsides into the whole place. It was quite a sight. About ten minutes before H hour, LCIs let go their rocket barrage which really messed things up. There were ships everywhere and of all kinds. The Japs had pulled back from the beach to escape the landing fire of the warships so there was little resistance at the beach. We moved on in about three to five miles the first day without much trouble. Had an air raid that night but the navy night fighters really tore into them. About five got through to the ships. Those navy flyers are really doing a fine job. There wasn't a Jap plane in the sky all day.

We are just laying around now doing bunk fatigue. Our household is some Jap ancestor's tomb. There are tombs all over this island, as the people worship the dead. (There should be a big boom in their religion after we leave.) Anyhow, it's not these Japs lying around here in these fancy urns that I'm worried about. I'll be sharing one of those urns with them if we have many more air attacks from their descendants, as that is a regular bomb proof shelter. These tombs look like a big horseshoe lying on the side of a hill and are the most notable thing about the island.

We found a civilian in a cave yesterday. The people have been living in caves since we started bombing them so extensively. We were prowling around and saw him stick his head up from behind a pile of baskets. We threw hand grenades fast and furious for about twenty minutes and succeeded in wounding one of our own men, but somehow missed the cave. The man was impressed by our display, as he came out and surrendered. He was healthy looking and pretty well fed it seemed.

The last letter I've had was dated February 15 so I ought to get lots of new [ones] when the mail finally gets here. At the rate we're going now the next letter will be from Tokyo.

Well, had better stop. I am feeling fine. Hope everything is alright at home.

> Lots of love,
> Bob

Okinawa
April 8, 1945

Dear Mother,

Things are going along nicely here. It is so much colder here than Leyte that we all have a cold, including the monkey. It gets real cold here at night. I sleep under three blankets and I wish I had more. The Japs are getting more planes thru at night and they keep us awake a lot but all in all we have been fairly well off from raids, as we are well protected.

The island is very pretty, what is left I mean. It must have really been pretty before the war. All the houses are either thatch construction or of limestone and coral. The latter are really nice with their red tile roofs, up turned corners, sliding panels and so on. The one railroad was a dinky affair, being horse drawn and very narrow gauge. Their farms are all terraced affairs and they have good crops of cabbage, tea, rice, beans, peanuts, wheat and oats all in a little plat about the size of our garden. The roads were cobblestone, and they have a big two-wheel cart pulled by one horse as their only transportation. Their pigs are sway-backed affairs but fat and healthy. We ought to know. The one we ate was almost too healthy, as we chased him for miles. I saw a bunch of the natives in a camp and they are clean, dignified and seem to be intelligent. A lot higher class people than the Filipinos. The women wear kimonos, beautiful silk things, and wear their hair in a knot. The men are short and look like any Jap. These people are not true Japanese, and the Japs consider them inferior, as they do everyone else, but the Okinawans consider themselves Japanese and resent the attitude of the other Japs.

The amount of lead that is slung into the air when a Jap comes over is terrific. All the ships, beach defenses, tanks, and individuals for miles around open up and tracers light up the whole country. It's quite a sight, especially at night.

No mail yet, but we are expecting it every day. It will probably be a good while yet though, I suppose. It's been nearly two months since I've had a letter.

I sure hope you are all alright. I am fine. With Russia at outs with Japan this war should end up pretty quick.

Write a lot. I'll get them some day.

        Lots of love,

        Bob

Finally, the trip was over, and we arrived off the west coast of Okinawa on Easter Sunday, the first of April 1945, April Fool's Day and all.

GQ came blasting out over the sound system at three A.M. but most GIs were already up, packing up their gear. There was certainly an air of expectation and nervous tension as the call to breakfast came, and what a breakfast it was! Steak and eggs—not powdered eggs, but real eggs—all you wanted! The shipboard doctors shook their heads at such folly, thinking of having to treat abdominal ailments in the near future. There were also many black, sick jokes bantered around at the breakfast table about the condemned's last meal or of being fattened up for the kill and so on. This attempt at humor seemed somewhat in poor taste and the forced-sounding laughter was short and rueful.

After breakfast, the packing up of all personal gear was completed and the duffel bags, which had the name of whomever they belonged to stenciled on the sides in big black letters, were put aboard various designated vehicles that would take it all ashore. In the early morning darkness, our tank-laden ship began to slowly circle with many other craft to await the dim pre-dawn light before going in to land in its prescribed place on the Hagushi Beach. Now, time was hanging heavy as we waited, fully dressed and equipped for battle. Word was passed over the sound system that religious services would be held immediately below in the tank deck for anyone wishing to attend.

It seemed many were interested in doing this as a large group soon had gathered in the heaving, dimly lit steel cavern filled with the hulking tanks. Their motors hadn't been started yet, so the air was still clear. (Soon, when all the tank engines were started, it would be hard to breathe in the tank deck before the exhaust fans were started up and the front doors opened.) It may have been an incongruous setting for a religious service, but few have ever been more fervently attended.

After brief sermons and prayers of reassurance given by both Catholic and Protestant chaplains, a trunk-like case was opened up to reveal a small but complete GI, olive-drab-colored pump organ. It soon became apparent that we had an organ but no organist. After a long pause, when no one else volunteered to play, I hesitantly said I might try pumping out a few hymns, but they would have to be only in the key of "C" as I played strictly by ear and couldn't read music. After another pause, it appeared that mine was the best offer that was forthcoming, and one of the chaplains invited me to give it a try.

Paperback hymnals were passed out while I sat down on a stool and pumped up pressure with my feet and began to play. The noises being made by the moving ship of war were now joined by the reedy sounds of the little organ as I began to play the hymn, "Holy, Holy, Holy." The singing was enthusiastically led by one of the chaplains who knew all the words by heart and sang very loudly. It was pretty disjointed at first, but improved rapidly. We did "Holy, Holy, Holy" again, and it sounded pretty good the second time around. "Early in the morning," our song was rising just like the words of the hymn.

Sailors and gear-laden soldiers, many carrying guns, heard the singing. Curious, they drifted in, and then, surprisingly, most took a hymnal and joined in singing. It was a pretty tough looking choir. Before long it began to sound like a Baptist camp-meeting was going on down in the tank deck as we moved on and loudly rendered with real feeling, "Oh God our help in ages past, our hope for years to come" followed by "Leaning on the Everlasting Arm." Then someone suggested "You've Got to Walk That Lonesome Valley," and even though it was not in the hymnal, it was such a hit, we sang it twice. "Onward Christian Soldiers," "Rock of Ages," "Fairest Lord Jesus," and "I Need Thee Every Hour" followed—along with any other old, simple hymn that I knew the tune to, could play, and whose words happened to be in the paperback GI Hymnal. But before long, word came that we were preparing to land and everyone should go to their assigned places on the ship.

Now those watching on the upper deck could just make out a dim line low down on the eastern horizon. That was the island of Okinawa where the Japanese were awaiting our arrival. To end up, we sang that old hymn of parting, "God Be With You till We Meet Again," and I swear there weren't many dry eyes in the whole tank deck when we finished. The meeting broke up somewhat emotionally with everyone vigorously shaking hands, slapping each other on the back, and issuing fervent wishes to each other for "Good Luck! Good Luck!" Indeed, after all these many years, I still can get a little emotional thinking about it. It's a memory I will take with me to the grave.

After our religious service ended in the tank deck, they began starting up the tanks. I hurried top side to the starboard side of the LST where Corporal Stone, an enlisted man from A Company, was waiting with a SCR–300 radio slung on his back like a field pack. I had been assigned by Lieutenant Colonel Edmondson, the Commanding Officer of the 763rd Tank Battalion, to take a radio man and go ashore with the 1st Battalion of the 383rd Regiment of the 96th Infantry Division. 763rd tanks, which were carried in several LSTs, were slated to support this infantry unit if and when they were safely ashore. Colonel Edmondson had briefed me in detail about my mission the day before. Upon reaching the beach, I was to find and report to Lieutenant Colonel King, who was in command of the 1st Battalion of the 383rd Infantry Regiment of the 96th Division.

Once I made contact with Lieutenant Colonel King, I was to discover what his intentions and needs were. I was then to contact Lieutenant Colonel Edmondson back here on this LST by way of the radio we were taking with us and keep him informed as to the situation on shore. I was also to relay any messages that might be forthcoming from Lieutenant Colonel King to Lieutenant Colonel Edmondson. This close communication between the infantry and tanks was thought necessary to coordinate their actions. The SCR–300 radio, which weighed about forty pounds, was equipped with crystals specifically assigned to be used by only the 763rd Tank Battalion. The various infantry units had their own radio networks that were on different channels specifically assigned to them. So, serving as what the military called "a liaison" officer, I was to be the go-between for these two small components of our gigantic army.

A control boat had been ordered earlier to pick me and my radioman up off this LST at the proper time and take us in to the beach where I could meet up with Lieutenant Colonel King. Control boats were really pretty small, about the size of some of the larger recreational boats I had seen on big Texas lakes. They had been unloaded off large ships in the early morning, and their name came from their function, which was to help line up and "control" the long line of Amtrac and Landing Ship Vehicle Personnel, or LSVP, that were now forming up to move in to the beach. When fully in place, the line of LSVPs and Amtracs that comprised the first wave for the landing of U.S. forces on the Hagushi beaches of Okinawa was an unbelievable eight miles long. Amtracs were amphibious tracked vehicles used to ferry troops from ships to shore. After reaching the beach, they could continue traveling inland, unlike the LSVPs which were strictly nautical.

The control boats were periodically spaced out at intervals in this line. By using pennants, semaphore flags, and blinker light signals, they tried to "control" and keep the line straight and its speed adjusted. There were several trouble-shooting control boats racing around to handle any unexpected problems that might arise. Now, one of these trouble-shooter control boats had pulled along side our LST. After its coxswain conferred with the officer in charge of the deck of the LST, he waved my radio man and me into action. We clambered down a cargo net that had been lowered down the side of the LST and managed to get into the bobbing control boat. After we were aboard, it sped away to join up on the end of a long line of LSVPs, which were carrying elements of the 1st Battalion of the 383rd Infantry Regiment toward the shore.

The beaches were still being bombarded by all sorts of naval ships. Destroyers, cruisers and big battleships were all just blasting away and rocket-firing Landing Craft Infantry, or LCIs, really caused a spectacular sight as literally scores of their big rockets flashed and roared off their decks in a slanting barrage toward shore. Soon the barrage lifted and a huge wave of navy planes zoomed over us at low level and strafed both the beach and the land behind with withering gun fire.

The control boat we were on now joined the long line of LSVPs in moving in to the beach and soon grounded on the shore. Ramps dropped down from the front of the LSVPs, and infantrymen sprinted out through the shallow water to shore. The coxswain of our little boat hollered to me, "You get off here. This is as far as I'm going." I waved my arm in answer and helped Stone, with the ungainly radio on his back, to get over the side where we dropped down into waist deep water and hurried ashore as the control boat backed out seaward and sped away.

"Where the hell is Colonel King?" I wondered, as I looked at the hundreds of GIs rushing inland under the lashing commands of their officers and non-coms. So far as I could tell, there had not been a shot fired at us from any enemy as we turned and followed the infantrymen while they pushed on inland through holes that had been blown in a masonry seawall.

Soon the infantrymen began to form a perimeter line some several hundred yards inland, and there I saw what appeared to be a group of important looking officers intently studying a map. I quickly approached this group and asked a captain if Colonel King were around. He nodded his head toward a very nervous looking lieutenant colonel, who was looking wildly from his map to the country side and then back to his map again. I walked over and said, "Colonel King, I'm the liaison officer for the 763rd Tank Battalion and was told to report to you when I reached the beach."

He wheeled on me in apparent fury and said through clenched teeth, as if I might be the cause of whatever the problem might be, "They put us ashore in the wrong Goddamned place! We're on the wrong f-----g beach! Don't you bother me now!" Turning his back on me, he wheeled around to join a huddle of other worried looking officers, all pointing in different directions and referring to their map.

I had recoiled at this unexpected reception from Lieutenant Colonel King and stayed back out of the way. After I continued to be completely ignored for quite a while, I shrugged at Stone and got on the radio. I reported to Col. Edmondson, who was still on the LST, that the 1st Battalion of the 383rd Regiment thought they were in the wrong place and that they now seemed to be getting ready to move somewhere else and that Lieutenant Colonel King was too occupied to talk to me and what should I do?

After a long static-filled pause, he finally replied, "I have that information about them now and yes, they are in the wrong place. We're going to put their tanks ashore some other place. They won't need them until they get straightened out. I'm just not sure where the other place is right now so you just come on up north ...." and here the transmission ended as the radio gave out a belch of sound and went dead.

After many futile attempts to re-establish contact, Stone finally said the obvious. "It's quit working." Then he added laconically, "I guess it got wet when we got off the control boat. I kind of fell down once."

So there we were, armed only with two puny carbines and a radio that no longer worked, afoot on a hostile shore. Of

Photograph courtesy U.S. Army
Scene of Hagushi Beach on L-Day, April 1, 1945.

course, it wasn't like we were alone. There were literally hundreds of armed-to-the-teeth soldiers rushing all about us with many more on the way. Since the last thing I had heard on the radio was the words "you just come on up north," I motioned to Stone to come on and started to trudge north up the beach that was rapidly becoming a mad house of activity.

Soon Stone began to complain about carrying the non-working radio. "We better keep it a while in case it dries out and starts working," I said. I began to be very worried about being a liaison officer without a working radio and every now and then, we stopped walking to try it with no luck. It remained as dead as the proverbial door nail. Now we had come to a stretch of beach where many Amtracs had come ashore leaving deep tracks in the sand. Looking inland, we could see the Amtracs still moving that direction, followed by hordes of our infantry. No Sherman tanks were in sight, however. I didn't know what to do. Without the radio, we were completely out of touch with our outfit.

Now, many more LSTs began to come ashore, opening up their big doors and dropping their ramps. They began disgorging all kinds of vehicles, men, and material. The beach was getting very crowded with LSTs. All at once, far to the north, a plane came zooming along headed south down the beach at a fairly low level. It was obvious to me that it was one of our own Navy Wildcat fighters, but it evidently wasn't obvious to gunners on many of the beached LSTs. Some gunner far down the line started shooting, and then, as the plane proceeded down the beach, everybody did. A tremendous fusillade of anti-aircraft fire from the beached LSTs now followed the plane. The pilot began to wildly wave his wings up and down to better show his insignia and that he was a friendly. His efforts were to no avail, however, for no plane could survive long in that hail of bullets and down he went. He crashed nearby us on the shore in flames.

We watched in stunned amazement as now some of the beached ships continued to fire on this plane, even after it had crashed. Even more incredible was when some of the ship-board gunners traversed their guns to follow the plane down. Their streams of bullets tore through the upper-rigging, funnels, and higher super structures on some of their neighboring ships. It was total chaos. Later on in the day, we saw two more of our planes shot down by friendly fire while flying down the landing zone of the beach. One of these crashed into the sea, but the other one, an SBD, made a nice belly-landing on land nearby us, and as the pilot and rear gunner were hurriedly getting out of the smoking plane, some idiots on the ships were still firing at them. We heard later that the air-space over the beach had been designated as a "flash red" condition, which meant to fire on anything that flew over,

Photograph courtesy U.S. Army
Aerial view of Hagushi Beach showing Amtracs advancing inland.

but this information came from a navy officer and might have been an excuse for the trigger happy sailors. Evidently the hapless pilots were not aware of this "Situation Flash Red" condition, and they were certainly navy themselves, but *c'est le guerre.*

The real question was, however, where were the Japanese? There still was no resistance of any kind, although it appeared there were bunkers and gun emplacements on a rise of ground a little farther inland. Our Amtracs and infantry had already passed them by without stopping, so they must have been empty. These Amtracs would soon be replaced by Sherman tanks. Then the Amtracs would return to the beach and be used in ferrying more support troops, equipment and supplies of all kind from ships off shore to the beach.

In the first hour of the invasion, over sixteen thousand troops were safely ashore without meeting any opposition. Before nightfall, there would be over sixty thousand ashore, along with a great quantity of artillery, tanks, and anti-aircraft guns behind an arc of a beachhead twelve miles long and a few miles deep. Engineers had unloaded bulldozers, and they were making more openings through the sea wall that paralleled the water front. This sea wall was made of masonry and in some places was as high as ten feet, but it had not been much of an obstacle for the U.S. invaders because of all the holes that had been blown in it.

Photograph courtesy U.S. Army

The 96th Division Infantrymen coming ashore at Hagushi Beach.

Stone and I continued to walk northward, agog at all the frenzied activity that seemed to increase the farther we went. All at once, Stone cried out, "Looky there!" Up ahead Sherman tanks were rapidly coming ashore from an LST that carried 763rd tanks. As happy as I was at that sight, I was even happier to see Lieutenant Murphy with some other headquarters people standing in a group watching the tanks come out of the tank deck. Lieutenant Murphy greeted me warmly and after hearing my tale of woe, to my great relief, told me that Colonel Edmondson had instructed him to watch out for me and take Stone and me inland with him to wherever headquarters would be situated.

That sounded good to me and for the first time in several hours I began to relax. I had been afraid that I might be in trouble for not fulfilling my mission with Lieutenant Colonel King. Late that evening, we loaded up in some jeeps that came off the LST, left the beach, and drove inland.

We passed by several of the peculiar horseshoe shaped tombs in which the Okinawan people buried their dead. They were very old and one of the more significant things about the island. Some of the larger ones had low-walled courtyards in the front of the tomb itself, which was usually built into the side of a hill. There was a small, square opening at front center that had a closely fitting stone door opening into the actual tomb. Inside, on several stepped-up ledges, were large crockery jars that contained the bones of long dead Okinawans. The interiors of these tombs could be fairly spacious, large enough for several people to move around in although the ceilings were low, preventing you from standing erect.

We didn't know it at the time, but over the next three months, these tombs would be utilized by all the different varieties of human beings on the island. Many Okinawan civilians had already used them as bomb shelters during our pre-invasion bombardment, while the Japanese soldiers had turned many of them into redoubts for machine guns and mortars. American soldiers would soon place a high value on them as a refuge from Japanese artillery and mortar fire. Lieutenant Murphy now decided to make one temporary headquarters. He got on the radio to see if that was OK with Lieutenant Colonel Edmonson, who was up ahead with the advancing tanks. He replied over the radio that it would be fine with him, so we pulled in and started unloading gear to set up housekeeping.

This housekeeping was to be in the courtyard of a big tomb built into the side of a rise of ground. We opened the tomb and, peering inside, made sure there were no Japs hiding in it. We found nothing alive in there, just big ceramic jars that were as big as one of our stoneware churns at home. There were thirty-five or forty of these jars and each contained human bones that had been carefully cleaned and stored away. Each jar contained more than one set of bones, many of them yellowed and very old. The jars had intricate designs on them and were very beautiful. They were aligned on three steps or tiers inside the tomb

Photograph courtesy U.S. Army
Lyre-shaped tomb, used by Okinawans for burial of the dead. We spent the first few nights in the courtyard of a similar tomb.

proper. The courtyard in front of the big horseshoe-shaped tomb had a low rock wall enclosing an area about forty feet square, which gave some protection. That was where Lieutenant Murphy had decided to establish temporary headquarters.

We were inland about one and one half miles or so, very near a big Japanese air base called Kadena, which the troops of the 7th Division had overrun earlier in the day. There was a nice looking set of farm buildings nearby. The main house was built of rock, with a tiled roof that had turned-up corners. This house had been badly damaged by our bombardment, but hadn't burned. There were sheds and out buildings connected by rock walls to the damaged main house, and a well was in the center courtyard of the complex.

These farmhouses were very old, some as much as 250 to 300 years. Many had stayed in the same family all down through the centuries. We had learned this from the briefings held aboard ship that described the island and its history, as well as warned us about a very venomous snake called a Habu. I never saw a Habu while on Okinawa, but some of the city boys were more afraid of confronting one of them than they were the Japs. It seemed to me very likely that there was a connection between the big tomb where we had chosen to become squatters and the complex of nearby farm buildings. I was of the opinion then, and still am today, that the same family had possessed and used both the tomb and the farm. You could tell the fields and gardens around them had been carefully tended before our arrival, but now all was in disarray.

Lieutenant Murphy thought the farm buildings should be searched before dark to make sure Japanese soldiers weren't hiding in them. I took three well-armed men and carefully approached and entered the house. The interior was in shambles, but it obviously had been pretty nice at one time. Sliding panels, now askew, had once divided the house into rooms. The floor was covered with straw *tatami* mats, but there was no furniture other than a few very low tables and some built-in wall drawers. Clothing and bedding were strewn about.

It was kind of spooky, and we cautiously looked about, guns at the ready. There was a muffled buzzing sound that seemed to be coming from a pile of clothing, which I warily approached. Then for the first time on Okinawa, I caught the cloying scent of death. That odor would become commonplace in the days ahead. With a shock, I realized that a pile of clothing on the floor was not just a pile of clothing, but a pile of clothing that included a dead man as well. He had been dead for quite a while, long enough to be greatly swelled up. He had also been bald-headed and the top of his smooth head was split wide open. Black flies and white maggots were wriggling about and covering this grievous wound. The flies were making the buzzing, droning sound as they swarmed about the blood-blackened head. There was a big hole in the ceiling, and it appeared that a rocket from one of our navy planes had blasted through the tiled roof and killed the man as he had been gathering up some possessions, which were scattered about him on the floor. He was the first of many, many more dead men I would see in the near future.

We carefully searched the other sheds and outbuildings, but found no one. I was intrigued by what was obviously the outhouse. In a little shed near the back door of the main house was a bench made of a black stone slab. This stone bench had two round holes in it just like one of our old outdoor privies in Texas. We used to call them "two holers." A large stone jug was placed under each hole, and we discovered later that these containers of saved excrement would be removed periodically and carefully emptied out onto the garden. There it would be worked

Photograph courtesy U.S. Army
An Okinawan farmhouse similar to the one in which we found the dead man.

into the loose soil, with bare feet, to act as a fertilizer. The surface of the stone slab around the two holes was as slick and smooth as glass from being polished by untold generations of Okinawan rear ends.

After our search we left the farmhouse with its bloated, dead inhabitant and returned to our nearby tomb-camp. An anti-aircraft battery was busily setting up four guns nearby, 90 mm it appeared, whose long barrels pointed skyward. We had a good, clear view down hill to the Hagushi beaches and all the frenzied activity still going on there as nightfall approached. As the sun went down, the weather now seemed very cool after the muggy tropical heat of Leyte. Some other units from the 763rd had arrived from the beach and camped around us. Now a guard system for the night was organized. Several machine guns in half-tracks, jeeps and weapon carriers were manned.

The ridiculous ease of the day's invasion had everyone giddy with relief. Rumors were rife, such as someone hearing from someone who knew someone on one of the command ships, where the word was that the dumb Japanese had miscalculated and moved all their troops that were to defend Okinawa over to Formosa. We supposedly had foxed them into thinking that was where we were going to invade instead of Okinawa. There were many other ballpark assessments, all wildly optimistic, about what the easy, walk-in-the-park landing of today had meant. Alas, these happy visions for the future would soon savagely be proved wrong.

Most everyone dug a slit trench to sleep in that night. The temperature dropped to fifty degrees which seemed terribly cold after the Philippines. Next morning, my little monkey, Suzy-Q, who had come ashore with the maintenance sergeant in his half-track, was shivering violently, so I took an olive-drab GI sock and cut the toe off for her head to stick through and then made two holes in the sides for her arms. When completed, it made a fine turtleneck sweater of which she seemed to be exceedingly proud. She would spread out her tiny fingers and rub one little hand and then the other up and down over her sock-covered body with a feminine preening look of admiration on her little smiling face.

The next morning, we began to get ourselves better organized. Tanks of the 763rd were still advancing east with the 96th Infantry Division, which was in line abreast with the 7th Infantry Division and the 1st and 6th Marine Divisions. On this second day, these four assault divisions had reached the east coast against scant opposition. The two marine divisions now wheeled to their left and were ordered to clear the northern part of the island. As there were few Japanese troops in this northern part, they made rapid progress.

The 7th and 96th Army Divisions, after they reached the east coast, had wheeled to the right and formed a solid line across the south-central part of the island. After getting properly lined up, and getting their artillery and other support groups ashore organized and coordinated, they were to advance in a solid front as quickly as possible to the south. The 7th Division's zone would be from the east coast to the center of the island and the 96th's zone from this center line to the west coast.

It took a day or two to get the proper alignment of these two divisions worked out. Since our little headquarters group was now camped near the center of where the 96th Division was soon going to be, we were ordered just to stay put at our tomb-camp while the divisions wheeled ponderously about us.

The big Japanese Kadena Air Field was nearby, so several other guys and I walked over to look it over. It had been a large Japanese installation that our infantry had overrun on the first day of the invasion. We found several of our antiaircraft units were setting up shop around the perimeter of the airbase, and U.S. Army engineers were already busily at work with heavy equipment repairing the runways, which had many craters blown in them by our naval bombers.

A bunch of our little artillery observation planes, which we called "grasshoppers," had already flown off a carrier and landed here. They were now taking off and landing, busy at work directing artillery fire on suspected targets. Looking back down slope toward Hagushi Beach, we saw that the Seabees or engineers had already started blading-up roads inland and were topping them with crushed white coral to make them all-weather roads. As all supplies needed by the huge invasion force had to come from the supply ships at the Hagushi beachhead by truck, all-weather roads were of utmost importance. The planners for Operation Iceberg had tried to think of everything.

Walking onto Kaden Air Base, we discovered under some trees and shrubbery several strange-appearing little aircraft placed around. Looking them over, we found them to be rocket-powered suicide vehicles, each of which could carry a huge load of over two thousand pounds of explosives in its nose. We knew from the intelligence bulletins we received from time to time that the Japanese were developing such weapons but, so far, had not used them. They were called "Baka" by the Americans, which supposedly meant "stupid," but the Japanese officially called them "Ohka," or "Cherry Blossoms."

They were incapable of taking off by themselves. To get airborne, they had to be attached to a Betty Bomber and carried aloft to a target area such as Hagushi Beach. After selecting a target, the Baka was released, and

Photograph courtesy U.S. Army
Baka suicide rocket, similar to the ones we found. Kadena Air Base.

dropping down from the Betty Bomber, the rocket engine was fired up. This propelled the Baka at great speed, up to 550 or 600 mph, while the pilot attempted to dive it into the suitable target he had selected, such as a big American navy ship.

It evidently was very hard for the pilot to control, so it wasn't too successful as a weapon, although I did see a Baka hit one of our destroyers at a later date. It must have been a wild ride for the pilot as it streaked through the sky.

So we had heard of them and now suddenly here they were, and that made us interested in looking them over pretty closely. One guy, after checking for booby traps, even got into the cockpit of one. They were so small they were almost toy-like.

The next day, we returned to show them to some friends and found MPs had cordoned off the whole area and wouldn't let anybody near them. It seems the high brass had heard about them being here and considered them to be such a new secret weapon that they wanted them loaded up and flown off for our experts to evaluate. In hindsight, we know now the high brass was worried about their use when we invaded the home islands of Japan. But then, we just laughed at the MPs and told them they needed to have arrived much earlier, as a bunch of guys had been getting in them and having their pictures

Photograph courtesy U.S. Army
A Japanese decoy airplane made of bamboo. Kadena Air Base.

taken yesterday. This made them mad, of course, but the baiting of MPs by front line troops was customary.

There were a lot of wrecked Japanese planes about, but we were surprised to see a great many artificial planes made of bamboo wood and paper as well. These phony decoy planes looked pretty realistic on the ground, so I'm sure they really did from the air. The Japanese were obviously hopeful that these decoys would draw the fire from our attacking navy planes away from their real planes, which were nearby in revetments.

On the way back to our tomb-camp, we walked along the side of a deep ravine and someone said, "Hey, I saw a Jap running down there." We raced over, and peering down, sure enough caught a glimpse of a running figure disappearing into a hole dug into the side of the ravine near the bottom. We warily approached the hole and threw several hand grenades. But they all missed the hole and when one exploded, a fragment flew up and hit the thrower. He wasn't seriously injured, but while we were gathered about him administering first aid, a figure clamored out of the hole and, climbing up out of the ravine, approached us with his hands held up over his head. He obviously was not a soldier, but a civilian and seemed healthy and intelligent. A couple of guys took him back to Kadena Air Base and turned him over to the MPs, still vigilantly guarding the Baka rocket planes.

As we walked past the farm buildings where I had seen the dead man the day before, a black and white swaybacked pig came grunting out of a shed and stood eyeing us suspiciously.

"Green, do you know how to butcher a pig?" asked the laid-back doctor who had sedated my monkey on Leyte.

"Well, hell," I replied, "you're the one trained to cut on people—that should be your job." He laughed and said something like, "We aren't supposed to eat anything produced locally, but barbecued pork ribs would sure beat the hell out of K-rations." We all quickly agreed to that and the chase was on.

We finally hemmed the pig up in a corner of the rock wall and shot him in the head. I borrowed a K-Bar fighting knife that was as sharp as a razor and cleaned and butchered the pig, as not only was I the only one who had even seen it done, I was quite familiar with the process. Growing up on the ranch, hog killing time was an annual event.

After the pig was gutted, skinned and washed, we built a fire, made a grate out of an iron gate and began cooking. Soon the wafting aroma smelled simply delicious and, before long, we had a crowd gathered about from down-wind. Actually, it smelled better while cooking than it tasted later on when it was done, but we cut it up into many pieces and passed them out. It tasted pretty good, although it would have been a lot better with some salt and barbecue sauce. Even so, it didn't last long, as everyone around wanted some.

Up until now the invasion had been almost a lark. The two marine divisions were still enjoying a romp, as they and their big entourage of correspondents and photographers swept northward against scant opposition. We at our tomb-camp could hear occasional gunfire to the east and south, but we still hadn't heard a shot fired at us.

By the third day after the landing, the 7th and the 96th Infantry Divisions had completed their wheeling to the right and now were emplaced in a solid line across the island facing south. They received orders to advance in line abreast in that direction as quickly as possible. The unanswered question about where all the Japanese defenders were located was about to be answered.

The third ranking Japanese officer on Okinawa was Colonel Hiromichi Yahara. His position was similar to an S-3 intelligence officer in the American Army. It was his idea for the Japanese not to defend the beaches, although this meant enduring the great losses that were sure to ensue from the punishing bombardment the Americans would place on the sites they had selected to land. The Japanese had correctly figured out the landings would be made on the Hagushi beaches.

Colonel Yahara's idea, which had been accepted by his superiors, was for practically all the 140,000 available Japanese soldiers on Okinawa to man a highly sophisticated defensive line of underground emplacements that had been constructed from the east coast to the west coast across the southern one-third of the island. This defensive line had been skillfully built over the past two years and was completely unknown to American intelligence.

Subscripted miners, some from Korea, had hollowed out the emplacements. Using copious amounts of concrete, they had made underground barracks and gun emplacements that would later prove to be all but impregnable. The Japanese had designed and constructed an inter-locking defensive system, all connected by tunnels, with strong points able to support each other. The system, known as the Shuri Line, stretched in depth from one side of the island to the other. It was by far the most elaborate defensive system ever faced by the Americans in the Pacific Theater and compared favorably to any in the European Theater. To top it off, this system was fully manned by crack Japanese troops of the 32nd Army awaiting the Americans, and they were backed up by many big artillery pieces hidden in caves to their rear. Of course, the Americans were completely unaware of any of this. It was not until Colonel Yahara wrote a book seventeen years after the battle that all these details were revealed.

During the very last days of the battle of Okinawa, Colonel Yahara had asked for permission to commit hari-kari along with other high ranking officers. Instead, he received special orders from Lieutenant General Ushijima, the Japanese commanding officer on the island. Ushijima would shortly commit hari-kari, but his orders to Colonel Yahara were that the Tokyo high command wanted him to work his way north through the American lines, disguised as a civilian. After reaching the sparsely settled northern part of the island, he would make contact with a small fishing boat that would take him to the home islands of Japan. There he was to report to the high command in Tokyo, and tell them what, in his observations, had worked the best for the Japanese in their fierce defense of Okinawa. Those tactics could possibly be improved on and used against the Americans when they invaded the home islands of Japan. The Japanese high command was well aware that Okinawa was being taken in order to be the advanced base for the build-up of American forces that would be used for the invasion of the home islands, as England had been for the invasion of Hitler's Europe.

Colonel Yahara successfully made it through the front lines, but was discovered when the group he was traveling with was taken to a camp for civilians and interrogated. Seventeen years after the war, he wrote his memoirs, which were published both in Japan and the U.S. Colonel Yahara was an intelligent, educated man who wrote his book concerning the battle for Okinawa with the cool, analytical outlook of the staff officer he had once been.

This book was of the greatest interest to me in later years, as it revealed so much about the Japanese side of the battle of which we, of course, had no inkling. While we were fighting them, we never took into consideration, or at least I never did, the situation as seen through their eyes. We became utterly frustrated with their unrelenting, dogmatic fight to the death, which we considered to be senseless and the cause of unnecessary deaths for both sides.

In our frustration, we developed the somewhat calloused attitude of "OK boys, if that's the way you want to play the game, we'll do our best to try and accommodate you in your desire to join your honorable ancestors as quickly as possible." We never did take into account, much less appreciate, the incredible discipline and dedication of the Japanese soldiers on Okinawa that enabled them to live underground under the most terrible conditions and continue to fight to the death or commit suicide when there was no hope of victory.

That type of behavior was incomprehensible to the minds of us American soldiers, as was their seemingly eager willingness to die for their Emperor. We American youths, on the other hand, desperately wanted just to get the war, which in our eyes the Japanese had so treacherously started, over with. All we really wanted was to remain in the land of the living until we could someday return to our homes and families, and also in my case, the Texas ranch that I so dearly loved.

So now, with these two completely different philosophies, the two armies squared-off for the no-holds-barred fight to the death. The fanatical, heavily armed Japanese troops lay hidden and waiting in their underground fortresses for the Americans who were coming south, completely unaware of what they were facing. The stage was set and the curtain going up for the beginning of the blood bath that the battle for Okinawa became.

The trail up to an observation point on top of an escarpment such as Maeda.

Chapter 6

KAKAZU RIDGE
TO THE MAEDA ESCARPMENT

"Cease this dreadful war and settle the matter at once without further blood shed."

The Odyssey

Okinawa
April 14, 1945

Dear Mother,

... We've been hearing rumors for the past two days that the war with Germany is over, but haven't got it confirmed yet. We finally got a confirmed report on the president's death. If we ever needed him it would be now.

I am acting as liaison officer between the tanks and the 96th. It is exciting at the least but you would be amazed at the small number of casualties we have had. It is almost unbelievable. As usual, Infantry has it pretty rough. I sure feel for old Jones. Haven't seen or heard of him yet.

The Japs shelled us the other night for the first time. It was the first barrage our outfit has been in, and you should have seen us dig in. A foxhole would have been a gross under-estimate in my case. A well would have been more appropriate. However, they didn't hit anything and the only harm done was a loss of sleep.

It's warmed up a lot now, and I am glad. The Infantry didn't even have blankets and had to stay up on the front in all that rain with only a poncho. I certainly have all the respect in the world for those boys. They are the ones who really have it rough....

Everybody is all pepped up over the rumor about Germany and Russia. We heard the Russians declared war on the Japs, and if that is true we ought to wind this up over here in pretty short order. I doubt if either is true, though.

I guess I'm too chicken-hearted, but I can't help but feel a little sorry for these civilians. They sure are taking a beating. Nearly every family has had some killed, and they are a pathetic looking bunch. They try to be friendly but of course we can't be friendly with them and are far from it in fact, but they are but a few out of the many innocents that have been caught in it all. This island never will be the same, though. It is really torn up.

It's getting dark so I had better stop. It keeps me pretty busy keeping up with the elements of the 96th and the tanks both, but I am safe so don't worry. From the looks of things, I'll be home for my birthday. Can you feature me being able to vote?

Hope you are all fine.

Lots of love,
Bob

Okinawa
April 21, 1945

Dear Mother,

Sorry I haven't written sooner, but I really haven't had time. I have been getting mail right along now, and, oh, do I love it. Two packages got here too. It seemed strange to be eating those cookies in the middle of all this.

We are still with the 96th Div. and are up against some mighty tough, determined resistance. Hirohito would be real proud of these guys. I mean you really have to root them out and kill them personally.

Ernie Pyle got it the other day but suppose you know that. This rock is a shade different than any battle he ever saw in Europe. They don't play by the rules over here. If they would put all these correspondents in one place, I think the Japs would run clear off the south end, there would be such an army. The marines, of course, are getting the credit. I don't believe any marine here has seen ten live Japs, as they weren't on the north end to begin with.

Met John Turberville in a hole up here the other day. He is a general's aide and looked right dapper. He went to school at Roswell.... He even had a crease in his fatigues, but I think he lost it before he & the general took off. These generals give me a pain in the neck. They swagger around trying to act like Patton, but in estimation wouldn't make a fair squad leader. You ought to see them take off when the buzz bombs start.

Those buzz bombs are terrific. They make a hole about forty feet across and anywhere from twelve to twenty feet deep, and this is really some hole. They are about ten feet in length and two feet thick and have fins on one end as well as 1100 lbs of explosives. I imagine the Germans taught them how to make and use them. We knocked out two of their landing ramps today.

… try to write a little everyday to you as I will take my paper with me. We leave before day & come back after dark so it is pretty hard to write, as we can't have any lights on at night.

… I look just like an ape, as I haven't shaved, bathed or had a hair cut in some time…. Been wearing my duck hunting boots for several days, as we had a big rain.

If you even can, try to send a can of pickle peaches. I've been thinking of them every time I open a can of this stew. A boy also got a can of fried chicken which was absolutely wonderful. I don't know if you could do that or not, though.

Have a few souvenirs I'll try to send home when we get a break. You probably won't think much of them as one is a Jap Nambo machine gun but it will be good for Stinky to play with.

I'm feeling fine and doing fine, so don't worry. I wanted to be right where I am so am well satisfied. The guys I am with are really swell, and we should have some better luck pretty soon. When we do break through, it should end pretty fast.

Give everybody my love as I think of you all the time.

> Lots of love,
> Bob

Okinawa
April 23, 1945

Dear Mother,

It is just after sunup and we have just finished breakfast. Have a little time now as we are going to wait till it gets a little lighter. Looks like it might rain but I sure hope not. It's funny how we always wanted rain so at home & here it's the worse thing that can happen, just about.

Took some pictures yesterday that ought to be real good. I missed the best shot. They made a direct hit on a jeep with a 150 m/m, and I didn't have my camera out. From where I was, the only picture I would have taken would be the bottom of a deep, dark hole.

They brought back a wounded Jap yesterday & were giving him plasma. He was a stout, husky fellow and no runt by any means. That's about the third prisoner I've seen yet.

Read *Time* magazine of April 9th. It says the southern end of the island is hard to defend. He must mean the last 100 yards of beach on the southern tip. The Japs are on ridges about the size of one mile hill west of Albany but a little steeper. Their pillboxes have been there for years. Some have big trees on them. The whole hillsides are honeycombed. We threw a W.P. smoke shell into one pillbox & the hill smoked in about a dozen places. *Time* also said the people were "undernourished beyond description." The ones I've seen are about as undernourished as a lard hog. I don't know why they can't write the truth. I guess it's too drab and unglamorous, and it is sure that. That correspondent better not come up here popping off about it being hard to defend. Some of these boys who have been here day & night for some time might take it the wrong way.

… I'm feeling fine. I've sure been scared a time or two, but so is everybody else & that doesn't hurt you.

Lots of love,

Bob

Major General John Hodge, 24th Corp Commander of the Army Divisions, now had the 7th and 96th Divisions in the position where he wanted them, which was on a strong line across the island with their artillery and other support groups in place ashore and ready to participate. It seemed now that everything was ready for the U.S. forces to roll on south.

General Hodge had quit worrying about a Japanese counterattack. One might have caused trouble if it had come before the artillery was emplaced, along with the consolidation of the strong line that the two infantry divisions had established across the island, cutting it in two. General Hodge's main concern now was to sustain the momentum of his army's advance. On the afternoon of April 3, he ordered the 96th Division to move south and take the Urasoe-Mura Escarpment that dominated the western side of the line, which his two divisions had established across the island. He ordered the 7th Division to take Hill 178 that dominated the eastern side of the line. General Hodge had no idea at the time that he was sending these two divisions against the strongest defensive position American troops ever faced in the Pacific Theater during World War II. To make it even worse for the 96th Division, the Kakazu Ridge sections of the main Japanese Shuri Line, which was in their

Photograph courtesy U.S. Army
Tank/infantry team advancing. Notice water cans on rear of tank—these were used by infantrymen. Bed rolls are piled in front of water cans.

sector out ahead of the looming Urasoe-Mura Escarpment, was probably the strongest of all.

The Japanese high command, to give them credit, had so far correctly assessed the movements that the Americans might make if they invaded Okinawa. They had foreseen that the American landings would probably be on the Hagushi beaches. They knew the next phase would come when the Americans started advancing southward. So far, the Americans were doing just as the Japanese had predicted they would do and had prepared for accordingly. The Japanese had constructed their elaborate Shuri Line defense across the route the Americans must take in order to move to the south following a Hagushi Beach landing, and there the Japs intended to make their stand.

General Ushijima, the Japanese commander, had no illusions as to their chances. The Japanese high command in Tokyo wanted him to tie up the Americans for as long as possible while they prepared to send down hundreds of kamikaze planes from the home islands and from Formosa to attack U.S. ships at anchor off Okinawa. They hoped this great multitude of suicide planes, many times what had previously been used, would damage the U.S. Navy to such an extent that the support vessels they protected would have to be withdrawn.

They knew these support vessels were essential as they provided the flow of supplies that made the American invasion possible. Without incoming supplies, the American forces on the island would soon suffer quickly from dwindling ammunition, rations and all the myriad other things that had to be brought in by ship. When the U.S. ground forces had been weakened by a lack of supplies and the protecting ships of the U.S. Navy forced to withdraw to avoid the kamikazes, then, in a glorious counterattack, the Japanese forces could roar out of their underground redoubts and gain a great victory. At least, that was the pipe dream that the high command in Tokyo wished would happen. But General Ushijima was no fool.

It was good that his ordinary soldiers seemed to take great stock in hearing about this glorious plan from Tokyo, but he knew it was not going to happen. However, he also knew that a delay of the Americans in taking Okinawa would give his countrymen back home some more time, and additional time was what was greatly needed for the now frantic preparations taking place in Japan to defend their beloved home islands from the American invasion everyone knew would come next. So General Ushijima intended to do his uttermost to delay the Americans on Okinawa as long as possible while inflicting on them as many casualties as he could. In truth, as it turned out, he was greatly successful in doing both of these things, for he really was a very good general.

The 96th and 7th Infantry Divisions made sweeping gains on the 4th of April, advancing over two miles to the south on a broad front. General Hodge was greatly encouraged by this and envisioned his infantry that had turned south might sweep quickly across the high ground of south central Okinawa and seize the badly needed port of Naha, thus taking the island in record time. But our intelligence had sadly underestimated both the number of troops and the elaborate preparations the Japanese had made to defend the southern part of Okinawa. In fact, they knew absolutely nothing at all about the Shuri Line where the main Japanese forces now awaited the Americans.

General Yahara told in his book how the Japanese troops that manned the Shuri Line were unusually well equipped. Besides having the standard issue infantry weapons, each rifle company also contained nine Nambu light machine guns and nine 50mm Knee mortars. In addition to that, they were backed up at battalion level by ten Hotchkiss heavy machine guns and two squat infantry howitzers. This was more firepower than an American infantry company possessed. On top of that, independent 81mm mortar platoons added additional firepower, while to the rear, well hidden in caves, was a plentiful supply of large caliber artillery with ample ammunition. Also, a large number of high velocity anti-tank guns were skillfully hidden all along the line, and many mine fields were in place, some made of 500 pound aerial bombs. But probably most important, according to Colonel Yahara's account, morale was extremely high among these underground well-trained, well-equipped, completely indoctrinated veteran soldiers. They were grimly determined and fully intended to fight to the death in defending this island.

As the 96th Division now continued moving to the south as ordered, Japanese resistance began stiffening from outposts they had placed in advance of the main Shuri Line. Three tanks from C Company in our own 763rd tank battalion were set afire by a strategically hidden 47mm anti-tank gun. In an ominous example of good shooting, the gun had knocked out the three tanks with an expenditure of only twenty rounds. This scenario would be repeated many times in the days ahead. Our tanks, out ahead of our infantry, would be allowed to approach very close to a hidden 47mm anti-tank gun. These high-velocity, flat-trajectory guns were relatively small and could be easily hidden underground, but at close range were able to penetrate our tanks' armor. They proved to be deadly tank killers in the days ahead.

Two other 763rd tanks had been disabled by mines with no lives lost. Nevertheless, the flaming loss of the three C Company tanks sent a chill through the ranks of the 763rd tankers. I was now ordered to resume my role as a liaison officer between the tanks of A Company and whatever unit of the 96th Infantry Division they were supporting.

So now I bid adieu to the headquarters group that I had been staying with at our tomb-camp where we had barbecued the swaybacked pig. Now, at night, I stayed wherever A Company tanks bivouacked. Every morning, Corporal Stone and I would take an SCR-300 radio and drive in our jeep to the infantry regimental or battalion headquarters or to an Observation Post, or OP, as they were called. These OPs were always changing as we advanced, so we were constantly on the move. It was exciting seeing the waves of our infantrymen moving out across the fields following behind our tanks. It was somewhat scary, too, looking at the higher terrain in front of us and realizing that the enemy was out there right now, watching us.

Hard-boiled Colonel Eddie May, C.O. of the 383rd Regiment of the 96th Division, sent his troops following some distance behind a motorized patrol of the 96th Reconnaissance Troop as they headed south down the road that led to Shuri Castle. The five vehicles of this mechanized cavalry recon patrol, headed by a half-track, soon came under heavy fire from an anti-tank gun and several machine guns. The leading half-track and two other vehicles were quickly destroyed, with two men killed and six more wounded, but the cavalrymen had done their job. They had located the enemy and the Okinawa honeymoon was over.

Kakazu Ridge was to be the first part of the Shuri Defense system the Americans would encounter. Overshadowed by the higher, more massive Urasoe-Mura or Maeda Escarpment just behind it 500 yards to the south, Kakazu Ridge did not appear to be a significant defensive terrain obstacle to the Americans, but its looks were deceiving. It turned out to be one of the strongest Japanese positions on Okinawa.

Now the 96th Division, supported by the 763rd Tank Battalion, encountered heavily fortified outposts in advance of the hidden, Japanese defensive line centered on Kakazu Ridge. After a strong Japanese position on Cactus Ridge was taken by elements of the 96th Division, small scale, probing attacks by the 383rd Regiment failed to advance and took heavy losses as they now encountered the main Japanese defenses on Kakazu Ridge.

As I mentioned earlier, my position as liaison officer for the 763rd Tank Battalion and whatever element of the 96th Division A Company tanks were involved with entailed going up to the regimental or battalion headquarters of the infantry or one of their OPs on the front lines. My job was to be available to transmit radio messages from the infantry to A Company tanks or sometimes to those in higher command of the tanks.

At this stage of the game, the infantry high command of the 96th Division was still full of aggressive assurance in their ability to rapidly overcome the enemy. I think now, in looking back on it, the easy, unopposed landing and rapid advancement of the four assault divisions across the island probably led the American high commanders into being overconfident. At any rate, they now made plans for the 7th and 96th Divisions to attack south and sweep the Japanese defenders quickly aside. There was an air of fierce optimism among the staff officers of the 383rd Infantry Regiment when I arrived at their headquarters on the 8th of April in the midst of their attack preparations.

Their headquarters were set up in a rock house, and as I started to go in to report my presence to Colonel May, I was stopped by a guard. He told me to leave my M-1 carbine outside as Colonel May had given orders that no loaded weapons were to be brought inside his headquarters. This was the same new carbine I had been issued at Fort Ord. I had been warned that Colonel May was one tough hombre, so such an order didn't surprise me. I leaned the carbine up against a rock wall and went inside the small house filled with officers busily making plans.

Just as I was getting ready to report to a staff officer, a tremendous explosion outside rocked the whole house and ground like an earthquake. Pieces of the ceiling crashed down and the house filled with dust. For the first time, the Japanese had begun using their huge Spigot mortars and had lobbed one that struck very close outside. They were awesome. These projectiles were 320mm and traveled through the air so slowly you could actually see them coming and follow their trajectory through the air. We soon called them "Flying Boxcars" or "Buzz bombs." They made a huge crater in the ground.

Photograph courtesy U.S. Army

Rescue attempt. This tank ran over a buried, 500-pound Japanese bomb. Unfortunately, the tank blew up before the crew could be rescued.

Everyone in the house rushed outside where the guard who had stopped and disarmed me was lying on the ground, badly injured from a piece of shrapnel from the Spigot mortar projectile. I was now greatly disturbed to see my new carbine scattered about in several pieces with the barrel badly bent.

Now, someone shouted an alarm and everyone quickly looked toward the Japanese lines in amazement as a long, writhing, twisting column of green and white smoke made its way across the sky. That was followed by another arcing Spigot mortar shell that ascended up from behind a hill to our front. Its slow, arcing path through the sky was apprehensively watched until it dropped down and exploded some distance away in a rice paddy. Now a staff officer looked up from an intelligence book and said that the green and white smoke trail, according to his intelligence book, was called "Twisting Dragon" by the Japanese and was a signal that meant "enemy sighted, preparing to advance."

Well, the Japanese had that right, of course. It was a little eerie to know that they were watching our every move from their higher ground and were setting off smoke signals like the Indians used to do in our Wild West to alert their forces that we were preparing to come at them.

As I was gathering the pieces of my carbine in a pile, a medic who had been working on the injured guard came over and handed me the guard's carbine. "Here," he said, holding out the gun. "Take this one. He won't be needing it anymore." I saw they had placed the injured guard on a canvas stretcher but had quit administering to him and covered him completely with a green poncho. He became the first American I saw killed by enemy action, but not the last by a long shot. I quit fooling with the pieces of my ruined carbine and took the one he was holding out. It was not nearly so nice and new as mine had been, but it was all in one piece, and I sure didn't want to be running around unarmed. So I took it and thanked him for the dead man's gun.

Now Colonel May gave the order for the 1st and 3rd Battalions of his regiment to move out and seize Kakazu Ridge, rising up before them. That was to be easier said than done. Running along in front and parallel to the ridge was a deep natural gorge which was impassable for tanks, so the infantrymen were to proceed without armored support.

The Japanese had developed The Kakazu Ridge position so supporting fire from many strong points such as the Maeda Escarpment could be focused on the area that had to be crossed by the attackers. Mortars on the reverse slope of Kakazu Ridge were zeroed in on the gorge, as were the relatively inaccurate Spigot mortars. A complex, interlocking system of coordinated fire-lanes from pillboxes, tunnels and caves on Kakazu Ridge covered all direct approaches and made them killing grounds. Artillery pieces to the rear were sighted in to lay down pre-registered barrages. It was a deadly piece of ground intended to wreak havoc upon any attackers, such as Colonel May's two battalions, now approaching.

My old nemesis from the landing, Lieutenant Colonel King, was in command of the 1st Battalion whose objective was the Kakazu Ridge proper. The 3rd Battalion was to attack and take the west side of Kakazu Ridge, called Kakazu West. The two battalions were to jump off without artillery preparation to try and achieve surprise. Little reconnaissance had been done and only a vague knowledge of the terrain ahead of them was available.

At first, all seemed to be going well. The 1st Battalion infantrymen reached and crossed the deep gorge and some had actually reached the top side of Kakazu Ridge when the roof fell in on them and they were suddenly assailed by a storm of artillery, mortar and machine gun fire. The two companies that had reached the top of the ridge were pinned down and isolated. The supporting companies were unable to move up and reinforce them. Fierce hand-to-hand combat took place as the Japanese suddenly launched a counterattack.

As casualties rapidly mounted, Lieutenant Colonel King asked Colonel May by radio to allow him to withdraw his troops from the top of the ridge, since they could not be supported and were running low on ammunition. Colonel Eddie May not only refused this request, but accused Lieutenant Colonel King of being "jumpy" and relieved him from command over the radio and put the executive officer in charge. He ordered him to hold their position on the ridge. That was tough talk, but it did the men on the ridge little good, as poor Colonel King's estimate of the situation had been accurate and the position could not be sustained.

Under cover of a smoke screen laid down by our 4.2-inch mortars, the men were finally able to withdraw, bringing their wounded back with them. Of the eighty-nine men who had reached to the top of the ridge, fifteen were killed and only three were uninjured when they at last returned to safety. Colonel May's regiment suffered 326 casualties that day and the Kakazu Ridge position of the Japanese was still firmly in place, so the American advance to the south was stymied.

Brigadier General Claudious Easley was a Texas A &M graduate from Waco, Texas, and the scrappy executive officer of the 96th Infantry Division. He, along with two of his regimental commanders, Colonel May and Colonel Halloran, were now smarting under the failure of their infantry division's attack upon Kakazu Ridge and still were of the opinion that a strong determined infantry assault, supported by artillery, ought to be able to take the position. The deep gorge in front of the ridge prevented tanks from accompanying the infantry, and flooded rice paddies prevented them from wheeling around the ridge in a flanking movement. Since the 763rd tanks were not to be employed, they didn't have much to do, but I was sent up to be with the infantry just the same, in case they changed their minds. Therefore, I had the opportunity to observe their actions from close up.

Easley, May and Halloran now came up with a new plan. Instead of using just one regiment to attack Kakazu Ridge, they would double the size of the attacking force and use two regiments in the assault, after pulverizing the position with a tremendous artillery barrage. It looked good on paper and sounded good when describing it, so the plan received approval from on-high, and it was on with the show.

On the morning of the tenth of April, after American artillery laid down a tremendous artillery barrage on Kakazu Ridge, the two regiments moved out to attack and gain the position that the one regiment had failed to take the day before. Heavy fighting took place all day and, again, the Americans gained the top of the ridge, but that was all.

As was to be repeated many times in the battle for Okinawa, the reverse slopes were where the Japanese were hardest to deal with and overcome. To make matters worse, steady rain began to fall. General Easley, aggressive as always, continued trying to reinforce the men on top of the ridge, but all came to naught in the pouring rain and a most miserable night was spent by the disorganized, dispirited and widely spread out infantrymen.

The attack was continued on April the 11th and 12th, but with little success and high casualties. In the middle of the battle on a rainy April 12th, news came of the death of President Roosevelt. I still vividly remember standing in my poncho in the pouring rain by the back door of a communication half-track and listening to the news of his death come out of a crackling radio speaker. It was sad. Roosevelt was the leader we were used to, and who in the hell was this Harry Truman, our new Commander-in-Chief?

In spite of the changes back home, the battle on Okinawa raged on, untouched by the sadness of the nation's loss. The 27th Infantry Division, a New York National Guard outfit, had previously seen combat on Saipan and Guam. Their actions there had been considered to be woefully inept by the navy and marines who were loudly critical of them. Up to now, the 27th Division had been a part of the floating reserve, but with the stalemate of movement before Kakazu Ridge, they were brought ashore and by the 15th of April, had been put in position to the west of the 96th Division.

On the 18th of April, the 27th Division attacked the west end of the Japanese line by secretly emplacing Bailey bridges and pontoon foot bridges at night across an inlet of the sea. Their infantry crossed over these bridges in the dark and by dawn were moving rapidly eastward down the top of the Urasoe-Mura Escarpment toward the static Kakazu Ridge area. They surprised Japanese soldiers squatting around their breakfast cooking fires and sent them scurrying south.

Encountering heavy resistance and counterattacks, they began to dig in and try to consolidate their hold onto this high ground to the west and slightly behind the Kakazu Ridge area, which had become such a thorn in the side of the American advance to the south. Hopes were high that the Japanese position was being out-flanked and might be taken. Now, the greatest concentration of artillery fire ever employed in the Pacific War began. This barrage came from over 360 guns from the twenty-seven battalions of various corps and division artillery that thundered away for twenty minutes, laying fire upon the Japanese front lines.

Then the barrage was shifted 500 yards to the rear while the American infantrymen faked making an attack, hoping to draw the undercover Japanese out of their deep redoubts to man their guns. When the American infantrymen quickly withdrew back to cover, the artillery once again was placed heavily upon the Japanese front lines for another twenty minutes of savagery. The artillery fire ceased after forty minutes of bombardment, and once again the assault lines of American infantrymen began to snake out and advance toward Kakazu Ridge. They hoped to find that the Japanese soldiers were either destroyed or so shell-shocked this time as to be incapacitated, but to their dismay, they found that was not the case. Again, fierce, withering fire and a blizzard of falling mortar shells riddled American formations all along the lines and before long, the attack by the 7th and 96th Divisions had run out of steam and was again stalled.

It was even worse for the Americans to the west, where the 27th Division had attacked with three battalions of infantry supported by the 164th Tank Battalion. Before the day was over, twenty-two American tanks were lost to mines, anti-tank guns, and satchel-charge teams for the greatest loss of armor in one day suffered by the Americans on Okinawa. We could receive the radio messages from the tanks of the 164th on our radio as they were being decimated by anti-tank guns and their protecting infantry teams were stripped away from them, leaving them vulnerable to swarming suicide satchel-charge teams. It was heart-rending to listen to their agonized radio transmissions pleading for assistance as they became cut off, isolated and under constant, violent attack.

Many of the tankers left their knocked-out tanks and hid out in no-man's-land, some for as long as forty hours before successfully making it back to friendly lines. The day had ended in a complete failure for the all-out American attack. Everywhere along the line, the Japanese still held, and the Americans had suffered 700 casualties and lost twenty-two tanks. It was now beginning to sink in on the Americans that the taking of the island was not going to be fast and easy as the landing had been, but instead, slow and very costly.

For the following five days, furious fighting raged all along the line of the 96th Division sector. I'm sure it was much the same for the 7th and 27th division infantrymen, but as I was only in the 96th Division sector, I was limited to my area, and it was really bad there. Nights became terrifying, as infiltrators tried to reach our tanks and blow them up with satchel-charges, while there were now air raids every night and periodically, Japanese artillery barrages rained down. Sleeping became a scarce luxury.

Photograph courtesy U.S. Army

Night air raid—the sky would be completely filled with tracers, beams from searchlights, and drifting parachute flares.

The air raids brought on spectacular displays of anti-aircraft fire that filled the skies with tracers and search light beams. The search lights would seek out and lock on to the planes, and when they did get one in their beams, it was usually a goner. Sometimes as many as four or five lights would converge and bracket the tiny looking plane in their brilliant beams. The plane would try to jink and dive and escape from the illumination, but usually, once it was found and caught by the beams, the rapidly converging lines of tracers would tear it to pieces. I found myself wondering about what it would be like to be the pilot of a plane imprisoned in the clutch of brilliant light, watching the lines of tracers begin to converge on you. I decided it would be like being a fly caught in a web and watching the spider coming out to get you.

The fighting during this four or five days had to be some of the most bitter infantry fighting of the whole Pacific war. But at last, Kakazu was taken, or at least the wily Japanese realized it would be, and to save their troops, pulled them back to their next prepared position, which was fully as deadly.

This was the looming Urasoe-Mura Escarpment, just south of Kakazu Ridge and squarely in the battered 96th Division sector. Although the Okinawans called this escarpment by its true name, Urasoe-Mura, because of the village of Maeda nearby the American high command called it the Maeda Escarpment. It was called still different names by the many GIs of the 96th Division, who now looked up at it in dread—Hacksaw Ridge, Sawtooth Ridge, or simply "the big escarpment." It was one of several high, steep ridges that ran from east to west across the south central part of the island of

Okinawa. Many of these terrain features became well-known and required ferocious battles to take them.

The Japanese had made these ridges into intricately fortified bastions over the years. Some of the more famous ones in addition to Maeda were Kakazu, Shuri, Sugar Loaf, Conical Hill and Yazu-Dake. Their underground installations, including this one, had several floors of tunnels, barrack rooms, electricity, running water and cunningly camouflaged gun ports and mortar patios.

Some historians who later wrote of the battle of Okinawa, described these heavily fortified positions as being like underground battleships in their ability to withstand the punishment of U.S. air and sea bombardment, as well as the constant battering from artillery and tank cannon. The destruction of their defenders cost the Americans dearly, with the loss of hundreds of lives before eventual victory.

The construction of these underground complexes had been completed long enough previous to the U.S. invasion, that the abundant yearly rainfall around sixty inches had caused copious vegetation to completely cover over all signs of anti-tank and machine gun apertures. These hidden emplacements had skillfully been arranged to provide pre-registered mortar fire and interlocking infilading and crossfire lanes of automatic weapons that created killing grounds for any would-be attackers.

Such almost impregnable positions were backed up by pre-registered large caliber artillery pieces hidden in caves farther back to their rear, which would periodically be rolled out to fire. This usually happened at night to avoid being seen during the day by our watchful artillery spotter plane.

The Japanese employed far more artillery on Okinawa than in any other Pacific Island battle. They were able to place concentration barrages of long duration upon chosen targets, something new for them in the island warfare of the Pacific Theater. Their underground fortresses were manned by fanatic Japanese soldiers who were completely reconciled to the fact that they were going to die soon, fighting for their emperor. These soldiers never even entertained the thought of surrendering.

This made a formidable and deadly situation for the GIs and marines of the American assault forces, whose advance to the south had now been brought to a bloody stand-still by the incredible Shuri Line and its grimly determined defenders. Now the U.S. high command began to press hard to get on with the show and get it over with.

This encouragement to move on and end the battle for the island sooner rather than later was particularly strong from Admiral Nimitz and his staff. They were greatly concerned by the rapidly escalating U.S. Navy's ship losses to kamikaze planes. An average of nearly two naval vessels a day were sunk, while many more were badly damaged. The concentration of navy ships required to supply and protect the Okinawa invasion made tempting targets for suicide bombers who flew down in waves from the Japanese home islands only three hundred and twenty miles away. Admiral Nimitz had good reason to be concerned.

As it turned out, the U.S. Navy would lose more ships around Okinawa in the next ninety days than it had lost in all the previous wars in its history put together. Alarmed at these rapidly mounting losses, Admiral Nimitz and his staff came to the island from their Guam Island headquarters to warn army Lieutenant General Simon Bolivar Buckner to his face that as the over-all commander of U.S. ground forces on the island, he would be replaced by someone who could and would move the campaign along faster if he could not. This ultimatum caused General Buckner to apply great pressure on his division commanders to move faster. So down the chain of command came the exhortations to get going until, finally, the pressure reached the kids on the front lines. While, in the security and comfort of the wardrooms of their command ships, the high brass fumed and fussed at the slow movement of colored pins on their maps, the kids at the front looked, with deep misgivings, up out of their muddy foxholes at the looming cliffs of escarpments like Maeda.

Brigadier General Easley now became the man delegated to getting and keeping elements of the 96th division moving forward. Most of the brooding bulk of the Maeda escarpment was in the 96th Division's sector and was the immediate problem holding up the advance of the U.S. ground forces.

Following prolonged bombardment by naval guns, artillery, tanks, and air strikes, elements of the 96th Infantry, after suffering terrible casualties, gained the forward slope and top of the Maeda Escarpment, but were unable to make any progress on the reverse slope at all. The tenacious defense of reverse slopes was now recognized as a Japanese defensive specialty developed to a high degree of proficiency on Okinawa. Under overwhelming pressure, they would give up the forward slope and even the top begrudgingly, but then defend the reverse slope to the death. The reverse slopes were more or less immune to our overwhelming artillery fire, whereas the forward slopes and tops of the ridges were vulnerable to it.

Rising 500 feet above sea level with its upper third over fifty feet of sheer cliff, the Maeda escarpment was about 4200 yards long and twenty to fifty yards wide on top. At its East End was a rocky spire that thrust up above everything and soon was called "The Needle Rock." One end of the escarpment ended just east of this Needle Rock, and off this end, which was a sheer cliff, there was good level ground for the movement of tanks and infantry teams. Now the Americans were trying to take advantage of this ground, better for maneuvers, by bringing their tank/infantry teams around the end of the Maeda Escarpment in a flanking movement. They hoped to then be able to work their way behind the ridge, where some of the 96th infantrymen had gained the top and had established an OP (Observation Post). The flanking maneuver of tanks and infantrymen might now enable an attack on the reverse slope positions by using direct tank-cannon fire and direct infantry action, including satchel-charging the openings of the embrasures. It was tough, bloody work but seemed the only way to neutralize the Japanese position.

General Easley and his aide, a friend of mine from NMMI—Lieutenant John Turbeville—were now constantly at the front conferring and planning with the infantry officers as to the best way of tackling the problem of this reverse slope of the Maeda Escarpment. This flanking plan that now evolved was undoubtedly General Easley's idea. Many of the infantrymen, unaware of the extreme pressure General Easley was under to get the front line moving, thought it very likely he was going to get them all killed with his plans and hated to see him coming.

The aim of the Japanese commander, General Ushijima, was not to win or even hold out, but to simply inflict the most casualties possible on the Americans. His soldiers, who espoused the old code of the Samurai warriors of fighting to the death and dying with weapons in hand, would have to be killed before there could be an American victory and the island secured. After that happened, the navy could disperse its concentration of ships from around the island, and they would be much safer from the kamikazes.

As a liaison officer, I would accompany my company commander, Captain Kennedy and the three A Company tank platoon leaders to the headquarters of the Infantry Regiment we were attached to. We would go just before dark each day. The headquarters were always located just behind the front lines, usually in a blacked-out tent, but sometimes in a captured underground Japanese bunker. There maps were studied by the officers and plans formulated to coordinate the use of our tanks with their infantry in the next day's activities. This was done under the hissing light of a Coleman lantern.

After all these years, I can still remember vividly how strained the faces illuminated by the yellow light looked as they pondered what to do. With heads bent down, faces frozen in intense concentration, their fingers traced proposed routes on the maps. Then they debated the pros and cons of each proposed plan. They knew full well whatever they did was going to mean the deaths and wounding of many of the boys they commanded, but this couldn't be helped. Great pressure was now being applied to them by General Easley and the higher ups to get moving regardless of the opposition, for Admiral Nimitz was applying great pressure on them.

So it was a hard game they were playing. Unlike the big brass, issuing orders from their sanctuaries on high, in the morning these officers, getting up out of their holes in the ground, would be faced with giving life or death orders to the young men in their command while looking them right in the eye. It was a tough, unenviable job. But it was war; it was *their* job and they were doing it, although their haggard faces and sunken eyes betrayed the toll they were paying for doing so.

After plans for the next day were finally hammered out and agreed to, we would return in a jeep to our bivouac usually less than a mile or so behind the front. There battalion maintenance would be busy as ants, refueling, repairing, reloading and preparing the tanks so as to have them ready to go at daylight for their crews to continue fighting the war.

At dawn, as liaison officer, I would go in a jeep with a radioman to the present forward OP. These OPs were located on or very near the front lines, as they moved forward when the front line did. At this time the OP of the infantry we were working with, which was the 381st Regiment of the 96th Division, was now on top of Maeda Escarpment. We would park behind this brooding ridge on the American-held side and trudge up one of the steep, winding trails to the top. OP sites were always selected to be on the highest ground, which provided the best visibility of the front lines. My radioman carried an SCR-300 radio on his back.

Reaching the top we joined quite a group of forward observers (FOs) who were the air coordinators for navy planes, navy gunfire controllers for ships off shore, and artillery coordinators. There were also infantry brass present such as regimental and battalion commanders who, with their radio crews and assistants, were trying to expedite activities. General Easley and John Turbeville would stop by from time to time to assess the situation, also trying to move things along at a faster pace.

This particular day, our tank/infantry teams were involved in carrying out the flanking movement General Easley had envisioned. Our infantry had circled around the east end of the Maeda Escarpment with A Company tanks and had moved toward us, approaching the reverse slope of the ridge that the OP was on. Soon, our infantrymen were fighting just below and to our left, following the tanks and being led in this attack on the reverse slope by junior officers, captains and lieutenants. As usual, the attrition rate was really horrible. Japanese snipers, who had been well-trained and were adept in picking out officers by watching them in action, concentrated on shooting them first.

The top rim of the escarpment where the OP was situated was a little higher on the back rim, more toward the Japanese, which gave those of us on top some protection from sniper fire, although mortars were an occasional hazard. Trenches had been dug along the higher back rim and a company or so of riflemen and several machine guns were emplaced in them, spaced out all along the rim to guard the top against a Japanese counterattack. If a target of opportunity presented itself down below them, they would be able to fire down into the valley, as well. Many of the forward observers were also in this trench looking through binoculars or spotting scopes and talking on radios to adjust the fire of the big guns, which were either on off-shore navy ships or from our artillery farther back to the rear. The air coordinators could call in navy planes to hit targets that they selected themselves from the OP or targets that the infantry requested. The gull winged Corsairs F-4Us fighters strafed and placed rockets on these targets, while the bigger, slower navy SBD and TBF bombers dropped large bombs.

At the bottom of the American-held side of the escarpment, where we parked our jeep, big 6X6 trucks were steadily coming and going, bringing supplies up to the front lines from the big dumps on the beach. The supplies were unloaded along the base of the hill and piled into high stacks of all kinds of equipment, water cans and boxes of ammunition and rations. There was a forward medical aid-station set up nearby to render immediate first-aid before sending the wounded to field hospitals in several jeep ambulances. These jeeps had no tops, but did have racks for stretchers built on them and they could carry several wounded men at once. Unfortunately, they were usually kept busy.

The triage system was used at this forward aid-station, and off to one side there was always a row, often a long row, of green poncho-covered dead bodies—our boys lying on stretchers. Their boots were sticking out, but their heads were covered by the ponchos. These bodies represented the daily toll of death being exacted on the infantry in this area. They were lying there awaiting grave registration crews to come up and collect them for burial. Most of the living, me included, tried to avoid looking at them as it was a disconcerting sight and a reminder of our own mortality. Sometimes, though, someone might be seen kneeling beside a stretcher and even holding a hand of a dead buddy, or with lowered head and hands clasped, saying a prayer for the soul of a lost friend, completely indifferent to the noise, tumult,

Photograph courtesy USMC/National Archives
Grave registration crew at work collecting dog-tags before the men were buried. One tag remained with the body for ID, and one was used to notify next of kin with the dreaded telegram beginning, "We regret to inform you...."

and chaos surrounding them. A steady stream of men, many with their shirts off, labored up the well-worn trails to the top, bringing up wooden boxes of rifle ammunition, hand grenades, and metal cases of belted machine gun ammunition. Mortars, 81 and 60mm mortars were set up at the bottom of the hill, off to one side. Their crews were steadily firing and looping mortar shells over the hill, attempting to make them fall and explode ahead of our advancing tank/infantry teams as they worked their way along the reverse slope in the flanking maneuver.

So the OP area on an active front line was always an anthill of intense activity, plus the fact that the ever-present sound of our own artillery shells moaning and whistling and howling overhead in a constant barrage blanketed everything. My radioman and I usually got into the topside trench near one of the water-cooled machine gun emplacements when we could. These gunners usually prepared deeper, sand-bagged positions that gave a more secure feeling than the simple, shallower trench that snaked off along the ridge top.

We watched today down into the valley to our left where we could see some of our A Company tanks, which we stayed in radio-contact with, leading the flanking attack. They had worked their way around the east end of the escarpment as General Easley had planned and were headed along the reverse slope of the ridge toward us. The valley just below us was filled with dust, smoke, and exploding shells. It looked dirty and messy, much like a big city dump does today. Debris, raw dirt, dead bodies of people and animals, and wreckage of all sorts littered the ground. The remains of houses that had been shelled or bombed were smoking. Once in a while, Japanese soldiers, mostly runners carrying messages, were sighted scurrying and darting like cotton-tailed rabbits, usually just running from one hole to disappear quickly into another.

When Japanese soldiers were sighted, our machine gun crews in the trench quickly adjusted their guns and tried to cut them down. When they succeeded, there was cheering all along the ridge from everybody, as if we had scored a touchdown. I wore earphones attached to the radio and listened in on the approaching tank crews' conversations. Periodically, an infantry officer of field rank came over and had me relay a message to a tank platoon leader to move his tanks this way or that. Often this evolved into an argument between them, with me in the middle.

When I would relay the request to the tank platoon leader, he would often come back angrily with something like, "Hell, they're flat crazy! I can't go any farther up that way! There's a deep ditch there!" Then I would tell that to the infantry officer, and after conversing with his men on his radio, he would reply with equal animosity, "You tell that tanker that my men say that ditch is nothing, and there is absolutely no reason the tanks can't go farther up that way. My men say they are being pinned down by machine gun fire and are beginning to take casualties from mortar rounds, so they need the tanks to try and put a stop to that—so you tell them to get moving!" And so, on and on it would go.

Finally, the approaching tanks of A Company began to crawl farther up into the valley toward us, followed by our darting infantrymen. Soon, they were fighting very nearly right below us as they worked at mopping-up the reverse slope. Suddenly, the tank lieutenant I had been relaying messages to screamed into the radio, "Green, get a medic and bring a stretcher down here. My platoon sergeant's been shot! Hurry!"

This particular officer, who was much older than I, had never been one of my favorites. In fact, we had previously had a run-in or two because he always acted like he resented my relaying the wishes of the infantry officers to him, requesting the movements they wanted him to make. He had openly accused me of siding with the infantry more than once, and he was probably right about that. My first-hand experience of being up on the line with the infantry every day and seeing how tough they had it had convinced me they needed all the help they could get from the tanks or anyone else.

Secretly, I considered this officer to be somewhat of a chicken as well as a first-class horse's ass. What had really teed him off was that I had openly accused him of deliberately turning off his radio. (Even today, I still think he did!) But he, nevertheless, *was* my superior officer, so I handed the radio handset to my radioman and told him to monitor the calls, as I had to go down to the lieutenant's tank. The radioman looked up at me with wide eyes. The valley was now resounding with the booms of tank-cannon fire, the fierce rattle of our infantry gunfire, and the explosions of their hand grenades and satchel-charges as they mopped-up along the reverse slope. Now the sound of increasingly answering Japanese gunfire was added.

"Down there?" he asked incredulously, nodding his head toward the noisy valley.

"Yep," I answered, "he wants me to come down there to his tank."

I scrambled up out of the trench and ran to where a couple of medics stood by a big stack of folded-up canvas stretchers and said, "Would y'all bring a stretcher and go with me down there?" I pointed to where the tanks were. "A tank just radioed they have a badly injured man down there who needs immediate attention."

Typically, they never hesitated. As far as I am concerned, the medics were the real heroes of the war. One of them picked up a folded stretcher, put it over his shoulder and said, "Let's go."

I trotted down the top of the ridge with them following me until the tanks were just below us. We passed through the line of entrenched infantrymen on the rim and then started zig-zagging down the steep face of the reverse slope toward the intended tank. The fierce rattle of an ongoing firefight began to sound very close. Before long, the three of us were moving among our infantrymen, who had come from the east with the tanks. They were frantically firing their guns and putting hand grenades and satchel-charges into any and all suspicious looking places as they cautiously advanced along the reverse slope.

Suddenly, as the two medics and I came trotting by, an infantryman reached out and grabbed my arm. "Don't go that way," he said excitedly. "There's a machine gun firing out of a hole beneath that big rock. He's already shot a couple of our guys." He motioned toward two crumpled GIs lying downhill.

He warned us just in time; we had been about to run directly in front of that rock. We waited as another GI carefully climbed on top of this rock and, widening his legs, suddenly swung what looked like a small backpack down beneath the rock. "Fire in the hole," he yelled as he ducked back, and there was a ground-shaking explosion as the composition-C explosive contained in the twenty-pound satchel-charge went off.

Immediately following that blast, a stocky soldier carrying a Browning Automatic Rifle (BAR), leaped right in front of the still smoking hole beneath the rock. With his BAR gun on full-automatic fire, he sprayed a clip of bullets into the aperture and quickly stepped back, as another GI instantly darted forward and hurled a grenade into the opening. It was savage, deadly business but the two medics and I left them busily at their work and hurried on to where the lieutenant was standing on the back of his tank, violently pumping his arm up and down in the signal to hurry and shouting for us to come on.

More of our infantrymen streamed past us on the attack, and there was suddenly an increase in the sounds of shouting and firing as we reached the lieutenant's tank. I looked intently at the still form of a soldier lying on the back deck of the tank. He was wearing a leather tanker's helmet, but upon getting closer, I could see a round bullet hole in his forehead over one eye and that the back of the leather helmet was in bloody tatters. One of the medics stepped up on the tank's bogey wheel and looked closely at the man, then said loudly, "He's gone. He's had it."

I looked up at the lieutenant and shouted over the noise of the rapidly increasing din of firefight nearby, "He's dead, Lieutenant."

"Dead?" He screamed back "Goddamn it! I told you to hurry, and you just messed around, and now he's dead!"

He was highly agitated, and his eyes were wild-looking, so I refrained from pointing out the obvious fact that the man had undoubtedly been killed instantly, being unsure of how he might react to that. He stood on the back deck of the tank, hands on his hips, glaring back and forth from the dead man to me. I glared back at him, thinking to myself, "Quit looking at me like that! I didn't shoot him!"

The two medics had unfolded the stretcher and pushed it up on the back of the tank next to the dead man, and now all of us remained frozen in our various positions, mulling over the situation and contemplating our next move. The noise of the nearby battle had greatly intensified. It was obvious the Japanese were now resisting fiercely.

Suddenly there was a loud, hollow pop, like the sound of a watermelon being hit hard with a board. The steel helmet of the medic standing on the bogey wheel went flying off as his head, exploding in a mist of blood, bone, and fragments. He slumped to the ground. The other medic and I dropped and lay as flat as we could on the ground behind the body of the just-killed medic. We now experienced a rising crescendo of sounds—shots, screams, explosions, the electrifying snapping crack-crack-crack sounds that bullets make when they are passing very close by your ears. It's a sound which once heard is never forgotten, for it means death is passing just inches away.

Now to make things worse, big 150mm Japanese artillery shells began moaning in and exploding nearby, inching their way toward us. "Christ, we've got to get out of here," the lieutenant screamed, as he quickly disappeared down the hatch in the turret of his tank, which immediately zoomed off, the other tanks of his platoon following. The dead man and the stretcher on the back of the tank slid down to the ground in a pile as the speeding tank made a violent turn. The other medic and I remained stretched out as flat as we could behind the dead medic as Japanese bullets snapped and crackled all around and over us.

Our infantrymen who had been moving forward on the attack, now had reversed direction and began to retreat, rapidly running past us. "They're coming!" one shouted at us excitedly as he sped by in retreat.

"Who's coming?" I thought fearfully as I raised up my head and looked in the direction our boys were now withdrawing from at top speed. Sure enough, my heart leaping at the sight, I saw a whole gaggle of little, uniformed, bandy-legged men carrying rifles with long, gleaming bayonets, led by two sword-waving officers running madly toward us, shouting hoarsely in a wild counterattack. They were not very far away from us.

Where they had come from I do not know. It was as if they had simply risen out of the ground. The medic and I took off running as fast as I ever ran in my life, in the direction our infantry was retreating. We hadn't gone very far when we zipped between two prone-positioned soldiers, who, I now saw, were part of a long line of our infantrymen. Their officers and non-coms had quickly organized them to handle this Japanese counterattack. All the men in this line were silently lying flat and pointing their guns toward the oncoming Japanese. Two light machine guns were also in this line, manned by prone, alert gunners.

The appearance of this silent, unmoving line so grimly and confidently awaiting the oncoming Japanese was both ominous and menacing, but greatly reassuring to me. I fell flat on the ground behind these waiting men. I was winded from my all-out dash, but shakily pulled my .45 automatic pistol from its shoulder holster. As I did so, I heard a nearby bass voice with a definite southern accent, say loudly but calmly, "All right, boys, let them have it."

With that order the whole firing line opened up. I heard screams and strange-sounding shouts. I saw the crowd of running Japanese soldiers, not over thirty or forty yards away, simply melting away under the fiercely unremitting fire, many spinning and crumpling, but a few turning back in retreat. The firing continued until the only Japanese in sight were the crumpled pile of shot down ones.

At last the firing stopped. After a period of watchful waiting, the infantry line began to get to their feet. "That sword is mine," cried out the stocky boy with the BAR as he leaped to his feet. "I got that SOB," and he began to run, along with several others out to where the shot down Japanese were lying. Some were twitching and moaning, just wounded, but they soon received the *coup de grace* by the Americans, who then began to strip them of whatever they had that they wanted. Nearly all American soldiers were inveterate souvenir hunters, even at the risk of their own lives, and a Japanese officer's Nambu pistol or Samurai sword would fetch a high price from the navy boys back on the beach.

I left this group of infantrymen who had so competently demolished the Japanese counterattack. Under the urgings of their NCOs and officers, they had begun to advance again, firing and satchel-charging their way along the reverse slope in a continuation of mopping-up. I holstered my unfired pistol and trudged back up the slope toward the OP. As I drew nearer to the top, I waved a greeting up to the line of riflemen in the trench atop the ridge so, hopefully, they would not shoot me. They looked at me curiously as I passed through them and one of them said, "Hot enough down there for you?"

I felt a surge of anger at his flippancy, but he had a good-natured grin on his face so I just shook my head, denoting that it had been a SNAFU situation. Indeed, I was too winded from the climb and what I had witnessed to speak.

Photograph courtesy U.S. Army

Tank at work, buttoned up.

Chapter 7

LIAISON OFFICER BECOMES TANK COMMANDER

"The ghosts of other dead men stood near me and told me each his own melancholy tale."

The Odyssey

Okinawa

May 2, 1945

Dear Mother,

At last we have a little free time, as we have been relieved for a short time to get up to fighting strength again in men & machines. We haven't fared as bad as some of the other tank units but our company has been treated pretty rough anyway. I have one tank left in my platoon, but our casualties have been light. We moved out one morning early and operated in front of the lines as usual. It came a big rain all day and by night two of my tanks were hopelessly bogged down. We got all the men out and into the other tanks and took off. During the night the Japs blew the two tanks sky high, of course. The next day I took the assault guns over and calmly sat and blasted off the top of Sawtooth Ridge. It was like a section of the Maginot line as it had four floors, electric lights, and five feet of reinforced concrete covered with dirt and rip-rapped with blocks of coral. We blasted it for two days, the tanks on one side of the ridge and assault guns on the other. A lot of times we were ordered to cease fire and our infantry would move along toward it only to be met with heavy fire. It's remarkable how much those Japs can stand. We finally blew the tops clear off and the infantry dropped about a freight-car load of heavy mortar shells down through the top, which seemed to dishearten the inmates somewhat. I took several pictures of the ridge but I don't know how good they will be.

I got my first Jap at a thousand yards with a rifle. He was an artillery spotter I guess, as he would raise up & peer around through his binoculars. There was an observer with me who had a twenty-power scope, and he directed my fire. I shot enough tracers at him to kill a regiment of Japs. Since then my tanks have closed up, burnt out and blasted so many caves, houses and pillboxes [that] we've probably accounted for several hundred, but that first one really counted.

These Japs are no bandy-legged runts. They are husky, well fed and mean as they come. Every dead one I see gives me a feeling of satisfaction I didn't used to get until I saw our boys killed. There is no need for any pity whatsoever toward the Japanese.

I used to think that it was a lot of bunk about getting used to sleeping on the ground. I borrowed an air mattress the other night and couldn't sleep on it at all it was so soft. It felt like there was nothing under me.

Been getting your packages right along. They are supposed to bring PX rations in before long, and then we can buy stuff, but this sure tastes good. We all get a big kick out of the funnies.

I've had it proved to me time and again that something is surely looking after me. One time I actually got down and thanked Him right there on the spot. That may sound funny to a lot of people, but those who laugh have never been left unscratched when men close enough to touch have been killed. If you didn't feel as if someone was looking over you, I don't believe you could go back at all. Tanks are nerve wracking anyway. You're out in front, vision very limited, constant roar of guns, motors, radio and traversing motors as well as looking for your own infantry and trying to distinguish who is friendly and who isn't. They all look about alike through a periscope. When you multiply that five times you have the troubles of the poor platoon leader but then everyone has his troubles and I wouldn't change places with anybody. Not that I'm brave, I know I've been scaredest of anybody.

It should be all over pretty soon. We are all hoping Japan will see the light and quit. Surely she realizes what will happen when our European armies get over here, as well as all the bombers. If she quits now, she might save a little something, a lot of her people's neck[s] for one thing. I think they ought to keep a constant blanket of gas over Japan for about two weeks. That would do the same job in an easier manner.

It's hard to realize May is here. We sure used to look for that month to roll around. I wish I was still in about the third grade.

... Hope you are all fine. I am....

Lots of love,

Bob

Okinawa
May 3, 1945

Dear Mother,

We are all feeling much better physically & mentally now. It's sure easy to see how anybody could get combat fatigue. What helps most is to be away from the artillery. We've had Jap artillery shooting over us so long, we're about all deaf.

It's raining again but we have a big, new tent so don't mind. We are really fixed up pretty nice. We thought we were going to get canvas cots but didn't, but that is a very small item. I think I could sleep on a cattle guard now with ease.

I've seen three of the boys I came over with, but still haven't seen Jones. I'm kind of worried about him. Infantry officers take a beating in this kind of fighting.

We are back up to strength now in tanks and are getting replacements in men, so we will be all fixed up pretty soon. I have the 1st platoon now.

Lots of old mail is coming in now .... It comes by boat from Leyte so it takes a good while.

Sure enjoy getting mail. That's the most important part of the day.

Lots of love,

Bob

Okinawa
May 6, 1945

Dear Mother,

This is a quiet, peaceful Sunday morning. It would almost be time for church if there was a church.

We've been taking it easy & enjoying ourselves the last few days. Not anything to do and that's my idea of fighting a war.

This place is a mad house every night about twelve. There are a bunch of Jap infiltrators running around loose & it's just like a wild western with all the shooting, yelling & chasing you ever heard. To want to die so, these Japs can sure get up and make tracks. We couldn't even catch one in a jeep the other night. Another time we chased a horse about 2 miles. He sounded like a whole platoon of Japs.

These navy anti-aircraft gunners need some additional training or something. If I were the guys who work the search lights, I'd quit. They keep the plane right in the light, and you never saw such shooting. They hit everything, but the Japs. There will be lines & lines of tracers going up somewhere in the vicinity of the plane, & without fail there will be about half a dozen lines going the other way, just blazing away. Then, if the plane does make a suicide dive every, ship in the harbor paints another Jap flag on the bridge. It's no wonder we are doing so well when every ship in the harbor shoots down two or three planes apiece. The navy fights a hard war, though I'd hate to have to crawl into a top bunk at night & try to remember which of the myriads of silverware to use for which course. It's so much simpler to fall in a hole at night and open a can when you're hungry.

I've got to do a washing today. We have us a barrel cut in two pieces to boil our clothes in. We go through all this motion, but I really don't think it does much good.

I'll sure be relieved to hear from Jones.… Hope everything is alright. I am fine.

>Lots of love,
>Bob

Okinawa
May 3, 1945

Dear Sis,

… I have a platoon of tanks now & like it much better than being liaison with the infantry. We are supporting the 96th Inf. Division and have had it fairly rough. I've had two tanks knocked out from under me so I'm beginning to think I'm a Jonah or something. Anyway I've got a full craw of fighting for a while. I believe I was more excited over killing my first Jap than anything I've done yet. I borrowed a Garand off a doughboy while I was with them. It's great sport, all except them shooting back. They are really dug in.

I should have some good pictures. I looked like one of these correspondents running around taking pictures. Most of the correspondents are with the marines so we don't expect much of a write up.... I'll enclose a picture of a now good Jap. I'm wearing his belt and have his cap, bayonet & gun. They all have a lot of pictures & carry all kinds of notebooks. They seem to be fairly educated. I found one notebook full of analytics & calculus.... They had a wounded Jap the other day giving [him] blood plasma. When they stuck the needle in his arm he jumped & tried to get up. One of the medics yelled, "Lie down there. You're a Jap. You're supposed to be a tough s.o.b." He lay down & said "OK, Joe," and everybody laughed & somebody gave him a cigarette which is very unusual, as they usually don't bother with Japs at all.

Guess I had better stop. It is getting dark & we can't have any light.

> Lots of love,
> Bob

The next day at daylight, my radioman and I returned to the OP on Maeda Escarpment. Much of the reverse slope had been occupied the day before by our infantry who had dug in and spent the night near where I witnessed them demolish the attempted Japanese counterattack.

Today our A Company tanks had returned and were working just under the hill, having again circled around the east end of the Maeda Escarpment. They were heavily engaged in firing on the reverse slope in support of our infantry who were following them. These tank/infantry teams were continuing to mop-up the reverse slope, carefully firing into and using satchel-charges to blast any suspicious looking nook or cranny as they cautiously worked their way along.

Corporal Stone, still acting as my radioman, and I were again up on top at the Maeda OP and in the trench along the back-topside of the high ridge, along with many other observers from the Army and Navy. Someone with a twenty-power spotting scope had located a Japanese forward observer across the valley who would periodically rise up in a cave opening and peer intently through binoculars at our tanks and infantry. When he did that, the guy looking through the twenty-power scope would shout, "He's up! Shoot! Shoot." Then some of the infantrymen in the trench would blaze away, but it was a long shot, and no one was even coming close to the Jap observer's cave opening.

I had always been a crack shot, even before the army, so I decided to get involved. I borrowed an M-1 Garand rifle from a soldier in the trench with us who had been shooting to no avail whenever the spotter said the Jap was standing up and exposed. It soon was obvious to me that the borrowed rifle was not sighted in properly at all. I told the spotter with the twenty-power scope to watch my shots as I aimed and fired tracer bullets at a white-colored rock off to one side of the Jap's hole. He did so, and while I fired shots of tracer ammunition at the rock, he would report where they were hitting, and I moved and adjusted the sights. Soon, I was hitting the white rock every time I fired, even though it was quite a long shot. We estimated it to be at least 700 yards, maybe just a little farther. Now I aimed directly at the top of the Japanese observer's dark hole and waited.

"Now! Now! He's standing up," cried the spotter and I quickly squeezed off a shot. "You got him! By God, you got him! Good shot!" the spotter cried and then let me look. Sure enough, a brown-clad body could be seen through the twenty-power scope, draped over the front lip of a hole. That was the first enemy I knew for sure I had done away with, although I would soon be responsible for the deaths of many more in the days ahead.

Today, I don't enjoy remembering that. In fact, I don't like to think about it at all, although when taken into the context of the times, it was certainly justified. Killing Japanese soldiers was what we were there to do. I can remember even then that I secretly had a nagging feeling of sadness or regret at the whole terrible mess of the war and what it was doing to so many people around the world, in particular, the civilians of Okinawa. It would have taken a really hardhearted person not to have been touched by what was happening to them during the battle for the island. They were truly between the proverbial rock and hard place.

The Japanese military would drive crowds of these civilians ahead of them into our lines, while Japanese soldiers would dress in civilian clothes and mix in with the true civilians. When the crowd would get near our positions, the Americans, seeing women and children, would hold their fire. That, of course, was what the Japanese military had counted on. When close enough to do great damage, the Jap soldiers dressed as civilians would produce weapons from beneath their clothing and kill as many Americans as they could before they, and often many civilians as well, were killed by American return gunfire. It was pretty bad.

In looking back now, I blame the Japanese, with their fanatical belief in "Fighting Spirit," much more than the Americans for the horrendous civilian deaths, estimated to be upwards of 120,000 people. That was more dead people than the combined total killed later at Hiroshima and Nagasaki by the two atomic bombs. The Japanese had tried to brainwash the Okinawans into believing the Americans were complete savages, and it was much better to kill yourself than be captured by them. Unfortunately, many civilians believed this ideology and wouldn't come out of underground positions where they were hiding and were consequently killed by us as the positions were neutralized. Many civilians who wanted to surrender to the Americans would be shot down from behind by Japanese soldiers as they tried to come out of their hiding places. The Japanese

Photograph courtesy U.S. Army
American GI feeding an Okinawan child.

soldiers, fully prepared to die fighting to be true to their Bushido belief, had little regard or feeling for any of the civilians who, in their eyes, were cravenly trying to surrender to the Americans and stay alive. They even began to brutally kill civilians for their food or whatever else they had that the soldiers wanted. The "Fighting Spirit" of Bushido, which the Japanese tried to adhere to, gave little mercy. On the other hand, the American soldiers I was associated with, except for a very few, tried hard to avoid killing civilians and often showed great concern and kindness toward them when they could, particularly with the little children.

Many times when reaching the front line infantry positions in early morning, I saw little children being fed by GIs. The kids had been left abandoned or their people had been killed, and they were just wandering about no-man's-land by themselves, which was highly dangerous. It was heart-rending to see these waifs being cared for tenderly by tough looking American soldiers until the chaplains and MPs could take them to the rear where civilian refugee camps were set up.

After my experience as a successful sniper with a borrowed rifle on the OP I returned the gun to its GI owner. He thanked me for sighting it in for him. "You can keep it if you want it," he said with a smile.

"No thanks," I grinned back, "it's too heavy." A loaded M-1 Garand did weigh over ten pounds.

Corporal Stone was sitting far down in the very bottom of the trench reading a dirty, wrinkled mimeographed sheet of paper. This paper, printed far behind the lines, contained current world and state-side events and was occasionally available at the front to keep the troops informed.

"You ought to read this," Stone said, holding it out to me. Nothing much was going on, so I sat down in the very bottom of the trench with him, and just as he handed the paper to me, all hell completely broke loose.

The very ground we were sitting on rocked and rolled, and my ears rang and hurt from the sudden roar of a great explosion very close to us. I was absolutely stunned from the concussion for several seconds. I felt something wet and warm suddenly drape across the back of my neck and shoulders, and something else wetly plopped down in my lap. Looking down, I saw a large, quivering, dark red mound of something that looked like raw liver in my lap. I remember thinking, "If that's mine, I've had it," but then as the dust and smoke cleared, loud, awful screaming began nearby, and I knew something really bad had happened to a lot of people. And it had.

At least two 155mm rounds from our own "Long Tom" artillery pieces that were located several miles behind us had for some reason fallen short and failed to clear the ridge we were on. They had struck squarely on the top of the Maeda Escarpment OP among the crowd of people there. One had exploded immediately behind the trench where I had just sunk down to read the news sheet. Two or three observers in the trench with me were sheared off at the waist by flying shards of steel shrapnel. They had been standing up and were exposed from the waist up as they leaned against the front of the trench to watch and adjust artillery fire in the valley below.

Seven or eight more men were wiped out or wounded when the other shells landed in their midst, as they were crowded into the open space behind us. As my head cleared, I stood up, greatly shaken, and brushed the bloody red clump, which was a kidney or liver, out of my lap and then saw that the wet feeling across my back, shoulders and neck was caused by a long segment of someone's intestine. I pulled it off gingerly and discarded it with stomach heaving. I still can remember how bad it smelled.

My radioman was still so dazed in the bottom of the trench, he couldn't move or speak. The part of the radio on his back that stuck up above his head was covered with blood and pieces of somebody's guts, but like me he was unhurt because we had both been down so deep in the trench.

"Let's get out of here," I said to him shakily and reached down to give him a hand up. We would be leaving our assigned spot a little early, but I felt like I had to get away from the mayhem all around us if I could. The terrible screams of the badly wounded always had an unnerving effect on me. They were horrible.

We left the trench and started back across the freshly churned up area where the friendly fire had just impacted. Those who had an instant ago been vitally alive men on either side of us in the trench were now just bloody, unrecognizable lumps and mounds of flesh and clothing. As we staggered across the top to get to the trail going to our jeep, I tried not to look at the blown-apart segments of what was left of four or five boys. Their parts were strewn along both sides of our route. Medics were already on hand and working on several badly wounded, screaming men. I gritted my teeth at this horrible chorus and then moved off to one side of the trail to let several other medics run by. They were racing up the trail from the aide-station below to help with the wounded on top.

At last we got down the trail and off the hill. When we reached our jeep, I helped Corporal Stone take the bloody radio set off his back. In doing so, I discovered that a piece of shrapnel had taken a big chunk off the top of it, rendering it inoperable. It seemed we were hard on radios, but this very likely saved the radioman's life. Though Corporal Stone made it through the war unscathed, in a perverse twist of fate, he was killed soon after returning home from overseas when a tractor turned over on him at his dad's farm near Robstown, Texas. Such happenings lead to a fatalistic belief.

Checking each other over, we found that we had escaped any damage, physically at least. I took off my stained and bloody fatigue jacket and pitched it on the ground beside the blood-covered radio. We didn't want either one any more.

We drove grimly in the jeep, away from the Maeda Escarpment and headed for our bivouac. When we arrived there, Captain Kennedy saw us and rushed over to the jeep. "Man, am I glad to see you two. We thought you all had had it. The tanks working down below you saw some big shells exploding right up there where you all had been staying, and then they couldn't raise you on the radio, so we imagined the worst. Are you guys OK?"

"Well," I said, "We had a close call but were very lucky and we're OK, but a bunch of poor guys up there were wiped out and so was our radio. It was a complete casualty."

"Well, screw the radios," said Kennedy, "but I'm really glad to see you all." With that he clapped me on my bare back.

I kind of smiled at him and thought to myself, "You're a good guy," and even today I still believe that.

Continuing in my job as a liaison officer several days later, I was up at an OP that had been moved forward with an advance of the 381st Infantry. It was a miserable, rainy morning, and our advance once again had been stalled by the ferocious Japanese defense on yet another highly fortified reverse slope of a ridge. Suddenly, I received an urgent summons over the radio from Captain Kennedy. He told me to hurry down to where one of his platoon leaders named Lieutenant Fielding [actual name has been changed to protect the identity of this lieutenant] had his tanks lined up on the narrow road behind the hill the OP was on. Lieutenant Fielding, a quiet Jewish boy from Chicago, had gradually begun losing it. A tank platoon leader normally leads his platoon of five or so tanks from the lead tank. Lately Lieutenant Fielding had been trying to lead his platoon from the rear tank, and that hadn't worked out very well.

As I hurried up, I saw a cluster of high brass gathered around the side of Lieutenant Fielding's tank in the steadily falling rain. I recognized General Easley, the second in command of the 96th Division, as well as the 381st Regimental commander, Colonel Halloran. I didn't recognize some of the other high brass in the group, but it was obvious they were all displeased about something. A distraught looking Captain Kennedy was standing dejectedly by Lieutenant John Turbeville, who had been a couple of grades ahead of me at NMMI. He recognized me and nodded a greeting to me as I hurriedly joined the group. General Easley had climbed up on the side of the tank and was talking sternly to an ashen-faced, fearful looking Lieutenant Fielding whose head, encased in a leather tanker's helmet, was protruding up out of the opened turret hatch. I heard General Easley tell Lieutenant Fielding something I have never forgotten.

"Son," he said, "a platoon of tanks is just like a piece of spaghetti. You can pull it from the front, but you can't push it from behind. Now I want you to listen carefully, because I am giving you a direct order. I am *ordering* you to take this tank and get in front of these other four tanks and lead your platoon through that cut in the hill," and here he pointed. "I want you to go down that road far enough so you can get in behind and fire on the reverse slope of this hill. Our infantry took heavy losses yesterday, because they didn't have any aggressive tank support from you. I don't want that to happen again today." Then with his voice rising, he finished up loudly with, "I want you to go down there and give them proper support and I mean I want you to do it *right now!*"

Fielding, with eyes tightly shut and tears streaming down his face, began shaking his head from side to side and said, "I cannot do that. I just can't," and then he sank down out of sight into the tank's turret.

Easley, obviously very upset, jumped down off the tank and turned on Captain Kennedy. "Get him out of there," he barked, "and then put someone in charge of these tanks that will get them going and do what needs to be done."

A shaken Captain Kennedy said, "Yes sir," and turning to me said, "Green, you've got to take over Fielding's platoon. Let's get Fielding out of there." So with the assistance of Fielding's tank crew, we pulled him up out of the turret. It was pitiful. He was weeping loudly and had soiled his clothes. Someone led him away, and I never saw or heard of him again. In the vicious fighting on Okinawa, hundreds of GIs suffered combat fatigue. Fielding was only one of many that this happened to. A special hospital had to be set up by the 10th Army just to accommodate those who suffered from this malady.

After Fielding had been pulled from his tank and led away, General Easley and Colonel Halloran unfolded a map and turned to me. With fingers tracing down the map, they showed me exactly where it was they wanted me to go. It looked easy on the map. "Just go through this road—cut over here and then on down the road until you can get in behind this hill. Then, lay all the fire you can on the reverse slope while the infantry tries again to advance behind you and over the top of this hill." They asked if I understood the plan, and I said that I did. Then Easley said briskly, "Well, let's do it. Let's get moving." He was not one to wait around.

So I got into Fielding's tank, put on his leather helmet, still warm from his head, picked up the mike and switched to intercom, the channel for communicating with the tank crew, and ordered the driver to pull around the four other idling tanks and get in front of them. When we had passed the lead tank, I switched the radio control to platoon channel that all the tanks could "read" or hear and said something like, "Ok, boys, follow me down this hill in single file. Stay in my tracks in case there are mines. We don't all need to hit one. They want us to get around this hill mass and put fire on its reverse slope while the infantry tries to follow us, so let's try and do what they want."

So now, like pulling a string of spaghetti, as General Easley had put it, I led the other tanks down the narrow road as off we went in the rain. We passed by a long line of strung-out crouching infantrymen, clad in their green ponchos to ward off the steadily falling rain, as they waited behind the crest of the hill. Several gave us a thumbs-up sign of encouragement as we went by, while others simply stared glumly up at the tank commanders. They dreaded having to follow us over the crest and go down the hill again into the killing ground where they had been so savagely repulsed the day before.

Our line of tanks now passed through the cut in the crest of the hill where our infantry had water-cooled machine gun crews dug in on either side of the road. From time to time these guns would place searching fire down both sides of the road as a deterrent for possible Japanese soldiers attempting to sneak up the road or bar ditches.

Passing by them and through the cut, I gave the order over the radio to "button up." All drivers and tank commanders who had their hatches open and heads out in order to see better, now lowered down out of sight inside the tanks and all the hatches were closed and latched. Now visibility was limited to the periscopes, and the rain made them blurry at best. As we proceeded down the hill, Japanese machine gun fire soon began to rattle off the front and left side of the tank. They were trying to shoot out our periscope heads, but so far had not been successful in doing so. If they were successful in doing this, we would have to quickly pull down the periscope and change the shot-out prism head with a new replacement head. There were several racks of these replacement prism heads located in various handy places about the tank's interior.

On down the road we trundled into no-man's-land. The landscape was getting pretty spooky looking. We now had to swerve to avoid running over a sad looking cluster of six to eight dead GIs, lying crumpled in the road. There were several more of our boys lying dead, strung out all down the left side of the road. They had been caught in a vicious crossfire and mortar barrage that killed them while they were trying to advance the day before.

Now clusters of Japanese mortar shells began to rain down and explode all around us as the rattle of their machine gun fire against the sides of the tank increased. Mortars usually wouldn't damage a tank unless it was a very lucky hit, and we didn't fear them as much as we did mines or the deadly anti-tank gun. Slowly we moved on down the road, deeper into the killing ground of the day before. I pulled my periscope down, wiped the raindrops off the head and quickly replaced it so I could see out better.

Tension mounted as we turned around the end of a spur of the hill and started moving in behind it to begin firing on the dreaded reverse slope. Now signs of current Japanese occupation and activities became easily apparent, with numerous large and small cave entrances and emplacements visible. We had fleeting glimpses of darting Japanese soldiers, obviously surprised at our appearance, hastily running along the well-used network of trails that snaked up the reverse slope to quickly disappear underground in a hole.

The valley floor was littered with equipment of all kind. Most of it was in bad shape or wrecked. There were three antique-looking made-in-Japan trucks that were backed up to a large cave opening and still partially loaded with boxes of something. They appeared to have been strafed into junk by naval planes.

As we continued to slowly advance, I talked on the radio to the other tanks saying, "Fire at will into all those cave entrances to our left when you can see them." The gunner in my tank let off a long run of machine gun fire from the coaxial gun. Every fifth round was a tracer, so in the dim, rainy light, it looked like red streaks of fire were plunging into the dark cave openings. Then with a loud wham, the gunner fired the tank's cannon, sending a round of 75mm HE into the cave.

The gunner had two buttons on the floor that looked exactly like a dimmer switch for car headlights. One was for the coaxial machine gun and the other fired the cannon when pressed by the gunner's foot. When the cannon fired, it recoiled, automatically ejecting the brass shell case, and the breechblock would remain open. The empty brass clanged and clattered to the steel floor of the fighting compartment. When the heel of the loader's right hand slammed in another shell, the rim of the new shell's brass case depressed a yoke as it entered the gun's chamber. This activated the immediate closing of the breech. As it quickly slammed shut, from right to left, it pushed the heel of the loader's hand out of the way. If you didn't load the right way, by using the heel of your right hand, with fingers to the left, the closing breechblock could easily sever a finger or two.

Japanese tanks were practically out of business at this stage of the war, as the Japanese had gone underground. But they had those good, high-velocity anti-tank guns that they took with them and cleverly concealed underground.

So now, still "pulling *my* string of spaghetti," I had led the other tanks through the cut, down the road and around behind the hill, and we began to lay fire on the reverse slope. I repeated the order for all the tanks to keep firing at will into the many caves and emplacements that now came into view as we moved farther behind the hill. All five tanks now vigorously began to lay all the fire they possibly could on this reverse slope as General Easley had requested. We slowly and cautiously moved farther into the valley, firing on the many targets that were now revealed. Suddenly, there was a loud noise and my tank shuddered. There was a furious clattering from its transmission as we ground to a halt.

"Green, you're being hit!" someone in one of the following tanks screamed in the radio. They had seen a shower of sparks radiate from the side of my tank where an anti-tank gun's armor-piercing round had struck us. Then another tremendous blow rocked my tank as we were hit again. This time I clearly saw through my periscope a quick wink of bright light on the bluff to our left as if someone had quickly flashed a spotlight on and off. I immediately knew it was made by the anti-tank gun that was firing on us. As I frantically looked through the murky periscope, I could see absolutely no sign of an opening on the hillside where I had seen the wink.

I quickly reached down, using the traversing control to turn the turret around until my sight hit the point where I thought the wink of bright light had been. In the tank model we had, the commanders had an open sight that was coordinated with the gunner's telescopic sight. A tank commander could traverse the turret to line up his open sight on a suspected target, thus showing his gunner exactly where to look through his telescopic sight.

"Fire right there!" I screamed at my gunner who immediately did so, first with tracers from the coaxial machine gun then with the cannon. "You other tanks fire where we are firing!" I shouted over the radio and they followed my orders, but then I saw the bright wink of light again as we were simultaneously whammed. The first two shots from the hidden anti-tank gun, although knocking out our drive chain and stopping our tank, had penetrated beneath our location in the turret. But this one came right through the side of the fighting compartment, removing one of the loader's legs just above his boot top as it did so.

Now it was pure bedlam, the loader screaming, his blood squirting all over everything, smoke filling up the inside and coming from God knows where, the driver shouting, "It won't move!" as he gunned the motor and ground and clashed the gears to no avail.

The gunner, a genuine Missouri hillbilly named Scoggins, was still tending to business, and he was as cool as a cucumber. He kept on lacing the hill with machine gunfire. "Keep firing on that hill where we are firing," I radioed the other tanks and then quickly reached up over the radio set for a morphine styrette. I went to the loader who was now down on the floor making horrible noises. I quickly removed the morphine styrette's needle cover and emptied it into his thigh. I then put my hand over the severed stump of his leg and squeezing tight, tried to stop the squirting blood. I remember being startled at seeing the round hole in the steel side of the tank where the Jap AP round had come through.

"Load me a round, Green, load me a round! I see the son of a bitch's hole!" screamed the gunner who was squinting intently through his telescopic gun-sight. The driver, good old steady Al Blomgren, had stopped trying to get the stricken tank to move and was looking back wide-eyed into the fighting compartment from his seat. I shouted at him to reach back and squeeze the stump of the loader's leg, as I was doing, so I could load a round into the cannon.

He reacted quickly, crawling out of his driver's seat until he could reach back and replace my bloody hand on the loader's leg. I jerked a yellow-nosed HE round from the ready-rack and slammed it into the cannon's breech. The gun immediately fired and recoiled, and I slammed another round in. And then another. I can still vividly remember how the ejected brass rounds that crashed down and lay on the floor looked with my bloody handprints all over them. The gunner, still calm as could be, now said happily, "I think we just settled that bastard's hash. Now what are we going to do?" Japanese machine gun fire rattled off the tank, but thankfully there were no more anti-tank rounds.

"We are going to get the hell out of this tank, but first get the fire extin-guisher and see if you can find out where all that smoke is coming from before we blow up," I said grimly. Picking up the microphone, I ordered the tank behind us to come up until he just bumped the rear of our tank, and then to open the escape hatch in the bottom of his tank. I told him that we were going to have to abandon our tank and get into theirs via the two escape hatches. I told the other tanks to start firing white phosphorous (WP) shells against the side of the hill to our left to blanket it in a smoke screen. I hoped the smoke might conceal us from Japanese machine gunners when we made our escape.

The other tanks immediately began to fire and soon had a pretty dense cloud of white smoke blanketing the hillside where most of the machine-gun fire had come from. I switched the radio over to intercom and told my bog (assistant driver) to open the escape hatch in the floor just behind his seat. That done, I quickly knelt down to the now semi-conscious loader who was slumped on the floor. The morphine had begun to take effect. I was surprised to see that the driver had tied a piece of cord, or maybe a shoelace, tightly around the stump of the loader's leg and the spurting of blood had mostly stopped. I also saw that the driver was bleeding all down his left shoulder. He saw me looking at his injured shoulder with concern and said, "I'm OK, I'm OK."

Photograph courtesy U.S. Army
Tanks in action. The center tank has been disabled, much as mine was, and the other tanks are coming in to rescue the crew.

"Well," I said, "if you're OK, let's get him to the escape hatch." I began to push the loader down through the cage opening of the fighting compartment. Both the driver and the bog reached over to help, and with me pushing from inside the cage, the floor of which was now slippery with blood, we got the comatose loader out of the turret.

"You two get him on out the escape hatch and pull him back under our tank, then get in the one behind," I said and then started pulling the crystals out of the radio and putting them in my pocket to render it unworkable. Meanwhile, the gunner was grinning and holding up a smoking rag wrapped around the anti-tank round. It had come through the side and crossed completely through the fighting compartment, where it had struck, but failed to penetrate the other side of the turret. The friction generated as it punched through the side of our tank had made it hot enough to cause a rag on the floor to smolder. How it had missed my feet and legs when it passed through, I will never know.

"Put that thing down and get the firing pin out of the cannon," I told the gunner as I demolished the radio. The firing pin assembly was a round cylinder about the size of a can of soup recessed in the back of the breechblock. You were supposed to be able to push it in, turn it a quarter turn and the whole "shebang" should come out in your hand. Sometimes it would and sometimes it wouldn't. This time, thankfully, it did. Without it in place, the cannon wouldn't fire. To leave a tank in enemy territory with an operational cannon was a big no-no. The Japanese had quickly turned some tanks that had been abandoned by another tank battalion into their own pillboxes and we wanted to avoid having that said about our battalion at all costs.

I had finished deactivating the radio, and he had the firing pin out, so we quickly squirmed down out of the turret cage and into the space behind the bog's seat. There, through the open escape hatch, we saw the muddy ground with a bloody trail showing where the driver and bog had dragged the injured loader. Quickly, we dropped down and crawled through the escape hatch and slithered on our bellies in the mud beneath the tanks. It was scary being outside the tank, deep in enemy territory. Thankfully, no machine gun fire came under the tank. Evidently, the smoke screen had successfully masked our escape. When we reached the open escape hatch of the tank waiting just behind us, we clamored up into the crowded interior. It was now a very full tank, but all of us were certainly glad to be there.

"Tell the other tanks to stay in our tracks and back out of here. You follow them," I shouted to the tank commander, and he radioed the other tanks behind to start backing up the hill we had started from. I was afraid to try and turn all the tanks around because of the danger of mines. The Japanese had buried many 500-pound aerial bombs to be used as land mines, and they were deadly to tanks and everyone in them.

When we got back over the crest of the hill and safely behind friendly lines again, we got out one at a time through all the hatches. Medics quickly took the unconscious loader and after quickly inserting an IV in his arm and starting blood plasma, loaded him on a stretcher, which they placed on a jeep. One medic got on board with him to hold the IV bottle up, then they sped away. I learned much later that he survived.

Medics also worked on the injured driver. Small pieces of steel were picked out of his shoulder then he was bandaged up, given a tetanus shot and declared still to be fit for service. As for me, I now began to get the shakes and had to sit down. The heavy, water-cooled Browning machine gun emplacements on either side of the road-cut were surrounded by sandbags, and I just sat down and leaned back against the sandbags while the guns intermittently fired away down the hill. For quite a little while, I shook uncontrollably as if I had a bad chill or malaria.

General Easley walked over, looked down at me and said, "Son, I need to talk to you and find out what you saw behind that hill, but I'll wait until you calm down and quit shaking." I meekly nodded, and then another medic saw the loader's blood all over me. He asked if I were hit. I shook my head and said no, I was OK, and that was true, but only up to a point.

[*Editor's note: Bob Green later received a Bronze Star for this action. He humbly says today that most everyone who saw a lot of combat received a Bronze Star.

The citation reads:

First Lieutenant James R. Green, 0557916, Cavalry (Armored), United States Army. For meritorious achievement in connection with military operations against the enemy on Okinawa Island from 13 April 1945 to 21 June 1945. As Liaison Officer between Tank-Infantry teams, First Lieutenant Green repeatedly exposed himself to enemy observation and fire to obtain better knowledge of the situation and targets. During the battle for Sawtooth Ridge, First Lieutenant Green was always present at the most forward Infantry Observation Posts, gathering information, transmitting it to the tanks, and coordinating their fire and movement with the Infantry. From 19 May 1945 to 21 June 1945, as a Tank Platoon Leader, First Lieutenant Green led his platoon in a superior manner and on many occasions made dismounted reconnaissance, under intense enemy fire, in order to employ his tanks in the most efficient manner. On one occasion, when his own tank was completely disabled, First Lieutenant Green continued undaunted from another tank. His continuous display of courage and devotion to duty under the most adverse conditions reflects great credit on himself and the military service.]

Chapter 8

SHERMAN FLAME-THROWING TANKS AND JAPANESE DEFENSES

"I long—I pine all my days—To travel home and see the dawn of my return."

The Odyssey

Okinawa
May 13, 1945

Dear Mother,

Well, we're back in again & it's not so new or exciting anymore. To tell the truth, I'm just scared, but I'm not alone in that respect. I take a new platoon up in the morning, so I'm a little nervous over that. Our company is in reserve & they needed a platoon leader in C Company so I'm over here. I will go back to A Company when C goes back and A comes up. I like A Company. They are a swell bunch…. Jones is OK. I went down to the 7th Div. to see him but he was gone somewhere. I'm so relieved to know he's alright. This country is rough on Inf. 2nd looeys. There is no definite front line & these Nips are quite willing to walk into sure death if they can get somebody. They kill a bunch every night trying to get into our area & throw satchel-charges on our tanks.

It's about dark so I had better stop. I'm first on guard tonight, thank goodness.

Hope everyone is OK. I am fine…. I sure miss that old ranch house & everybody in it. A quiet place like that would sure be heaven.

Lots of love,

Bob

May 14, 1945

Dear Mother,

Well, I'm back & got along fine today. As usual, it's just about dark. I feel like Genghis Khan tonight as we burned, blew up, ran over, covered up, sealed in caves & just plain shot around two hundred Nips—and I just had five tanks & two flame thrower tanks, but we had quite a good day. This is one place there is no bag limit on game. We go back in the morning but I'm full of confidence in the new men. They can drive, load & shoot to perfection. I really don't see how it could be done better. We got along fine today....

We built our own road today with a tank dozer. The Japs blow all the roads off the sides of these hills & it's practically impossible to get thru. We foxed them today though. We dozed the road thru & I ran a flame thrower down spraying the whole country. They would flush out of their holes just like a bunch of quail. They hide along the roads in spider holes. A spider hole has a top of grass & stuff & you can't see it at all until they pop out. We made a bunch of Japs good today.

> Lots of love,
> Bob

On the 19th of April, the Japanese defenders of Okinawa experienced the terrifying effects of a new weapon the Americans unleashed on them. This was the armored flame-throwing tank. The 713th Tank Battalion had been formed for and equipped and trained in the use of this new weapon on the Hawaiian Island of Oahu, where fifty-five M4-A3 Sherman Tanks had been modified to become flame-throwers. This was done by installing fuel containers that held 300 gallons of napalm and gasoline, along with a high-pressure pump inside the tanks. A pipe was inserted through the cannon tube and the high-pressure pump forced the napalm/gasoline mixture to shoot out of it in a solid stream.

These flame-throwing tanks also had a small copper tube that carried pure gasoline and ran inside the cannon tube along with the napalm pipe. The operator, before firing the main stream of napalm out the larger pipe, caused pure gasoline to come out of the end of the small copper tube and could then make it ignite. That caused a jet of flame to spurt down across the end of the napalm pipe. This jet of flame was called "the igniter," and its purpose was to set the big stream of napalm on fire when it passed through under high pressure. Then in a solid stream of fire, it shot far out from the tank in a fiery torrent. The two pipes carrying fiery death were concealed inside the cannon barrel to confuse the enemy as to which tank was a flame thrower.

All the tanks looked alike until a long fiery stream of napalm suddenly spurted out of a cannon barrel. It looked like a stream out of a high-pressure fire hose, except instead of water, it was flaming napalm. This stream of intense fire could reach out over 100 yards and splash napalm into gun ports and cave entrances.

These cave entrances usually had a ninety-degree turn just inside their openings and then, in a short distance, another ninety-degree turn that led back into the interior. These two ninety-degree turns prevented outside gunfire from being shot directly into the interior of the underground facility, but the flame-throwing tankers were not deterred by this

Photograph courtesy U.S. Army
A flame-throwing tank knocked out this Japanese 47mm anti-tank gun. The charred remains of a crewman is shown nearby.

for long. In just a short time, when facing such a cave entrance, the operators of the flame-throwers had learned to thin down the viscosity of their stream of napalm. Then, by positioning their tank at the proper angle in front of a cave entrance, they were able to ricochet this thinner-than-normal fiery stream at an angle so it would glance off the back wall just inside the cave entrance and then splash on down and around the next turn. This created such a roaring inferno in the cave entrance that it quickly sucked all the oxygen out of the underground emplacement. If the extremely hot fire didn't kill the unfortunate people who were underground inside the cave, the lack of oxygen did.

It was a horribly efficient method of dealing with the dug-in enemy, and as tough as the Japanese soldiers were, it became the one weapon they couldn't stand up to. I don't know of anybody who could.

One old boy in the 713th Tank Battalion, Niemeyer I think his name was, had rigged up a fire hose to his tank so you could also use it on foot. By dragging the fire hose up there among the rocks where a tank couldn't go, you could get in pretty close to where the Japanese emplacements were, if you could avoid getting shot. I used this one time at one of the major holdups at Yazu-

Dake ridge. The Japs were shooting down on our boys from apertures in the cliff where the ground was so rough we could not use our tanks to get up to where they were. The infantry guys said if we could stop them from shooting up there, they could go on with their advance. Niemeyer was carrying the fire hose that was attached to his tank, but nobody wanted to go any closer to this cliff

Photograph courtesy U.S. Army
Infantrymen guarding against satchel-charge teams while tanks work over a Japanese strong point. Notice tank to left of flame-throwing tank, furnishing close-in support.

because of the exposure to Japanese fire, and you couldn't quite reach the crevices with blazing napalm from our present position, even using the fire hose.

I popped off and said to Niemyer, "Well, I think if you would go right up the cliff over here—it looks like the direction that little ravine runs down toward that crevice—you could put some raw napalm in it up there, and it might run down the cliff into that crevice. Then we could throw a smoke grenade and set it off, and it would burn all the way down into the crevice. It would be better to try that than trying to get up close enough to where you could shoot the fire into the hole and get shot, yourself. Just let it run down that ravine and see if it doesn't go down where the Japs are."

He said, "If you want to try it, you're welcome to it," and handed me the hose.

The way that cliff sloped down it sure looked like it would run down into the hole, so that is what I did. I slipped on higher up the cliff with that fire hose, and I was doing great. That napalm was running down there just like I had hoped it would, and then, evidently, there was something on fire down where the Japs were, because all at once the whole damn cliff blew up from down below. You could hear all this terrible screaming from underground where the Japs were. It really sounded horrible. Anyway, that was the end of the resistance there, and the infantry was able to continue their advance.*

The Japanese soldiers soon learned to fear and dread the flame-throwing tank over all others. Many times as I watched alertly from my tank while in close support of the flame-thrower tank, I would see a flame-thrower tank in position in front of a Japanese emplacement light his igniter. When that little flame of the igniter appeared at the end of the gun tube, and before the big stream of flaming napalm came out, Japanese soldiers would literally come bursting out of the caves, emplacements, grass and wood work where they had been concealed, running like hell. Exposed, they could quickly be shot down by machine gun fire from all the tanks. It hadn't taken the Japanese long to learn what soon followed the igniter's little flame, and they wanted no part of it.

The fifty-five flame-throwing tanks of the 713th Battalion arrived on Okinawa on the 2nd of April, the day after we landed, but didn't see action until the 19th of April. They were in continuous action then for the next seventy days, being apportioned out to the regular tank battalions such as our own 763rd. This let each platoon of five regular tanks have at least one or sometimes two flame-throwing tanks as well. Due to losses, a platoon seldom had this many tanks for very long. Forty-one of the original fifty-five flame-throwing tanks were knocked out of action during the campaign. Twenty-six of the forty-one were repaired and soon returned to action. It is my personal belief that the use of these diabolical machines contributed more to the defeat of the Japanese on Okinawa than any other American weapon.

The regular tanks of the American army's armored force on Okinawa also suffered heavy losses. By just the end of May, almost a month before the fighting was over, not counting marine tank losses, the four army tank battalions had lost 221 tanks. I personally had to abandon four disabled tanks myself.

Photograph courtesy U.S. Army
Infantrymen mopping-up on Japanese who were flushed out of a tomb by a flame-throwing tank and killed in the tomb courtyard.

The 221 tanks lost constituted about 57% of the total number of U.S. tanks on Okinawa. It was fierce fighting.

Along with the 47mm high velocity anti-tank gun the Japanese used, our tanks and soldiers were also in danger from the 500-pound aerial bombs the Japanese had buried as anti-tank mines, which were deadly. But to me, the spookiest anti-tank weapon the Japanese used against us was the suicidal satchel-charge teams that would hide along the side of the roads in what we called "spider holes." These teams would usually consist of four to six men who would have a field-pack-like canvas satchel on their backs. Our infantry had satchel-charges too, also in canvas sacks, but ours usually weighed only about twenty pounds. This lighter weight made it easier to be swung into caves by using the carrying strap. The two-pound blocks of Composition C2 explosive we used in our satchel-charges were much more potent than the yellow picric-acid explosive of the Japanese, and more two-pound blocks could be added to our

Photograph courtesy U.S. Army
Division of infantrymen approaching Yazu-Dake Escarpment.

satchels if needed. The Japanese canvas satchel-charges usually were filled with forty or fifty pounds of their explosive, though, which made them pretty potent.

A spider hole was simply a hole in the ground big enough for a Japanese soldier and his satchel-charge to crouch down in. A woven wicker cover, big enough to cover the hole, had sod and grass placed upon it so that

when this cover was pulled down in place over the hole, the suicide bomber and his charge of explosive was completely hidden. When done properly, spider holes were hard to spot, even for someone standing close to them. Consequently, they were virtually impossible to be seen by someone peering through a periscope in a tank.

A satchel-charge team always selected what they thought was an advantageous spot for them to dig their ring of holes. Locations selected might be a sharp turn around a bluff or the end of a cut through a hill. Such places prevented the tanks behind the lead target-tank from being able to shoot down the team members with machine gun fire before they could complete their mission. The mission consisted of letting a tank get inside the center of their circle of spider holes, and then all the members of the team would suddenly throw the wicker covers aside and leap up out of their holes in a coordinated attack. Some were designated to dive out in front of the moving tank so it ran over them, and the resulting explosion very likely would break a tread. Others would climb quickly up on the back of the tank's rear deck where the armor was thinner and set off their satchel-charge by pulling a string that was attached to a detonator. Still others would dive inside the bogey wheels and suspension system to set off their charges. In a properly coordinated and carried out attack, a tank that was inside one of their rings had little chance of escaping serious damage.

At the height of an attack, when several exploding satchel-charges were going off at once, legs (complete with the two-toed *tabi* shoes and the leg wrappings Japanese soldiers wore), along with arms, heads (complete with helmets), and various other body parts would fly off in all directions. If the tank were disabled and isolated from other tank support, then other Japanese would take the place of their blown-up comrades and attack that tank. They would quickly swarm all over it with picks, crow bars and sledge hammers in an effort to pry up a hatch and drop a hand grenade inside.

I once lost a tank to a satchel-charge team, and I found it to be a completely unnerving experience. I was leading my platoon slowly down a narrow road. My tank had just come around a bluff and was temporarily out of sight of the other following tanks. Through my periscope, I just caught a fleeting glimpse of lunging bodies before there were several loud explosions and the tank suddenly stopped. They had been successful in breaking a tread, blowing themselves to smithereens while doing so, of course. After the attack had blown the participating team members all over the landscape, another lively group emerged from hiding. They began energetically attempting to hoist a huge package of the

yellow picric-acid explosive that was wrapped in fiber matting up on to the back deck of the tank. That fiber-matting package must have weighed at least 300 pounds.

Luckily, the tread that had been blown off the tank was on the opposite side from where they were struggling to lift their heavy burden up on to the back deck, causing the deck to slope much higher on their side.

Now, one smart-ass got the

Photograph courtesy U.S. Army
Aerial view of the Yazu-Dake Escarpment with tanks firing on Japanese positions along the cliff.

telephone that our infantry occasionally used out of its box on the back of the tank and in perfect English kept repeating, "Cease fire, please, cease fire, please!" Fortunately, before they got the tremendous charge up on the back deck of my tank and detonated it, the other tanks of my platoon responded to my frantic radio cries of "Mayday!" They turned the corner around the bluff and came roaring up behind us just like the U.S. Cavalry in a John Wayne movie. They quickly shot the Japanese attackers down, using machine gun fire. Why the big bundle of explosives wasn't set off is a mystery, but the Japs had a lot of trouble with duds, so maybe it was faulty or wet.

To American tankers, or especially me, at least, there was something particularly unsettling about satchel-charge teams. We found it hard to fathom the fact that so many young Japanese soldiers could be influenced or brainwashed to literally blow themselves to bits so nonchalantly. Such a small value placed on human life was hard for American boys to understand. Hard, dangerous fighting, yes, that was one thing we did understand, but deliberately killing yourself in droves was beyond the pale for the mind of the ordinary American serviceman to accept. It somehow didn't smack of fair play, if there were such a thing in war.

Photograph courtesy U.S. Army
American infantrymen satchel-charging an underground Japanese position.

The U.S. sailors aboard their beleaguered ships, which were being battered daily around the island, felt the same way about the kamikaze pilots that were attacking them. But now, nearly sixty years later, I find it surprising that we are once again experiencing suicide attacks by people who take over our air-liners and deliberately crash the big jet planes into tall buildings, killing themselves and hundreds of others in the process. The Israelis are daily being blasted by Palestinian terrorists who hide explosives in their clothing and join crowds on buses and in cafes. Then they deliberately blow themselves up in order to kill as many of their perceived enemies as possible. I still find it hard to believe that these modern-day suicide bombers are hailed as heroes and martyrs by their Muslim countrymen, just as the Japanese considered their kamikazes long ago, so I guess nothing much is new in this old world.

[*Editor's note: Bob Green received the Silver Star for his action at Yazu Dake Escarpment. His comment about it was: "Tanks were always in the limelight because they were more noticeable, being out in front and doing something. Decorations were always iffy. A lot of them were certainly well deserved, but many actions that deserved a decoration went unreported. A lot depended on who was watching, and who would go to the trouble of all that paperwork involved in writing it up. Some decorations were politically motivated or to seek publicity for a military unit. My getting the Silver Star seemed good at the time, and I am proud of it today, but for years I was bothered by the memory of how those poor old Japs sounded screaming down in that hole while I was pouring that napalm on them. But it did end their resistance to our infantry and let us move on, and that is what we were there for."

His friend Lewis also received a Silver Star. After the battle was over, they went to visit their friend Jones who had been assigned to the infantry and had been wounded three times. Bob said that Jones, his head still in a bandage, said to them, "If you two deserve the Silver Star, I ought to get the Goddamned Congressional Medal of Honor for what I went through!" Bob said they couldn't disagree with that.

Bob's citation reads:

SILVER STAR—AWARD. By direction of the President, under the provisions of the Act of Congress, approved 9 July 1918 (Bulletin 43 WD, 1918), a Silver Star is awarded by the Commanding General, United States Army Forces Western Pacific, to the following named officer:

First Lieutenant JAMES R. GREEN, 0557916, Cavalry, United States Army. For gallantry in action at Yazu Dake Escarpment, Okinawa, Ryukyu Islands, on 16 June 1945. As a medium tank platoon leader, First Lieutenant GREEN was assigned the mission of wiping out stiff enemy resistance originating from a series of caves, crevices, and pillboxes. Unable to reach the enemy positions with a flame-throwing tank because of the rough terrain, he voluntarily and with complete disregard for his personal safety advanced against enemy rifle fire, carrying a hose extension from the tank and sprayed the enemy positions with highly inflammable fluid which he intended to ignite with a smoke grenade. Despite intense heat, smoke, and the danger of flying fragments from exploding enemy ammunition brought about by the premature combustion of the fluid, he remained in the vicinity until it was apparent that nothing could possibly remain alive in the raging inferno. By his conspicuous bravery and inspirational devotion to duty in accordance with the highest traditions of the military service, First Lieutenant GREEN effected the destruction of the fanatically resisting enemy in this sector. Home address: Albany, Texas.

BY COMMAND OF LIEUTENANT GENERAL STYER:

W. A. WOOD, Jr.

Major General, USA

Deputy Commander and

Chief of Staff

Chapter 9

EXPERIENCES OF A TANK COMMANDER

"There will be no one to understand him if he talks about the war…. only those who shared its excitement and horror with him can talk about it."

The Odyssey

Okinawa
June 15, 1945

Dear Mother,

My platoon has today off. First day off we've had in thirty-eight days. I slept till about eleven & boy was it restful. Ever since we had a Gook run berserk in our area at one in the morning my sleep has been rather meager. I'm getting to where I really hate to see that sun go down. This Gook was right in the middle of us before anybody on guard saw him. The guard's tommy guns wouldn't work, so he ran under his tank to get another one and the Gook let out the most blood curdling yell I've ever heard (that's what woke me up) and ran right by me & another fellow. I got my pistol tangled up in my mosquito net & only succeeded in tearing my bed all to pieces. By that time everybody in camp was hollering & shooting but when the dawn came no dead Gook was found, so [I] guess he escaped. I sleep with an assortment of knives, pistols, rifles, hand grenades, tommy guns & my Jap Samuri sword all around me now. As soon as I can I'm going to send the Samuri sword home. It's a good one and I'd like to keep it after all this is over.

Heard over the radio that we were "mopping-up" Okinawa now. If this is "mopping-up," I'd sure hate to see the real fighting. We've fought harder the last few days than ever before, trying to end this up. It really shouldn't be long now. I was buttoned up in my tank for twelve & a half hours yesterday—the longest yet....

I keep forgetting to ask for more chicken & stuff but I sure won't this time. Send fifty pounds if you can....

Well, in another year I'll be eligible for a furlough. Course that doesn't mean I'll get it, but I'll be eligible anyway.

    Lots of love,

    Bob

A decision that affected us was now made by someone higher up, most likely General Easley, who was always working zealously at trying to solve problems and move things along. The new plan was that instead of tank officers going to the infantry regimental or battalion headquarters to be briefed on the next day's plan of action, they would instead drive up close to the front in a jeep in the late evening. There they would meet with the infantry officers in the sector where they would be working the next morning.

The new plan was for both the infantry and tank officers to look over the terrain and sometimes, if necessary, make an on-foot reconnaissance. This was done to try and get an agreement from both infantry and tank men as to where the tanks could or would be able to go the next day, without having a knock-down-drag-out argument over the radios during

Photograph courtesy U.S. Army
Last photo taken of Brigadier General Claudius Easley, who was killed by two shots to the head from a Nambu machine gun shortly after this photo was taken. I had great respect for him.

the battle. Due to heavy losses, the tankers had become much more reluctant and harder to persuade to go into places the infantry wanted, and needed, them to go. Often these places appeared to the tankers to be, if not impassable, at least highly questionable places to try to take tanks.

During the battle for Kakazu Ridge, the infantry had learned a bitter lesson and now no longer wanted to try to go it alone, but always wanted armor out ahead with them following in close support. The flame-thrower tanks of the 713th Tank Battalion had now become the main weapon in overcoming the

dug-in enemy. As previously mentioned, each regular tank platoon had at least one and sometimes two of these flame-throwing tanks attached to them under the command of the tank platoon leader. The flame throwers had to be closely guarded and protected by both other tanks and infantrymen when they maneuvered up close into position to fire their deadly napalm/gasoline mixture into caves and emplacements.

Photograph courtesy U.S. Army

Tank/infantry teams guarding a flame-throwing tank attacking a Japanese position.

These new, on-foot reconnaissance missions were often pretty scary and very dangerous. Many times they actually took place in the no-man's-land between the lines. On one earlier recon mission, Colonel Harmon Edmonson, the commanding officer of our 763rd tank battalion, had endured all the haranguing from General Easley he could stand about his tanks not doing all they should be to help the infantry. He had come along on a scouting mission to personally see if something was amiss and needed to be done differently by his tankers. It was to be the last thing he ever did. As we stealthily moved single file down a narrow road, the watching Japanese suddenly dropped several mortar rounds with great accuracy among us, and we all hit the deck.

The red-headed lieutenant who had called me down off the Maeda Escarpment OP to his tank and almost got me killed in a Japanese counter-attack had his big, fat buttocks ripped asunder. Lieutenant Colonel Edmondson didn't appear to be hurt at first, but we noticed, as we were attempting to extricate the screaming red-headed lieutenant back to safety, that Edmondson remained prone and very still. Someone crawled to him and rolled him over. We discovered he had been fatally wounded by a little shard of shrapnel that had made just a thin, bloody line in his forehead where it entered his head.

Another hair-raising recon experience occurred one evening when five or six of us were piled onto a jeep to go meet with our infantry compatriots. I was driving the jeep, and we had just pulled out. As I was shifting into second gear, a large shell from a 150mm, Japanese howitzer moaned in and landed right where our jeep had been sitting an instant before. To our good fortune, the shell

was a dud and did not explode on contact but bounced high into the air, cart-wheeling end over end completely over our loaded-down jeep. It came to earth again in the road right ahead of us, where it rolled and bounced wildly along. I slammed on the brakes to keep from overtaking it as my passengers ducked, clutched each other in terror, and all began shrieking many kinds of

Photograph courtesy U.S. Army

Flame-throwing tank at work.

advice and lamentations in my ears. I hastily veered around the shell, which, as we had been told many times, weighed over eighty pounds and gave it a wide berth as we shakily continued on our way with jangled nerves.

So, having already had those reconnaissance experiences, we were understandably on edge and tried to be on high alert while participating in subsequent missions, but a later one turned out to be the wildest of all. It began one evening with an on-foot reconnaissance just ahead of where our infantry had dug in for the night.

I was in the lead, followed by Captain Kennedy and four or five other officers as we entered the street of a little village. We quietly slipped along between the small buildings to ascertain if tanks could negotiate the narrow village streets the next day.

I had armed myself with an M-3 submachine gun, which was a cheaply built, mass-produced weapon made out of stamped-out metal parts. Everybody called it a "grease gun," which it really did resemble. However, it had a large magazine of .45 ACP ammo, and besides being compact and easy to carry, it was fully automatic, even if it was not held in high regard as a weapon.

Suddenly, as I crept along the silent, deserted street, there was a loud clatter. As my hair stood on end, three Japanese soldiers rushed pell-mell out of a doorway I had just passed and disappeared around the corner of a house. As I whirled around to shoot my "grease gun," the loaded magazine, which fit loosely at best and never was secured by a very good latch, used the centrifugal force of my sudden, violent turn as an excuse to come loose. It simply flew off the gun and skittered rapidly across the cobblestones until it disappeared with a splash into a hole filled with muddy water at the side of the narrow road.

I immediately shot off after it, and dropping to my knees, started fishing frantically with both hands under the muddy water seeking to retrieve it. Some of the other officers following along behind me evidently found my frenzied efforts to be funny as hell, because they let out with a series of strangled, suppressed-sounding snorts, soon followed by uncontrollable shouts of laughter. This proved to be contagious, for all at once, the whole little group following behind me burst out into loud, uncontrollable guffaws.

This crazy situation continued to rapidly escalate, and I, too, was suddenly struck with the notion that it was beyond a doubt the funniest thing that I had ever been involved in. I quit fishing for the magazine and slumped to the cobblestones, joining them in the wild, raucous laughter. Before long, it seemed to get even funnier and funnier, and all of us were just screaming and howling with unrestrained laughter. Captain Kennedy and the others had now dropped limply to the ground, holding their bellies and slapping the ground while tears streamed down their faces. I wasn't any better, and even though I was more or less the goat in the affair, that didn't matter to me.

We were all being incapacitated by a serious attack of the sillies. A Japanese soldier could have just walked up and simply knocked us all in the head with a hammer, and we couldn't have resisted. The only thing that would have made the situation even more surreal would have been if some Japanese soldiers had come out of the houses and joined in on the fun, holding their sides and roaring with laughter at the whole, stupid capriciousness of the lottery of life and death we now all found ourselves embroiled in.

In recalling that event today, I still have to smile at the complete ludicrousness of the situation and how quickly it had happened. It was as if a page had been turned, removing us from the deadly serious, dangerous position we were in and suddenly making us participants in a Marx Brothers slap-stick comedy. In discussing this event many years later with a psychiatrist relative, he tried to explain professionally what he thought about this more or less hysterical happening. He theorized that it was probably brought on by a sudden release of the constant extreme tension we had labored under for a long period of time. This tension had been building up inside us for days and had become a pent-up force awaiting a trigger to release it. That trigger, of course, being my frantic antics and efforts to recover the magazine of my "grease gun" when the Japanese soldiers startled me and my frenzied movement caused it to shoot away. The situation had instantly evolved into a period of behavior that got almost out of control before it ran its course.

There were other periods of seeming insanity. In one village we camped near, we discovered a kimono shop, and most everyone in my tank platoon helped themselves to a kimono. I wore a brilliant scarlet one with a golden dragon twisting all down the back. We were a gaudy-looking bunch for a while, but the kimonos were soon discarded, as they snagged and hung up on everything inside the cramped space in the tanks' interiors.

A more painful memory involves bringing my platoon of tanks up to the front early one morning and stopping near a group of four or five sleepy-looking infantrymen. They were squatting on their heels around a small fire holding their canteen cups by the handles over the flames. The "C" ration cans contained a small packet of powdered coffee that could be emptied into a canteen cup of water and heated. The infantrymen had made their fire by breaking off a chunk of the explosive Composition C, which looked like gray putty and was in their satchel-charges. The burning of this substance produced intense heat, but practically no smoke. As I looked down out of the turret of my tank at them, my eye caught just a glimpse of something hurtling down and dropping in a straight line out of the sky. It was a large Japanese mortar shell, and it exploded right into the center of their little fire, with disastrous results. Every man around the fire was instantly blasted into sudden oblivion.

Yet another time, stopping my platoon of tanks behind a hill and getting out in order to discuss plans with the infantry we were to work with that day, I noticed that everyone seemed to be greatly upset and in a foul mood, more so than usual it seemed. I thought maybe someone held in high esteem might have just been killed, but upon inquiring, discovered that was not the case. The cause of the unusual distress was a youthful-looking kid lying wounded and unconscious on a stretcher. His jacket had been opened and his unbuttoned trousers and drawers pulled down to reveal several grievous shrapnel wounds, but the cause of all the great concern lay in the fact that, in addition to his other serious wounds, his penis had been clipped off, right next to his belly. Now, that was the hit that every one of these testosterone-loaded, virile, young men found to be their very worst fear, and it was amazing to see how greatly they were affected. There were muttering discussions concerning this calamity among several little groups of solemn men. When finally a medic quit working on the injured youth and stood up with shaking head, indicating he was dead, several distraught looking soldiers in the discussion groups actually looked relieved, and all agreed that "the poor S.O.B. is better off."

Still another time, I had dismounted from my tank behind a hill on the front line. There was a mortar squad set up nearby, which was busily dropping shells down their tubes and looping them over the hill. As I stood talking to some infantrymen about our plans, one of our Navy Corsair F-4U planes zoomed over the hill from completing a bombing run on the other side and was seemingly struck by a mortar round just fired from one of the mortars close by. Shouts of "Heads up! Heads up!" rang out as one of the plane's wings came spiraling down like a big metal leaf to wham on the ground near my tank. The rest of the plane, with wild, uncontrolled gyrations, spun and twisted down to smash onto the ground, where it burst into flames. I will never forget seeing the stricken look on the face of the pilot, looking out at me as his out-of-control plane went hurtling by, carrying him to a flaming death. It still kind of chills me thinking about it.

There was another time a pilot looked down right at me, but this time he was Japanese. My tank platoon was circled like a wagon train one evening, just before dark, near the southern end of the island, right before it was declared secure. I had walked up on a nearby hill to see if the sea was visible off to the south. If the sea was in sight, then the battle was nearly over for that would mean the Japanese could go no farther. I looked down on my men busily loading machine guns on top of the tank turrets, preparing for night-guard duty, and I wanted to be sure and return to camp while they could still see me. You never roamed around in the dark. Suddenly I heard the sound of an approaching plane, and it sounded like it was coming on rapidly. I hastily scanned the horizon to locate it, and suddenly I saw it coming right toward me, very low down, much closer than I had expected and, without a doubt, very Japanese. I hastily crouched down and froze, hoping to avoid being seen by the pilot, but as the plane curved smoothly in a shallow bank around the little hill, the pilot looked right down at me. Our eyes met and locked.

He had his canopy pushed back, and I clearly remember his red and white *hachi-machi* cloth. It was a cloth pilots tied around their head, denoting them to be kamikazes, and although I didn't know about the *hachi-machis* then, it seems most likely now that that's what it was. I also remember he had on black gloves, and as he curved around me, he waved one hand from side to side at me. I could see his teeth glisten in a smile. I instinctively waved back before catching myself and hastily drawing my arm down. This all happened in just a heart beat, and then he was gone over the hill. His plane had appeared to be an old and somewhat slow one with a large bomb suspended beneath it. At any rate, for an instant I had really locked eyes with the enemy, only this time, he really didn't seem like an enemy at all. He seemed to wish me well with his waved greeting. It was strange encounter I have never forgotten.

Another strange incident took place close to the Yazu-Dake Escarpment, near the southern end of the island. I had positioned my platoon's flame-throwing tank in front of a cave entrance, with my own tank pulled up in close support. When the flame-thrower's igniter came on and jetted flame down in preparation to light the main napalm stream, suddenly there was movement in the cave entrance. An old, civilian man appeared, and he hesitantly, and with the stiff movements of the elderly, emerged out into the open. He now stood up very erect, raising his arms up high over his head with his palms open and spread out flat, as if he were warding off or trying to stop something. In truth, he was—something horrible. He had long, white hair, a scraggly beard, and was dressed in a white kimono and had a strange, boxy-shaped hat on his head.

"Hold your fire," I quickly ordered over the radio. "Let's see what he's up to."

The figure, whose stately bearing and attire signified an elder of Okinawan importance, stood rigid and transfixed with upraised arms until it became obvious to him that he wasn't going to be immediately killed. Then with slow, stiff movements, he turned and began shouting back into the cave. At the same time, he began to make exaggerated gestures with his arms and hands, as if he were fanning the air out of the cave. I will never forget the procession of people who tentatively and fearfully began to emerge out of the cave. They were mostly women and children, but the group included a few elderly men as well, and there must have been a hundred of them in all. Many of the women were carrying babies and leading little ones by the hand as they came out and clustered around the old man. He stood straight as an arrow and stared at the idling tanks impassively, as if the intensity of his gaze might prevent them from hurting his people. I really believe it was one of the bravest acts I ever saw.

I would like to be able to say that I opened up my hatch and, sticking my head and shoulders up out of the turret, gave them a friendly, welcoming wave. Then, that I motioned grandly and expansively for the old man to lead his group to safety behind my tanks, but I didn't. I was sure if I were to do that, a watching sniper would quickly shoot me in

Photograph courtesy U.S. Army

A group of lucky Okinawan civilians, such as the ones who emerged from the cave with their patriarch-savior.

the head. Instead, all of us in the buttoned-up tanks watched through our periscopes as the group of civilians fearfully emerged and huddled around the old man. It was with great relief that we soon saw one of the infantrymen step forward from behind the tanks and beckon the old man to lead his brood to him, which he did. Then the infantryman led them behind the tanks to the rear and safety. The vision of the frightened looks on the tear-stained faces of the women and children as they passed by our idling tanks is still vividly imprinted on my memory. It was as if they considered the tanks to be alive, like huge prehistoric beasts that might eat them up, and, in reality, that wasn't too far off the mark.

As they filed by, following their patriarch-savior, I was reminded of a full-page Doré woodcut I had viewed as a child in our big old family Bible back home. It was a full-page illustration of Moses or some other Old Testament patriarch leading his people to safety.

Watching that group following their patriarch past my tank that day struck a chord in my heart. Down through the long years, I have never forgotten the old fellow's actions. What he did when he caused a pause in the very midst of the chaotic bloodletting turned into something beautiful. For a brief interlude, before the killing continued, he showed how the human spirit could transcend all the boundaries of hatred men had erected between their races.

As the group of civilians passed through us to safety, I heard a buzz and click on my radio speaker that signified someone in another tank was pressing a microphone open to speak, but no one said anything. Instead, I heard a long, drawn out "Whew!" Then there was a great sigh of relief, which was soon joined by several others clicking in. I quickly added mine. It had been a near thing.

Chapter 10

THE LAST BATTLE

Still, death is certain and when a man's hour is come, not
even the gods can save him."

The Odyssey

June 24, 1945

Dear Mother,

... Well, the fighting is over. That sentence doesn't even come close to describing the relief that we all feel now. It is really over. It ended rather suddenly to me, as I expected it to last a little longer, but all at once they just gave up the fight, and we didn't worry about them doing it. We've spent the last few days cleaning up a few cane fields around here with flame throwers, and we've flushed out about forty. It reminds me of quail hunting the way everybody moves through the field behind the tanks, having a big time.

Now that it is over I don't know what we will do, but most probably go somewhere to rest up a bit before the next one. I don't see how anybody could have had as much luck or so many fortunate happenings of fate as I did. Something sure looked after me.

I have a flag, rifle, bayonet and Samuri sword I am going to send home as soon as I can. They haven't passed anything to go home yet, but now that it is over it shouldn't be too long before they will.

Guess John is getting ready to come over this way. He got a pretty good deal getting on a LST as the officers live swell on them and the kamikaze boys are not after them while there are bigger ships around. The LST I came up here on was pretty nice, even though it was an old ship and about ready to scrap.

We have a shower unit set up right over the hill from us. It is run by colored troops and they really are good guys. They were right up here when this was the front lines, and they killed several Japs at night when they tried to slip through. They also have killed two horses, several pigs and almost cut a bridge completely down with their .50 machine gun and we are right glad there is a hill between us.

... We pull guard with our tank searchlights now that the danger of artillery is over, and it is much better. That pitch dark guard pulling got very nerve racking at times.

Well, had better stop and clean up a little. Today is the first whole day I've had off in five weeks. All the other days I was suppose to get a rest (three in all) something came up and we would have to rush up and burn out a machine gun nest or clean out a cave of snipers or something to keep them happy.

Hope you are all fine. I will keep the letters coming as I should have lots of time now.

Lots of love,
Bob

June 30, 1945

Dear Mother,

... We went down to the beach and traded the navy some Jap rifles and radios and what not for some wire and sockets. We have a Jap generator we picked up and are going to have electric lights for the company, which will really be the thing. I don't know what we would do without the navy. They are usually very nice and give us everything they absolutely don't have to have.

We are still having infiltrators at night. We killed three last night. I don't know just what they think they are going to do, as most of them just have a hand grenade or two and don't have a chance of getting through all the guards, but they still try. These Japs are pretty hard to convince they are whipped.

Jones was wounded, but is OK now and back with his outfit. He was hit by shrapnel.

I went through Naha and Shuri today. They are absolutely leveled out. I couldn't even figure out where Shuri castle was. I had seen it at a distance before they started really bombarding it, and it was a huge looking thing but they sure changed the contours of things around there. Naha might have been a pretty nice town once. It had some right nice looking buildings in it but they are all gone now. I have never seen anything like it, but I have seen lots of things here lately that I never had seen before.

We have another show tonight. It is supposed to be a Laurel and Hardy picture. The other two we have had were the sorriest I believe I ever saw. I don't know what they think we are over here, sending us such tripe as that.

I am still sleeping on the ground but expect to get a cot shortly. I think the ground is about as comfortable as one of those cots anyway. I sleep very well on it.

It's about show time so will stop now. Hope you are all fine. I am OK.

> Lots of love,
> Bob

July 3, 1945

I didn't get to mail this the other day so will do it now. Guess the Stamford rodeo is going full blast now.

We aren't doing much yet, not that I mind.

Hope you are all fine.

> Lots of love,
> Bob

July 8, 1945

Dear Mother,

I've been running around here all day with Jones trying to get him in this outfit, and I think maybe we are going to succeed. I sure hope so. He has really been through the mill. He has been wounded three times and thought he just had to get out of that Infantry, for which I don't blame him.

I am sending my saber and a rifle home. I may send a flag and a pistol also, but haven't made up my mind for sure. The pistol is a beauty—brand new and very Gookanese looking. I'm a little scared to send it as they often take them up when they censor the box, but the others will pass alright.

... I went swimming the other day at the beach, and it was lots of fun. The beach was a lot better than we thought it would be, and we really enjoyed it. We can go every day now if we want to.

Jones has sure lost a lot of weight but I guess he has a right to. He was buried alive for fifteen minutes once when a shell caved a bank in on him. He said he was hollering so loud he blew most of the dirt off, and some guys dug him on out. His baby is six months old now and he has so many pictures of it, he can't carry them all. I sure hope he gets over here, but they probably won't turn loose of him.

The island sure looks different now than it did. They have a beautiful network of roads, and with our electric lights, movies and showers it is really a nice set up. This sure was a tough fight though. We see news reels every night of the fighting and all the pictures are of the marines, which makes us kind of mad as we killed twice as many Japs as they did and had the roughest terrain to go over, but our press agent is just not as good. The 96th killed more Japs than any other division here by a good deal. We went right down the middle the whole way.

Well, there isn't anything new happening that I can tell about.

Lots of love,

Bob

After eighty-two days of fierce fighting, the very last battle of World War II was officially declared to be over on the 21st of July, 1945. This last battle was, of course, the battle for Okinawa and we, who still were fighting vigorously on the island everyday, thought that the declaration was premature. In retrospect, I know now that it referred to the fact that all organized Japanese resistance had ended. Unfortunately, there was plenty of unorganized resistance to keep us busy from the thousands of Japanese soldiers who still were holding out underground. They mostly stayed out of sight during daylight hours, but would come out at night and create havoc as they roamed around in the dark. They were mainly trying to go north, looking for something to eat or merely wanting to raise all the hell they could by killing Americans before they themselves were killed. Their last orders from General Ushijima before he committed hari-kari was for them to try infiltrating through the American troops to the mountainous, sparsely populated northern part of the island, and there to carry on guerrilla warfare. Many tried to do this but few succeeded in escaping to the north. The American presence and tremendous build-up over the narrow mid-section of the island around the Kadena and Yontan air fields made such movements through the sprawling, semi-permanent U.S. installations almost impossible.

Nisei interpreters, most of them American commissioned officers, were brought in, and they began to attempt to talk some of these recalcitrant Japanese soldiers into simply surrendering instead of committing suicide or continuing fighting. And in fact, over time, nearly 11,000 finally did surrender on Okinawa, which was an astounding number for the Pacific Theater conflict. This large number indicated that there was beginning to be a breakdown in the former steely resolve of the Japanese soldier. Even they were beginning to have doubts about the rosy propaganda from Tokyo that still claimed grand and glorious victories over the Americans. But these Japanese troops, although they had nothing but small arms now, were still very dangerous.

The American front line infantryman, particularly those such as the 96th Division who had fought it out so savagely, weren't filled with much sympathy for these hiding-out Japanese soldiers. If they couldn't face up to the now very obvious fact that they had been defeated, let them commit hari-kari as their generals had done. If they didn't want to come out from underground and surrender peacefully, we ought to just securely close up their holes with demolitions or bulldozers and not give them any more chances to kill Americans. Seal them up, forget them, and let's get it over with was the way many looked at it.

The 96th Division had good reason to feel that way. They, along with the 7th Division, had borne the brunt of the battle down the center of the island. But headquarters' higher-ups didn't see it that way. With Okinawa now secured, the big build-up for the main event of the Pacific War, the invasion of Japan, was on deck. Since the European conflict had now ended, the eyes of the media had turned and were now focused firmly on the action in the Pacific Theater. That being the case, the high brass wanted everything handled with care, including the taking and handling of Japanese prisoners. And that led to me becoming involved in a most unhappy event.

One day, several jeep loads of non-combatant rear-echelon people from 10th Army Headquarters drove into our bivouac area. Soon, I received a summons to report to Captain Kennedy and found him talking with this group from headquarters. Captain Kennedy introduced me to them and told me the reason for their visit. Apparently, a sizable bunch of Japanese soldiers had been located holed-up nearby, and the big brass wanted to convince them to surrender. These people had formulated a plan to bring that about.

They had brought along with them a Japanese soldier who had already surrendered, and their plan was centered on using him. They also had with them a Nisei American officer and various other noncombatant people from headquarters. They were all neat and clean-looking. We were grubby and dirty-looking. The Nisei officer had been talking to this prisoner, and he had agreed to help convince the holed-up, still-armed-and-dangerous Japanese soldiers to surrender. This group had earlier tried out a similar plan using another Japanese prisoner who had surrendered, but they had run into a real problem, and that was the reason for their being here. They hoped we tankers might help prevent this problem from recurring in the future.

It seems the problem arose when they tried to send their prisoner, who had surrendered, in on foot to speak to the holed up Japanese. He was to tell them that by surrendering, good and fair treatment was in store for them. They would be well treated, as he had been. The mission was spoiled when the unappreciative Japanese soldiers hiding underground quickly killed the incoming messenger. Since these still-hostile holdouts were shooting at anyone who approached their position, the headquarters group now had come up with a new plan.

They first had to secure a new replacement prisoner since their original one had been blown away. This they had done and had brought him along. Their new plan was still based around using him to appeal to the renegades in their own language, but this time have him do it over a loud speaker, which they would rig up on the outside of a tank. That was where we came in. With him safely inside, the tank might drive up close to the ridge where they were hiding. Then, the still-hostile Japanese wouldn't be able to shoot him, but would be forced to listen as he appealed to them over the loud speaker. It seemed to be a well thought-out plan.

Captain Kennedy obviously had little enthusiasm for becoming involved in any of this, but since they were from high-headquarters, felt he had a duty to oblige them. He now proceeded to prove that the old-time army idiom of "rank has its privileges" was still alive and well. He ordered me, in a nice way, of course, to take my tank and try to help them do whatever it was they wanted to do, and then he quickly left the group.

After an enthusiastic major asked what I thought of the plan, I agreed it might be worth a try. Indeed, I really had no choice in the matter, but with my tacit approval, they got busy. A radio specialist rigged up and tested a loud speaker on the front of my tank. He soon had it working very well. They now wanted to know where their prisoner could ride in the tank, so I told my bog he could just stay in camp so the prisoner could ride in his seat. The bog seemed delighted with that part of the plan. The prisoner was scared to death of the tank, but after the Nisei officer barked at him sternly in Japanese he finally, apprehensively climbed into it through the bog's hatch. I got in the turret and over the intercom told Al Blomgren, my driver, to follow the officers' jeeps, and off we all went.

The jeeps soon led us to a location where a platoon of infantry from the 382nd Regiment of the 96th Division was lounging about, waiting on us to show up, and warily eyeing the rocky ridge where the Japanese were hiding. This infantry platoon had been through the mill during the recently finished campaign. They all looked like those two beat-up, slovenly, front-line-infantry characters named Willie and Joe in Bill Mauldin's popular cartoons in the *Stars and Stripes* publication. This platoon had been ordered to come here and take charge of any prisoners, if and when they surrendered.

I got out of the tank as the American Nisei officer began giving the woebegone Japanese prisoner some last minute instructions. In rapid-fire Japanese he told him how to use the microphone he had handed him, which the prisoner held as gingerly as if it were a venomous Habu snake. While that was taking place, I walked over and shook hands with the infantry platoon leader. He was a very tired, grizzled-looking staff sergeant named Constable and was much older than the members of his platoon, whom he referred to as his "kids." His description was apt, as they did look like tired, dirty kids that should be home, going to high school.

Constable and I began to visit and swap war stories. As I had been working with the 96th Division the whole time since L-Day, we quickly discovered we had been involved together in some of the same battles. He told me he was the fourth leader of this platoon—the three previous ones, all second lieutenants, having been killed. The members of his platoon, his "kids," had suffered over 75% casualties, and now there was only a fourth left of the original ones who had landed on L-Day. The rest of his platoon were new, green replacements that had been added as needed. As our conversation tapered off, he became quiet and reflective looking.

After a period of silence, he suddenly flicked his cigarette away and turning to me, started talking very seriously. I remember the gist of his long-ago conversation as going something like this. "I want to ask a favor of you. I have been overseas for over three years now, been wounded twice, but have lucked out in two invasions, and now I sure would like to live until this war is over and get back home in Georgia to my wife and kids." He paused now, staring off into space, then sighed and continued. "Now here's the screwy part. This morning I woke up with this funny feeling. I've never had one like it before, and it's got me a little worried. For some strange reason, I feel like I need to be very careful today. I've been in a lot of really tight spots before, but they never made me feel this way. I don't know what it is. Maybe I'm getting ready to crack up or something, but it's got me worried. Several times in the fighting I didn't think I had a Chinaman's chance of living to see another day, but I survived. Now that they have declared this island secured, the bad part must be over, and I'm still alive and kicking. So now I wake up this morning with this funny feeling."

He paused, looking off into space again, then turned and looked intently at me and said, "Now, I know this probably will sound silly to you, but would it be possible for me to ride in your tank with you today while we carry on with this goofy plan from headquarters, instead of me risking getting shot at this late date, fooling around outside? I still could stay in charge of my kids from the tank."

As he awaited my answer, I could tell he was deadly serious and his words gave me a prickly feeling. "Absolutely!" I told him. "That would be fine with me. Come on. Let's get in." So both of us turned, climbed up, he on one side and me on the other, and we entered the tank through the two hatches in the top of the turret. I stuck my head out of the one on the right and he, the one on the left.

All was quiet. We had gotten over our surprise at no longer hearing the swishing, moaning sounds of our artillery shells constantly passing over our heads, as they had done for weeks. Now all our artillery had ceased firing. Also absent was the distant rattling sound of a firefight, which was another switch. It really seemed pretty calm and peaceful, and it appeared safe enough with the heavily armed platoon of infantry all about us. For that reason, we kept our heads up and out of the turret hatches, as we could see immeasurably better that way than we could if we were "buttoned-up" and looking out through a periscope. Also, it made it easier for Constable to be able to watch over and stay in close contact with "his kids."

I told Al over the radio intercom to go ahead and approach the rocky ridge, and when we got fairly close—fifty yards or so from it—I had him stop the tank. I reached down through the basket of the fighting compartment to where the prisoner was sitting and prodded him on his back. He jumped wildly and looked back fearfully at me. I pointed emphatically with one hand at the microphone he clutched, at the same time acting as if I were speaking into my other balled-up fist. He understood that I was signaling him to invite his cohorts to surrender. Immediately, he began to yammer in a high pitched voice.

The infantrymen in Constable's platoon gathered around the tank, shaking their heads and grinning in derision at the shrieking of the prisoner over the loud speaker and waiting to see what would result from all the racket. Up on the rocky ridge, we began to see heads appearing out of holes and bobbing around. Then we saw one Japanese soldier and then another come out of the ground and stand upright, carefully watching us. When no one fired at them, they began to slowly file down the slope, hands over their heads and dressed only in a G-string loincloth, as they had been instructed.

At seeing this, the prisoner inside the tank was encouraged and increased the volume and speed of his tirade. I remember I leaned over at this change and told Sergeant Constable, who seemed much more relaxed now, that there must be a little ham in every human being on earth. He had laughed and said that the prisoner sure did seem to be enjoying his job. The prisoner's haranguing and high pitched shouting rang and echoed off the hill. Before long, there were at least twelve, or maybe fifteen, nearly nude Japanese soldiers making their way down the steep hill, while a lot more were beginning to move around up on the ridge. As the first ones got down off the rocky ridge and straggled down to the tank, they were met and closely inspected by our infantrymen, making sure they were not carrying grenades or small weapons. Stripped down to a loincloth, it was hard for them to hide anything.

Passing inspection, they were shunted off to one side and placed under guard in a compact group. They seemed to be complacent enough. It appeared all was going well and that the new plan was working successfully. There was a noticeable easing of tension all around. One of our infantrymen now climbed up on the left side of the tank and asked Sergeant Constable a question. Constable answered him at length, and then, as the boy was in the act of jumping down, evidently Constable thought of something else he wanted to add to his instructions. Constable leaned out and began to shout to the boy, while at the same time pointing at something for emphasis. The minute he pointed, a shot rang out from up on the hill and a bullet hit him right between the eyes. He dropped like a sack of sand down to the floor inside the tank.

I hastily ducked my head down into the tank, but just before I did I caught a glimpse of the dismay that flashed across the face of the infantryman who had just jumped off the tank. I quickly knelt down to where Sergeant Constable was slumped on the floor of the fighting compartment. His head was bowed down on his chest, while a full stream of blood poured out of the round hole in his forehead. Rivulets of red blood began to run across the steel floor as his head, legs and arms twitched and jerked involuntarily in the last throes of dying.

The loader and I exchanged shocked, head-shaking looks, and I wearily ordered Al to take us back to where we had started out on this operation. As we headed back toward the people from headquarters, who were clustered about their parked jeeps, the infantry platoon herded their prisoners along and accompanied us.

The minute we stopped, I was greatly startled by a strident voice suddenly booming loudly down into the tank. "Did they just shoot old Constable back there while ago?" the voice shouted. I looked up to see the infantryman who had been up on the side of the tank a few minutes ago talking to Constable. He was back on top of the turret now and looking wide-eyed into the open hatch that Constable had used.

"They sure did," I answered.

"Is he dead?" asked the youthful GI, staring down at the crumpled body on the floor.

"I'm afraid he is," I answered.

"Son-of-a-bitch!" the infantryman bitterly exclaimed through clenched teeth as he jumped down off the tank. "Hey you-all," I now heard him shouting loudly outside the tank, "I was right! They damn sure did shoot old Constable back there awhile ago, and he's dead!"

For a few seconds, there was utter silence. Then I heard a strange sound coming from outside the tank. It sounded like what I would imagine the noise of many big zoo animals, such as a group of lions or bears, might make if they all suddenly started growling together. Then, the growling noises were drowned out by the unmistakable staccato sound of a BAR being fired on full-automatic, accompanied by loud yelling and screaming. Hastily looking out, I saw that the prisoners, who had been put into a compact group, were now all crumpled together, dead. The infantrymen stood over them and glowered at them.

The American soldier holding the still-smoking BAR looked up at me as I stared down wide-eyed at them from the turret of my tank. He then earnestly and somewhat plaintively, I thought, shouted up an explanation. "One of them bastards shot old Constable back there and then dropped his rifle and ran down here with his hands up. We couldn't tell for sure which one it was that did it, after they all got mixed around down here, so we just shot the whole wad to make sure we got him."

I just continued to stare down at him, but didn't say anything. Frankly, I was at a loss for words. I didn't know what to say. What possible good would it do to say anything now? Constable was dead, the prisoners were dead, and I experienced a wave of sadness and remorse washing through me for everyone concerned in this crummy war. I was just so horribly tired of people being dead. I really felt like my mind was incapable of sorting out whether what had happened to the prisoners was good or bad. I had seen mountains of dead Japanese in all the combat I had recently been through, so seeing these lying in a bloody pile really didn't affect me a whole hell of a lot. But then, I guess it did in a way, for I also remember that I thought at the time, "My God! We're getting to be as mean as they are!"

The clean, dapper, rear-echelon noncombatant headquarters people were simply stunned and speechless over what they had just witnessed. I really think they were afraid to say anything at all in fear the enraged infantrymen might turn and shoot them, too. And at that time, I wouldn't have bet a whole lot against that possibility had one of them smarted off. There was no doubt that Constable's kids were killing mad. But after a pregnant pause, with everybody staring at each other, things started cooling down. Soon, without saying a word to anybody, the headquarters group just quietly retrieved their prisoner and loudspeaker from the tank, loaded up in their jeeps, and drove away. It did now appear that the chances of getting any more of the watching Japanese in the vicinity to surrender were probably pretty slim.

I stayed nervous for days in fear the group from headquarters would report what had happened, and I would become involved in some kind of investigation with possible repercussions coming down through channels. But it wasn't very long before the two atomic bombs were dropped, ending the war and killing over 120,000 Japanese men, women, and children, most of them noncombatants. In contrast with that, if a report had been made about our little handful of prisoners being shot down in cold blood, it would have seemed like such small potatoes, they would have pitched it in the wastebasket.

I consider myself to be as kind or, maybe, even more kind-hearted than most people. But as an old man, I can be perfectly honest now about a past no one has an interest in anymore. So, I can say that at the time, standing there in the turret of that tank with Sergeant Constable lying dead at my feet and his life's blood all over the soles of my boots, I didn't think the killing of those prisoners was an atrocity. I just thought of it as retribution.

I remember that I stared down at all those distraught American boys, "his kids," he had called them, seeing some wipe at their eyes in frustration over this

Here I am, proudly showing off my Namburi pistol. My weight dropped from 152 to 127 lbs. during the 90 days of fighting, making me look very thin.

senseless killing that took place while we were all involved in trying to carry out an act of mercy. The murdered sergeant had earned their admiration and respect the hard way, by being their platoon leader in the fierce fighting they had just come through. His steadiness and sound judgements, made quickly in the heat of battle, had often made the difference between whether they lived or died. In the hellish conditions of the no-quarter, infantry ground-fighting, they had grown to trust him implicitly. He had become more important to them at this stage of their young lives than their father or brother, their teacher or coach. They had suffered together through many dismal days and long, horrible nights on the often rainy and soggy front lines, fighting an implacable enemy. This enemy wouldn't give up when he should, but tried to take as many Americans along with him as he could when he was finally trapped and faced death.

There are all kinds of leaders in this world, in all sorts of endeavors. But, in my estimation, when our nation is challenged and has to enter into war, a good infantry leader at the platoon level, who vigorously and aggressively directs his men in fighting for their country and its beliefs, has the toughest job around. On Okinawa, I worked with many of them and developed great admiration as I watched them in action. Such men as Sergeant Constable, in prolonged fierce combat such as that the 96th Division experienced on Okinawa, would have to rank close to the top of the Order of Valor. I'm sure Sergeant Constable would have been embarrassed to have been considered in that light, but that is certainly the way I saw him and others like him. And now, at this late date of the fighting, he was lying dead on the floor of my tank, in which he had sought safety. So, in trying to recall long ago feelings that I have spent fifty years trying to forget, I think I agreed with "his kids" back then that the most important thing at the time was to be sure and kill the bastard that had bushwhacked Constable. And even today, after dredging it all up again out of my fading memory bank, I'm afraid I still feel the same way.

That premonition he had on the day of his death has always been spooky to me. Are we really capable of being warned of impending disaster? In Constable's case, if he were being warned by a guardian angel that morning, it did him little good. When death came looking for him, it found him just as easily in my tank as it would have outside with "his kids." But still, he sure as hell felt something was amiss that morning. That has long made me wonder down through the years, if there can be such a thing as a premonition. *¿Quién sabe?*

Many, many times, over the years since that day, I've thought about that Japanese rifleman, up on the hill, squinting down his sights at the two heads sticking up out of the turret of that tank. He probably aimed first at one and then the other—one of them mine and one of them belonging to Sergeant Constable— as he tried to make up his mind which one to shoot before dropping his rifle and running down to surrender. He probably thought he was pulling off a good one on the dumb Americans and figured by mixing in with all the others, he would get away with it. I had a fifty-fifty chance then and won out when Constable pointed off to something to direct one of his boys. The watching sniper thought that indicated he was an officer or, at least, someone of importance and quickly pulled the trigger.

I took this photograph off the body of a dead Japanese soldier. The soldier pictured is wearing the traditional leg wrappings and tabi shoes.

I still kind of shudder when I think about what a deadly roll of the dice that was. What if I had pointed instead of Constable? I stayed shaken-up for some time as I realized just how close I had come to death. So, I think I understood then, and know I do now, why the prisoners were shot without mercy by Constable's "kids." We were all just so sick and tired of Japanese obstinacy and trickery, their complete lack of respect for life, and their inability to admit defeat when it was so obvious they were completely whipped on Okinawa. All we wanted was just to get it over with without them killing us. Our attitude ran along these lines: If they don't want to surrender, well OK, so be it. Don't surrender. But then don't expect a lot of mercy from us when we try to give you a chance to live and you respond by killing us.

The whole thing left such a sad memory for me down through the years. I have always felt a little guilty in the fact that I was the one whom the fates decided to let live that day. I have never forgotten the fact that the crafty Japanese sniper had a choice of two heads, and I lucked out while Sergeant Constable lost. Even now, in recalling and writing about it, I still feel anger toward that Japanese sniper for what he did that day. In refusing a generous offer to live, he ended up getting himself and his associates killed, and he kept poor old, tired Sergeant Constable from ever getting back to Georgia, when he had come so close to surviving the war. But then somebody is always going to be among the last to die in any war, I suppose. However, I remain so thankful that by the hair of my chin, it didn't turn out to be me and that I got to live to enjoy my grandchildren.

I'm sure today, in our more enlightened age of multi-culturalism and one-worldism there would be hell to pay for such a happening. But I believe that before anyone, particularly a noncombatant, earns the right to pass judgement on those infantry boys for what they did that day, they first should have to walk in their shoes and experience a little of the hell they endured. Those who have never had to participate in a wholesale blood-letting such as Okinawa can never have a true understanding of just how really bad it can get. Old General Sherman surely did speak the truth when he said, "War is hell!" For all those young people who have had to go to war, that has really been a fact, regardless of which side they fought on.

Chapter 11

AFTER OKINAWA

"There's hope that you will see your loved ones, reach your high-roofed house, your native land at last."

The Odyssey

July 14, 1945

Dear Mother,

Well, my promotion came through finally, so I am now a first looey. I sure am glad to get rid of those shave-tail bars and sure am lucky to get them so quick. The order was dated July 9th so it took awhile for it to come down all the channels. After losing so many tanks, I'll probably have to be a thirty-year man to pay for all of them. It's a good thing I don't have to though, as I would be out about half a million.

All the officers in this battalion are old men with lots of points, so myself and the other boy I came in with have a good chance of going on up some day. I hope it is all over before that though....

We had fresh eggs for breakfast this morning and they were really good. We drew fresh meat for dinner today, so things are really picking up. That will be the second time we've had fresh meat since we've been here, so we are all looking forward to it.

I guess the rodeo was a big success as usual. Stinky should have gotten a big bang out of it. It sure is fine for Tom to have a furlough now that everybody is there. It shouldn't be too much longer before we can all be together again. That will sure be a great day.

Our monkeys are thriving on all this sunshine. There is going to be a blessed event pretty soon so we have to be a little more broadminded with the expectant mother when she tears up everything as usual. I would like to have a pet monkey at home but they get into everything. Their favorite trick is to sit very peacefully on your shoulder, the picture of sweet innocence, and before you know it they are sitting on top of the highest object around calmly chewing up your fountain pen or something similar. I rescued mine before it suffered anything more than both ends teeth-marked, but many have suffered a horrible fate. They have more curiosity then anything I ever saw and have to look into everything. They used to have to sleep with me when it was cold and would get scared and nearly choke me to death when something would make a noise. I think I am going to get some film so I will send you some pictures of them. If it is at all possible try to get me some of that colored film or any kind, but I know how hard it is to find any there. It is impossible to get any here without writing back to Oahu, and it takes so long for it to get here.

I guess I had better stop. I hope you aren't worrying about me now, as I am just as safe as if I was back at NMMI.

Lots of love,
Bob

Mindoro, Philippines
August 16, 1945

Dear Mother,

Well, the war is over. It was amazing how calmly everyone took it over here. There was hardly any celebrating at all. It sure was a pity it couldn't have happened in time to save all those boys on Okinawa. I guess that's what we are all thinking.

We had a very nice boat ride, best I've had yet. It's the first time I haven't been in the middle of a typhoon or some other kind of whirlwind. This place we are at now is nice and muddy and hot, but it's only a short stay anyhow....

I hope you are all alright. I've been awfully anxious to hear from you.

Lots of love,
Bob
P.S. Send some more chicken.

Mindoro Philippines
August 21, 1945

Dear Mother,

It's still raining. Never have I seen such a country. It hasn't missed a day since we've been here and doesn't look like it intends to. It is practically impossible to move a vehicle of any kind. Even the jeeps are stymied. I don't believe there is any bottom to this mud at all.

The war is officially over I suppose, but it just seems unbelievable. It will probably be some time yet before I can think about coming home as we are almost sure to be occupational troops, and if I have to stay over here I had a lot rather do that than sit here in the mud. That ought to be fairly interesting, seeing what Japan looks like.

I had a letter from my loader yesterday. He is back on his farm in Missouri. He was hit in two places when the 47 m/m knocked us out that day, but says he is alright. The loader lost his leg and has been home for some time. I never will figure out how all that missed me. The gun was on my side and it was just like a knife-throwing act as I had holes all around me. When I think back on it I get twice as scared as I was then, which is practically impossible. We've been fighting the battle of Okinawa over every night, and we sure get into some real arguments. I'm glad they gave up before we had to hit the home islands. That would have really been rough.

Old Jones and I have really been around the country since we got over here, but it doesn't seem like this year is as far gone as it is. He is sure anxious to see that girl of his. She is nearly seven months old now.

I hope you are all fine. I am gaining weight, even if we do have spam every day and am doing fine. I sure will be glad to get back again.

      Lots of love,

      Bob

September 4, 1945

Dear Mother,

Not much happening now. We are practicing drill most of the time and teaching classes on Japan the remainder of the time. We have got to be in super shape and do everything perfect in order to make an impression on the Japanese, so we are really having to bear down as we were all mighty lax in everything during combat.

We are now attached to the 43rd Division and 11th Corp and are no longer connected with the 96th in any way except still using their APO. Before long we will lose most of our old men as many of them have been over here for three years and many for over forty months. It's about time they let them have a break....

Lots of love,
Bob

Batangas, Luzon, Philippines
October 2, 1945

Dear Mother,

Here it is fall already. This year has really gone scooting by. I should be home before too much of another one has scooted. It's still rainy, sloppy and bore-some, but I can stand all of that now that the war is over. It certainly is a relief not to be sweating out another landing. We play bridge a lot and are trying to fix up a squad tent into the officer's club so we find a little something to do.

Jones is still in the hospital with his teeth. He is really having a time of it. They decided they would have to pull another tooth now. He set up a great howl to no avail as they are going to pull it anyway. I go down and see him every day or so and he seems to be enjoying himself what time they are not working on him. With his little gal at home and his three purple hearts over here he has practically enough points to get out now. He should get home before Christmas at least....

Think I will go back to Manila and see Stokes again soon. There isn't much left of the town. They really tore that place completely up. All the old churches came out fair but that is compared to the rest of the buildings which were completely flattened. The churches were just about half flattened. They look just like the old missions at San Antonio, same style and everything. I guess they were built about the same time. There are two big churches here at Batangas, one of them caught a thousand-pound bomb but the other one is alright and is beautiful. I climbed all over it yesterday and appraised it. They are trying to take it over to store Wacs in but I don't think the priests are going to agree. It must have been a convent at one time as they have several large dormitories or something. Anyway, the Wacs don't see how they could possibly live in tents in all this rain and mud and aren't there any hotels to take over like they told us, etc., etc. In my opinion, the Wacs are a waste of time, money, equipment, shipping space, chow rations and filing cards, and all they should do anyway is stay home and sell war bonds.

Thomas Weaver should be out of this organization by now or pretty near it. We Greens are definitely not army career men. I've been awful lucky in this army though. I've never been in a unit by myself. There have always been some guys I knew along with me, which helps a lot.

I suppose I've raved on long enough. I'm sure fed up with this country. I sure hope Kipling was right when he said never the twain shall meet. Everything over here added up isn't worth the life of one American boy but they sure threw away a lot of them.

> Lots of love,
> Bob

Batangas, Luzon, Philippines
October 7, 1945

Dear Mother,

I finally got some mail…. there should be quite a stack on the way somewhere. All our eighty point men left this morning and the sixty point men and officers with seventy-five and over leave the tenth, so the battalion has about reached the end of the road, and though it was plenty rough at times, this was really a swell outfit. I sure was lucky to get into it…. There are five of us officers left without sufficient points and so far we don't know what they are going to do with us, but we will probably get in some MP outfit, Quartermaster (God forbid) or some administrative job, and we wouldn't be worth our salt in any of them, but we could at least have a new audience for our wild and wooly tales. I am now S-1 so am on the Staff, which is a dubious honor, and I don't know one record from another, so I have a lot to learn, but there are a bunch of good non-coms there so as usual, they run the thing and we officers sit around to lend the place the proper atmosphere, I suppose.

My monkey has really grown. She sure gives me a lot of pleasure. I take her walking every afternoon, and we have a good time in general. She is the biggest show-off I ever saw and always is on the lookout for new victims so she can pick their pockets and run up a tree with fountain pens, cigarettes (which she carefully tears individually apart) and everything else she can get her hands on. I'm going to sure try and bring her back with me when I get to come home.

Jones gets out of the hospital tomorrow. I think he really hates to leave, as he has been having a big time with all the nurses and eating ice cream every day and what not. He's lost a lot of weight, but otherwise looks fine. He sure is a fine guy. I don't think I ever met such an all-around fellow besides my two brothers, and he reminds me a lot of them.

A bunch of naval officers from the LST that took us to Okinawa came all the way down from Manila to see us yesterday and we had a real reunion....

There isn't much out of the ordinary happening around here now. You should have seen the looks of those boys' faces when they left this morning. Most of them have been over here for forty-two months or more and they were at last on their way home. I'll sure be glad when I'm on my way....

Lots of love,
Bob

Batangas, Luzon, Philippines
October 15, 1945

Dear Mother,

All our high point men & officers left today so we now have about a hundred men & five officers left. I'm executive officer of the battalion, something I never thought I would be. I don't know what they will do with us but I imagine we will break up pretty soon. I really think I'll be home about January at the earliest or March at the latest so that won't be too long.

I've got my bronze star now, so will send it home. Guess that will have to be your birthday present....

You ought to be getting the box of souvenirs I sent from Okinawa pretty soon.... I sent two sabers and a rifle. Hope they didn't rust. Those Samurai blades are beautiful....

It's still raining. We were in the tail of the typhoon that hit Okinawa I guess, as it's about to drown us out.... I'll sure be glad to get out of this place. The roads are too muddy to try to go anywhere so we just sit in our tents and debate on first one subject and another-usually fighting the battle of Okinawa over again....

Had a letter from Cummins. He wants to go to Texas U. I'd kinda like to, too.

Guess that's about all for now. I'm fine. Hope you all are. I wish you would stop worrying. The war is over. I'm just as safe now as a person could be.

Lots of love,

Bob

Batangas, Luzon
October 23, 1945

Dear Mother,

We are still sitting here doing nothing. They can't deactivate the battalion unless they have a War Department order and no telling how long that will take. We have a good set up now, so I'd just as soon stay just like we are until we can go home. We all (the officers) have a jeep and a good place to go swimming & that's all Jones and I have been doing. We have us some underwater masks and spend all our time exploring the coral reef. They are the most beautiful, but the weirdest things I have ever seen. There are schools of big, brilliant blue colored fish everywhere & many other kinds. The water is clear as a mirror and is about thirty feet deep. We take our air mattresses out with us to rest on, and they are really nice. You can crawl on them & float around all day. Jones is an expert swimmer & has improved my swimming no end.

The LST flotilla that took us to Okinawa from Leyte, docked down here at Talaga beach and all the officers came up to see us. They are the best bunch of navy boys I've ever met. They practically gave us the ship when we were on it....

We really have a good tent now. That's been about all we had to do is work on our tent. We have a radio, plenty of light, clothes racks and just about everything. Suzy's house is right outside so I can keep an eye on her while I'm at my desk. We're up on the side of a hill and can look way out over the China Sea. Banana trees grow all around, and there aren't many mosquitoes, so you see it's pretty nice, considering other conditions we've lived in. It's funny how you can get accustomed to anything. I remember when I first got in the army. I was very much put out at the idea of sleeping between two wool blankets without sheets! I thought that was awful.

I never have told you too much about Okinawa. At the time it was all happening, I was just bursting to tell you so many things I couldn't, it was pitiful. I wish I had kept a diary now, but I never would have. I was always ready for sleep when I got back to the bivouac area. I had five tanks and two flame-thrower tanks in my platoon. We called the flamers fire engines and they really were.

Our radio procedure was atrocious. All the months I spent in school learning all the set ways to talk over the radio were to no avail. We called each other by our names & would scream & cuss and tell jokes and everything else. Every time one tank would kill some Japs all the rest would be just like a pep squad. When a tank was knocked out we would let the war go hang and spend the rest of the day getting the crew out.

I lost seven tanks out of seven. Four were my own & three my platoon sergeants'. The reason for that was that one of us was always in the lead and the lead tank always was the one that caught it. Especially from mines. Jap satchel-charge teams would usually wait for the rear tanks. Those satchel teams would scare me to death. There are about twelve men to a team and all have about forty pounds of explosives strapped to them and they try to jump under the tracks or run into the side of the tank. You could get a flash of them flashing from rock to rock through the periscopes and I would begin to wonder why I wanted to come overseas. I was satchel-charged once. They swarmed all over my tank like a bunch of ants. One got on the phone & said cease firing in perfect English. The gunner told him something that wasn't very nice and proceeded to fire instantaneous bursts all around the tank which pretty well settled their hash. It was really funny how the whole platoon looked after me. They all had a big brotherly attitude toward me & every time I would stick my head out the turret every tank commander would just bawl me out.

There is a picture of my tank in *Yank*. It is the one of old TK 20, later known as "shoot, you've faded." It had eleven anti-tank holes in it and looked like an old rusty bucket, but we loved her. We lost her at Conical Hill finally.

We turned in all our tanks last week. That was probably the last time I will ever ride a tank again, but I'm not grieving over it. I must say, everybody had a different look in their eye when the motors were roaring and the traversing motor crying. Like a bunch of old fire horses when they smell smoke.

I suppose I had better stop. I could write about Oki for days & besides you'll all be so sick of hearing about it when I get home—it will be pitiful. We have fought that battle over so many times we just about have a monologue down perfect.

Write a lot. Mail is coming in good.

> Lots of love,
> Bob

Batangas, Luzon
November 13, 1945

Dear Mother,

The days are still flying by. It sure doesn't seem like it is the middle of November already but this place is July all the time. I guess it is getting cold back there now, and it won't be too long until duck season.

We traded two extra jeeps we picked up on Okinawa for a crash boat so we have really been playing sailor at forty knots. It's about the size of a PT and is about as fast. We roared over to Mindoro yesterday and are planning on going up to Corregidor soon. They have about ten more crash boats they would like to get rid of, as all of their crews have returned to the states, and there is no one to keep them pumped out and serviced. I wish I could get one home to Possum Kingdom....

We like to have been put in the guard house last night. We have a gook neighbor right behind the officer's row of tents who owns no less than ten thousand chickens. We got pretty tired chasing them off our beds every time we came in, so last night Jones and I had a turkey shoot at chickens with our pistols. The engineers across the road thought it was a banzai, I guess, as they sent the MPs down, but we talked the boy out of it. He had been over here eight days and as Jones called me Colonel Green and I called him Major Jones we all got along fine. We fried the chickens and they were good. The engineers will probably paint another battle star on their sign out in front. We are going to build us one of those traps with a figure four trip like we used to do a long time ago and have chicken till we leave here. I think that would be a little quieter than the pistols. It sounded like the battle of Okinawa all over.

I really don't see much hope in getting home very soon. The points are counted as of September second. I have only fifty-six points as of then and officers need seventy-five so until they lower the score or advance the date, I'm here for a while. I figure now I might get home by March or April, but if they could ever get some ships over here for a change and get some of the three-year men with over a hundred and twenty points home maybe we low-point men would get there a little earlier.

They put out these huge figures, which is suppose to be the number of men to be shipped in some certain month and then that's all. The men are still in the various replacement depots and have been there for more than a month. This Pacific Theatre rates about as high as a Pfc in the Mexican Camel Corps. They get last on anything that comes out. We fought the battle of Okinawa in tanks built for the British to be used in North Africa. No wonder we lost so many of them. I think half of them blew up on their own accord. Well, anyhow don't expect me home for Christmas.

What I wouldn't give to sit down at our table and eat a meal. I'll bet I gain fifty pounds the first month I'm home, and I could use it. When I think of all the food I used to leave on my plate. And cold, sweet milk. I haven't had or seen that since I left Seattle. I'll eat you out of house and home when I get back.

Well, suppose I had better stop and take my siesta.

Lots of love,
Bob

Batangas, Luzon
November 27, 1945

Dear Mother,

We are all in a dither around here now as we just got orders to deactivate. We are supposed to be deactivated the second of December or as near to that date as possible. Then they take all the men and officers we have left and put them in certain categories based on the number of points they have. All the different outfits we will do to have a shipping date to go back sometime, but we don't know where we will go or what, so far. Jones goes to the 28th Tank Bn. which is sailing for home from Batangas Bay the 25th of December. There is another officer who will go with me in the 50-60 point class, and it is rumored that we will go to some antiaircraft battalion in Manila. He is battalion CO and is a good guy. We went to Manila yesterday to see about deactivating, and they told us we could have our captaincy if we would sign up for another year or six months, but we just laughed. If I intended to stay in the army I would do it, but I've had enough. All I want to do is get out and get back to school. We have our time in grade for a captain and might get it when we get back to the states, but I doubt it, as they are promoting everybody who is staying in first-which is right. The trouble with signing up for any more time is that you have to spend it overseas. If I was in Europe or Japan or some civilized place it would be different, but this place ....

... I sure hope I can get home before too much longer. If this war hadn't ended we would be fighting on Kyushu now. The 96th Div. was to be in the assault landing there in September. They told us that right after Okinawa, and we were to get ready down here. We all were really sweating that one out.

We had what was known or what we call, anyway, a Snooper Scope on Okinawa. It was brought up to us at night and taken back early in the morning so the Japs couldn't get a look at it and consisted of an infra-red light whose beam was completely invisible but when you wore special red lens glasses you could use it just like a search light up to two hundred yards. It was really amazing. On the darkest night you could spot that light out there and see the Gookanese just a-crawling around like a bunch of snakes, and they would never know they were being watched. Along the last days of the campaign they caught on to it, and every Jap we would kill would have him a pair of red lense glasses. We really had fun with it for a while though.

When I was Liaison officer with the infantry, I got to be great pals with a major. He was a battalion commander, and when we were just holding the line and not attacking, he and I would get two sniper rifles and go up on the OP and really have a time. Those rifles were beautiful things with a ten power scope, and if you ever caught sight of a Jap, he was with his honorable ancestors very shortly. The major was killed by a navy plane one morning while we were drinking our coffee. These navy boys came circling over and one dod hit his trip and the fifty calibers flew. The major was hit, and when you are hit with a fifty caliber that is all. I guess the pilots got another cluster when they got back, but they sure did away with a good dough-foot. His name was Morris, and he was from Louisiana. Our own planes made many mistakes, but I can't blame them too much as every time they would come near the island all the A.A. batteries and ships would open up on them, so I guess their nerves weren't any too good. On D-plus-three I saw the navy shoot down five of its own planes in forty-five minutes. Pretty good shooting but not very profitable. Those kamikaze boys had the navy so jumpy not even the sea gulls were safe. They weren't near as good at shooting down Japs as they were Corsairs or Avengers. Time after time they let them get in, but the pilot would be so excited or something that he would usually miss the ship and merely blow up the water. I don't think half of them knew how to fly. They would get in one straight line and stay there. I saw a cruiser, an APA, and a destroyer hit while I was there.

Well, I suppose I had better stop. I may be home in time for the stock show if I'm lucky.

Lots of love,
Bob

Batangas, Luzon
November 29, 1945

Dear Mother,

Have to get up early in the morning and go to Manila to see about this deactivation. I dread that rough road, but enjoy being there. It is a pretty interesting place, and I know it well enough to get around without the time and trouble it used to take me.

I sure would like to get home, but I don't want you to be one of those who write congressmen. As adjutant, I get about five letters a day from various congressmen requesting me to please see that Johnnie gets home for Christmas, etc. They might as well address their letters to Abraham Lincoln for all the good they do. If Congress would, they could get us home, but like most of the people in the world, they just pass the buck on down. I just hope I get in in time to have a vacation and start to school next September. I sure hate to lose the past years when I should have been in school, but maybe it is for the best, as when I go to school this time it will be to learn something. I am pretty sure I want to be a doctor. I may sound conceited, but I feel like I can choose anything I want to and do it, which is a good way to feel I suppose. I do want to amount to something though, as I feel like I was spared for some reason when so many others were killed.

I got two packages today. I hope this is the last Christmas I ever spend away from home. The vegetable soup was really good. I had that for supper. Good soup is rare around here.

I'll be glad when we are deactivated and moved to another outfit. I think a change would do us all good. I hope we can get in some decent outfit in Manila and get out of the jungles for a change.

We all went out and had target practice with our pistols today. I sure would like to get in on some of that hunting that is going on around there. I wonder whatever became of that flock of geese Tom and I stalked fruitlessly that morning? I wish we could get them started around there.

My monkey and I take a walk every afternoon just like you used to do with the dogs. She is quite an affectionate ape and lots of fun. She got a lot bigger than I ever thought she would and may be quite a problem if I try to bring her home with me. That's the trouble with me having a pet. I get too attached to them and can't get rid of them. She's such a baby I don't think she could shift for herself if I turned her loose. She can't even climb a tree too well and is always falling out.

Guess I had better go to bed and get ready for the trip in the morning. I may send you another cable from Manila.

> Lots of love,
> Bob

Manila, Luzon
December 17, 1945

Dear Mother,

I guess you have about given up hearing from me but we are finally moved and settled again. I am living in a building now in downtown Manila so it is much better than anything I have had lately. I am an O.D. & in charge of a bunch of guards as well as supervisor over a Philippine Inf. Battalion, which is some job.

Suzy-Q doesn't like this city life at all. I have to leave her over with Lewis, who is at Rigal Stadium, and I think she is about to die of a broken heart or she thinks I've forsaken her. I don't get to see her much but am trying to fix her a place over here.

This outfit has been over a good while but none of the guys have ever been in combat, so I am really the big wheel around here. I have all the officers having nightmares at night already. They seem to be a pretty good bunch but are pretty much G.I. (or strict). I was spoiled in our old outfit, as we had about as much discipline as a herd of rats.

We have moved seven times since we left Batangas, and I was just about ready to become a beachcomber.

Hope everybody is OK. I haven't had any mail here yet, but it should catch up before too long.

> Lots of love,
> Bob

Manila
December 26, 1945

Dear Mother,

Well, Christmas is over. We really had a good meal but other than that it didn't seem much like Christmas. We ate so much turkey and dressing I nearly died. I sure hope this will be the last time I spend Christmas away from home. I haven't had any mail in a long time, but they are supposed to have a lot tomorrow, so maybe I will have some.

I have moved three more times, and we move again tomorrow, I hope for the last time. This outfit is split up all over Manila and is doing a little bit of everything. Suzy doesn't like all this moving any more than I do.

The way things look now, I may get home in February and I don't feel too optimistic about it. All these old codgers who came over here about two months ago are going home on length of service so that keeps this place pretty well stripped of officers. I never dreamed of going home this soon till the war was over, but now that it is, I think we have a little better right to go home than these guys that spent four years in the states and two months overseas after the war was over, but there is no use complaining about it....

There is no place like the ranch to spend Christmas. I was just thinking back yesterday of all the ones we had. That is sure some home. If anybody in this army has a real home to go back to it's me.

There just isn't anything to write about with no mail and not doing anything but moving. I'm feeling fine and am actually gaining a little weight, as the food is much better up here. The best food I've ever had overseas and the living conditions are so much better than what we had in the past, that I think I will be able to survive till I get on that boat. That will really be the day.

I hope you are all fine. I just can't wait to get home again, and I really feel like it won't be too much longer.

Lots of love,
Bob

Manila
January 15, 1946

Dear Mother,

It is a hot, sunny, lazy day. The workmen have just finished putting a front porch on our establishment, so now we can sit on it in the afternoons and discuss the one and only topic of demobilization. I've come to the conclusion that all I can say for sure is to expect me home when you see me coming, but I can't get too upset about staying over here, cause I know I will get home eventually and in one piece, and that is an awful lot in itself. We really have an abode to live in now. I've had natives working on this shack ever since we've moved in, and McClure got us a radio and a record player and says he is going to get me an accordion in the near future, so life decidedly is looking better.

A barge loaded with oxygen tanks and parachutes blew up on the harbor last night, so we all rushed over to Dewey Ave. and sat on the sea wall and watched the fire. It looked so much like an air raid that Lewis and I kept one eye hunting a hole all the time. No one was killed, which was a great surprise to all the GIs and me too, as I don't see how anyone could have escaped that blast. It broke the monotony anyway.

John Turbeville was up last week from Mindoro. I guess he is on his way home by now as the 96th was suppose to leave the twelfth. He had never seen Manila before and wanted me to show him the town and I did. His hand is alright now but his fingers are still crooked. He was hit by the same burst of machine gun fire that killed General Easley on Okinawa. He was Easley's aide and is General Bradley's now. Bradley has the 96th Division....

Our jeep was stolen last night but the MPs found it this morning, minus the tires and a few other various items. We were lucky to get it back at all, as they usually don't. There are more black markets and gangs of racketeers in this town than I ever knew existed. They have stolen jeeps and stolen tommy guns and they have really been giving the MPs and police a bad time. The more American troops that leave the worse it gets. Nearly every night they have a wild chase down the streets, firing madly but so far I have only seen one hit out of several thousand rounds fired, and he was just hit in the arm. These Gooks are such poor shots there is little danger. The colored troops and Filipinos have it out with each other about twice a week too so all in all it's not very quiet in this town. And on top of everything, the GIs have mass meetings about every other night and parade down the streets screaming they want to go home and the majority of them just got off the boat. What disgusts me is that the leaders of the mobs are three no-good goldbricks who all three were leaders in the CIO back in Detroit. That is the last straw. I hope they keep them all over here till 1950. I agree that there has been a lot of bungling by the mighty muckity-mucks but all in all I think they have done a pretty good job in getting guys home.

When I heard one of the Unionist leaders wearing the patch of the Afwespac Special Service get up and say "we have won the War, now let's win the demobilization," that was enough for me. When General Styler asked how many men present (there were about 20,000 there) had been in actual combat and been shot at he was greeted with a chorus of boos. I certainly don't agree with the army in its ways, but the army isn't suppose to be a democratic organization anyway, and if the CIO starts running it as well as the country I'm going to go back to Mindoro and live in the rain and jungle. Thank God we didn't have that bunch of jokers fighting. What a rout there would have been.

Suzy is getting bigger, fatter, and sassier every day. She is certainly a one-man monkey. I never have a bit of trouble with her, and even when I chastise her she never offers to object, but she sure chases everybody else off. I couldn't bring her home because she hates women and children for some unknown reason, and there will be plenty of those at home. I sure have had a lot of fun with her though. She trusts me so completely and is always so glad to see me that I'm sure going to hate leaving her. I am going to take her up to the hills and turn her loose if I ever do get to come home....

My Christmas packages should get here soon, also. I hope we don't move anymore before we come home. I may have been too optimistic about getting home in February, but nobody knows, so maybe there is still a chance.

> Lots of love,
> Bob

Manila
February 3, 1946

Dear Mother,

I am now on my way to Japan or Korea. We are escort officers for a bunch of replacements they are sending up & will sure help to relieve the monotony of sitting around here. It will take between three & five weeks to get back here. Maybe by that time I will be ready to start home. The only thing I hate is that I won't get any mail, but I'll keep writing you from wherever we are. We will come back to the same outfit so keep using the old address.

Hope you are all fine. I am.

> Lots of love,
> Bob

Jinsen, Korea
February 9, 1946

Dear Mother,

It's 30 degrees outside and we are all about to freeze to death. Somehow I always thought of Korea as being hot. We got here last night and are still sitting out here in the harbor. We get off tomorrow & go by train to Seoul, where we catch a plane to Osaka or Tokyo. Then we catch a plane from there back to Manila. It has been a nice trip. We are each in charge of one hundred men and have to see that they clean up the troop compartments, etc., so we usually don't have much to do and are getting to see some more of the world. This sure is a bleak looking place. There is snow on the tops of mountains and this old Yellow Sea is really & truly yellow. We came right up the coast of Formosa & it sure is rugged. I had seen it once before when we came from Okinawa, but we came a lot closer to it this time. We have about three thousand troops on board. They all have just got over & think they are being abused terrifically being sent up here & maybe they are. I'd sure hate to be stationed up here. I've been spending most of my time in the hot shower. It's the first hot water we've had since the last time I was on a ship, and I sure do love it. I just wish this thing was headed stateside. This sure is a nice break in the monotony though. We were lucky to get the job of escort officers, and there were officer's clamoring to go, but they gave us priority. It sure seems funny for it to be so cold. We just can't get used to it. I think we'll all be glad to get back to Manila and warm weather.

The food here is wonderful. We have soup every meal, but breakfast and all kinds of salads, desserts, rolls, muffins and everything. I'm about to flounder.

We had some real rough weather coming up, but I didn't get seasick, although most of my boys did. I haven't been seasick but once, and that was the first board from Seattle to Oahu, and then I liked to have died. This is my sixth boat ride, and I haven't got home yet, but there shouldn't be too many more. The big rumor has it that my category will start home in March, but don't believe it. Don't believe anything till you see me walk in.

I don't think we will stay in Seoul long, but I'll write & tell you about the sights.

> Lots of love,
> Bob

Manila, Luzon
February 19, 1946

Dear Mother,

Back to good old Manila again. I didn't appreciate it till I got up north and froze to death for two weeks. We left here on the Marine Adder, a big troop transport run by the Merchant Marine and went to Jimsen, Korea. We got up there in a little over three days. We went right up the shore line of Formosa and had a good look at it, and it is really rough. I thank my lucky stars we didn't have to hit it. We had twenty-eight hundred troops on board, boys who had just got overseas, and it took about three days to unload them, as there were no docks, and we had to unload them in small boats. It sure was a cold job. We were escort officer and in charge of about two hundred men each. We had to see that they kept their compartments clean while on the boat and stuff like that. There really wasn't much to it. We finally got them all off (it was below freezing and snowing all time. I like to have frozen.)

We went in to Jimsen and looked around awhile. The people look just like the rest of these Orientals except they are larger. They have a good many large factories up there and seem to be quite industrious. It sure is a poverty-stricken land though. All the houses are covered with coal smoke and look like the slums of our own Yankee land. I'm sure glad I'm not stationed there. We left the ship and went to Keipo airport, which is about sixteen miles from Seoul (pronounced Saul) and spent one night there in a barn-like building the Japs left. I have never been so cold. I spent most of the night running around the room wrapped up in a blanket like an Indian in a six day race. We got on a C 47 next morning and took off for Japan and I ran all the way from Korea to Japan inside the plane as the heater was broke, and it was ten below inside.

We flew to Hyushu first and then went right up Honshu. We flew right over Hiroshima, and the pilot went down to five-hundred feet and circled for about ten minutes to give us a good look. It looked like our field in the dead of winter. Absolutely nothing there. Hard to believe it used to be a city larger than Fort Worth, but some mighty plain writing on the wall as to what will happen if this old world doesn't quit behaving like a bunch of spoiled brats.

Then we went right over Mt. Fuji, and it was so pretty it was breath taking. It stuck up out of the clouds in a perfect cone covered with snow. Easy to see why the Japs thought Gods lived there. We landed at Atugi airport and hopped on a bus, not knowing where we were going, but just out to see Japan. We got off in Yokahama and spent the night in a Casual Camp. It wasn't as cold in Japan as in Korea, but it was still mighty cold after being down here so long. We set out next morning and saw all there was to see of Yokahama and then got on the intra-urban to Tokyo. They have more of those things there than anything. Soldiers have special cars to ride in so we didn't have to get in the way of the stampede of Japs. I never have seen such crowds. The intra-urban really went fast, but I was scared to death all the way. I think it ran half off and half on the rails all the way to Tokyo, and sounded like a worn out thrasher thrashing rocks. All the buildings between Yokahama and Tokyo were conspicuous by their absence. The B 29s did a pretty good job.

We got off in Tokyo and were besieged by red caps. One about three-feet high carried my bag which weighed not less than twice his own weight, but I gave him a basket full of sen which added up to about two bits, but he was all smiles and knocked on the floor three times with his bald head, hissing like the snake he was. By this time it was dark, and we went to the A.T.C. hotel and got a room. It was real nice and I stayed in the hot shower about three hours. It was the first time I had been warm since I left Manila.

We took off again next morning to see the town and hired us some rickshaws to ride in. My substitute for a mule came about to my waist, and if he hadn't been a Jap I would have felt sorry for him, but I rared back and tried to look like a Roman Emperor riding through a conquered city. We went up to the Imperial Palace and watched the noble subjects come up and carefully take off their coats, kneel down and Kow Tow three times toward the palace. In that weather I wouldn't have taken off my coat for Hetty Lamar. It was dubious about my pacer getting me back to the hotel, but he made it.

The large buildings of Tokyo are still alright, and they have some nice looking ones. Their street cars are still running, but look like they should have stopped doing so in 1920. And people! The town is packed. I was still very apprehensive about walking down the streets with all those slant eyed apes all around me, as we didn't get along so well on Okinawa, but they seem to accept the fact that they are no longer the big wheel over here. We saw the Emperor coming back from an inspection of bombed-out areas. If he inspects them all, he will be a mighty busy god for the next fifty years, but all the people lined the streets and bowed their mangy heads as he went by.

The country of Japan is beautiful. Much more so than any I have yet seen over here, and I hope I will soon be through seeing anymore. Their fields are all just like gardens they tend them so well. There are lots of pine trees, lakes, mountains and all the rest that makes up beautiful scenery, but all the time I was looking, I was visualizing how easily they could have defended it. Thank God the war ended. I remember how the correspondents talked of Okinawa's beautiful scenery too. A good old mesquite flat will satisfy me from now on.

We went back to Atugi on a bus run by the army and took off once more, this time in a C 54. It had a heater, so I took off the top three layers of clothes and made it alright. We landed at Osaka, but it looked about the same as the rest. All the rest of the way down the inland sea, we could see components of the Jap fleet sticking half out and half under the water. They really got caught with their pants down in there. We left Atugi at six-thirty in the afternoon and landed at Naha airport on Okinawa at about midnight. We spent the rest of the night there and left at noon the next day, today that is. I had seen enough of that rock so I didn't bother sight seeing there any. I was sure glad to land here at Nichols Field and feel that good old hot air. I'm glad I got the chance to go up there, and it was a very nice trip.

I have fully recuperated from the loss of my tonsils and feel fine. Now don't get too optimistic (I'm trying not to) but I should start home this next month if everything works out. I think this might really be it this time, but have been fooled so many times am trying not to bank too heavily on it, but I sure do want to get home.

Hope you are all fine.

Lots of love,
Bob

It was weeks after the island had been declared secured that all fighting finally ceased on Okinawa. Shortly after that happened, the 96th Division and the 763rd Tank Battalion wearily loaded up on LSTs and other transport ships and sailed south, headed for the island of Mindoro in the Philippines. The original plan had been for the two war-ravaged units to be completely refitted on Mindoro and brought back up to full strength with new equipment and replacements to get ready for the invasion of Japan proper. But now the war was suddenly over, and it was a new world.

On the way down, our convoy was in mountainous seas on the edge of a terrible typhoon off Formosa. No one was allowed on deck and although the LST was not nearly as loaded as we had been when going to Okinawa, it still did creak, groan, bend, buckle and shake as it rolled and wallowed in by far the roughest seas any of us had ever seen. It was pretty scary. The typhoon moved on to strike Okinawa dead center and wreaked even more destruction on that poor, battered island.

After that rough trip, our LST unloaded near the town of San Jose on Mindoro. It was a very primitive place, and we were there during the peak of the rainy season, so our stay there was not a very pleasant one. The constant rain made the ground so soft that every time the wind blew, the pyramidal tents we lived in would blow flat down because all the tent pegs were useless and just oozed out of the muck. After a short stay, we were elated when orders came to load up on LSTs once again.

After loading up, we had a short ride up to the southern part of Luzon Island where we unloaded and set up camp near a fairly large town named Batangas, about ninety miles south of Manila.

Left to right: David Paul Jones, former University of Arkansas football star, and I relaxing on Mindoro. Jones earned three Purple Hearts and was allowed to return stateside soon after the war ended.

Now all the older officers, NCOs and enlisted men who had been overseas for four years began to receive orders to go home. Before long, Jack Lewis and I were the only officers left who had been with the 763rd Tank Battalion on both Leyte and Okinawa. Many new junior officers and enlisted men arrived from the States to replace some of the old hands who were happily leaving everyday for home.

Jack Lewis, by some quirk of army-paperwork fate, received his notice of promotion from second lieutenant to first lieutenant three days before I did. Because of that, he now out-ranked me by those three days and that made him the highest ranking officer in the battalion, and he became the 763rd Tank Battalion commanding officer. I now became the executive officer, adjutant, and practically every other position that required a commissioned officer until we could saddle the newly arrived officers with some of those we didn't want.

It was pretty heady at first being in exalted positions as the commanding and executive officers. But we discovered the battalion was slated to be deactivated very soon, and we were the ones who were going to be responsible for handling that job. It was going to be a monumental task. We also discovered that there was something related to deactivation called a "Table of Organization" or a TO. As lowly platoon leaders, we had never been concerned with this bookkeeping device, indeed, had never even heard of it. Now, in our new elevated positions, the TO had suddenly become extremely important in our lives. We discovered it contained a listing of every single thing that had ever been issued to the battalion, from tanks to toothbrushes.

The former battalion headquarters staff of old NCOs, who understood how the army expected its records kept, had, by this time, all happily gone home. They were the ones who had always kept the reams of paperwork connected to the TO list of government property in proper and up-to-date order. They could easily produce and show an officer from the Inspector General's Office the

correct paperwork that showed where every piece of listed battalion equipment was located or else produce a record showing what had become of it if it were missing. Neither Lewis nor I had the foggiest clue about any of this. But we could line up the new officers and replacement men to get all the tanks, trucks, jeeps and half-tracks that were on the list cleaned up and ready to be checked off the TO.

After this was done, we had to turn them in by driving them to a gigantic motor pool located near Nichols Field. The day we delivered them was the last time in my life that I rode in a tank. We then turned in all the machine guns, side-arms (most of them), all the maintenance

This was taken after I was named Executive Officer of the 763rd Tank Battalion. Taken at Batangas, Luzon, P.I.

equipment and tools, tents, cots, sleeping bags, kitchen equipment and various other things that were listed on the TO.

Finally after all the major items listed had been identified and turned in, we said, "to hell with it," and declared everything else had been "lost in action." We now began to give all the equipment that we had left to the Filipinos. An

NCO of Italian descent, who was a devout Catholic, had become friendly with a group of Italian nuns who ran a big orphanage and convent adjacent to a big old cathedral.. This sergeant told us about these nuns and their orphanage down the Batangas road and what a rough time the Japanese had given them, so we decided that Christmas should come early for them.

We proceeded to load up and haul a mountain of stuff that wasn't listed on the TO down to their convent and presented it to them. A lot of this excess equipment had been acquired when the 763rd had been fighting on Leyte near the airstrip where the Japanese paratroopers had descended one evening from thirty-eight Betty Bombers. As the Jap paratroopers floated down to land nearby in the jungle, the air corps personnel, who were living in comfort in a nice camp at the air strip, simply jumped in vehicles and madly fled the premises, abandoning the camp and all their equipment.

Much of the 763rd personnel were emplaced nearby, and when they saw the air corps group skedaddle, they immediately let the war go hang and rushed in their vehicles to the abandoned air base. They quickly loaded up and helped themselves to what they considered to be an over-abundant supply of opulent equipment for the air corps. Among the air corps' liberated items that they "borrowed" and took along with them on all their later travels were several gasoline burning Servel ice boxes (when possible, ever after kept full of beer), many fine air mattresses (I later ended up with one of these), two large generators for electric lights, some folding tables and chairs, and much fancy, extra kitchen equipment.

We also gave the nuns many other larger handy things, such as several jeeps of doubtful pedigrees that had been picked up and "accidentally" loaded on LSTs at various places. There was also a mint condition weapons carrier and a perfectly good 6X6 truck that had been "borrowed" from the navy on the beach at Okinawa. The nuns were overwhelmed at our largesse and to show their appreciation, invited Lewis and me along with several NCOs to come to the convent one night for an Italian dinner they cooked. We went, and it was simply delicious.

The Mother Superior was a tiny old lady who spoke good English. She told us how she had volunteered to leave Italy and come halfway around the world in 1915 because she knew Europe was getting ready to have World War I, and she wanted, at all costs, to avoid being involved in a war. Spreading her hands expressively upwards in a graceful gesture, she then exclaimed, "And look what happened! War found me even over here! But it took thirty years to do it!"

The Japanese had certainly treated them miserably, raping many of the younger nuns whenever they wanted to, as well as raping some of the not so young ones and many of the orphan girls who were cared for there, too. The nuns spoke of the Japanese with great anger and bitterness, but then would always ask God's forgiveness for having expressed themselves in such a manner. Their old buildings were badly damaged by the Japanese who, mean as snakes to the end, had tried to blow them up before they were forced to leave by the approaching Americans. We felt virtuous for having so benevolently dispensed the government's property to such deserving people who were doing God's work, as well as being capable of preparing great Italian food on short notice for honored guests.

Jack Lewis, Commanding Officer of the 763rd Tank Battalion, with his bride, Evelyn. Lewis was awarded the Silver Star for his service on Okinawa. After leaving the service, Lewis returned to Cody, Wyoming, where he became a rising political figure, until one morning when he slid on black-ice on the way to his office and was killed.

So with some exceptions, which I won't fully go into at this late date, the equipment of the battalion had now all been successfully turned in somewhere, and the hated TO paperwork officially rectified and approved. To finish up, we placed the official paperwork concerning all the actions of the battalion while it had been in existence in a large trunk-like container, and Lewis and I drove it up in a jeep to the huge army headquarters in Manila. When we turned that in, they gave us a notification that stated the 763rd Tank Battalion was now officially declared to be deactivated and no longer existed in the service of the country. *Sic transit gloria!*

Lewis and I were now assigned to various units in Manila on a temporary basis. He started dating an army nurse from Buffalo, Wyoming, named Evelyn Vonberg and before long, I was best man at their wedding in a small Manila church.

One sad day, Suzy-Q managed to untie her leash, and as she was running running across the street to get into my jeep, she was hit and killed by a truck. I stopped making arrangements to bring her home with me and instead drove her several miles outside Manila into the jungle and buried her beneath a banana tree in an ammunition box. In her little coffin, she wore her GI olive-drab sock-turtleneck sweater she was so proud of, and I pinned her campaign ribbons on her sweater. These included the Purple Heart ribbon we awarded her the time she got her tail cut off when a two-inch-thick steel tank hatch closed on it. (She had accidentally caused it to slam while climbing on the tank.) I have to admit there was a lump in my throat as I covered the small box with red volcanic dirt. With her funny little antics and sunny disposition, she had been a great source of enjoyment, not only for me, but also for many others during the almost two years she was with us. I still smile when I think back to how she loved to ride spread eagle on the steering wheel of my jeep and would grin delightedly when I turned a corner, causing her to revolve head-over-heels.

Chapter 12

HOME

"It really is your fate to make it back alive and reach your
well-built house and native land."

The Odyssey

Finally, I received orders to board a huge troop ship named "General Pope" and along with a multitude of other soldiers, spent sixteen days crossing the old blue Pacific to sail under the Golden Gate Bridge one early morning. Never had a bridge looked so beautiful. It had been quite an odyssey, but I had made it safely home.

When we disembarked from the General Pope at the Oakland dock, a brass band was playing Sousa marches and pretty USO girls were passing out doughnuts and coffee. All officers, including me, were directed to a building where there was a long row of pay telephones, and many of us began to call our homes. I called the ranch at the old 9012-F-3 number that, when everything was in order and working, caused the operator in Albany to plug in and make the old crank telephone in the ranch house ring three long rings.

I can still remember the joy I experienced when I heard the faint noise of the receiver being picked up and my mother's voice answering. She had a peculiar way of saying "hello." It kind of came out "HAL-low," with a stress always placed on the first syllable of HAL, and this always instantly identified her to those who were well acquainted with her.

I still remember her first words, "You're home—you're home." And my answering, "Well, not yet, but I'm sure a whole lot closer." Then my dad's voice came on and in my mind, I visualized his familiar voice traveling along that single wire, nailed on the top of all those twenty-three miles of mesquite fence posts from the ranch to Albany. I had repaired that line so many times when broken, putting it back together with a tightly wrapped "telephone splice."

Dad now said, in a well remembered, all business-like tone, "We are going to have to drive 1,200 steers from the ranch to Albany to put on the railroad next week, and we need you to help. Bill has a new horse for you to ride, which he thinks you're going to like. So hurry on home." It was a happy conversation.

First I had to go through another physical examination, but it was somewhat cursory and not nearly as rigorous as we were usually subjected to. After that, we were directed to a BOQ (Bachelors' Officers Quarters) building and then, after checking in there, entered an officers' mess hall nearby, where I nearly overdosed on fresh, sweet milk. Talk about ambrosia! I hadn't realized how much I had missed cold, sweet milk for the two years I had been overseas. They also had broiled T-bone steaks for us, but I drank so much milk I couldn't eat mine.

The army people really tried to expedite all the necessary paper work. They asked if I had any desire to remain in the army, and I just smiled and shook my head no. It finally was beginning to sink in that I was getting close to the end of my military career and would soon actually be a civilian again. The next morning I received orders to go by rail to El Paso, Texas, to be discharged at old Fort Bliss. Almost four years earlier, I had gone by rail to get to Fort Bliss to enter the army with my NMMI class, so a closure of sorts was in the making.

As I rode the train across Arizona and New Mexico, my excitement at the prospect of soon being back to civilian status and actually being with my family once again on the ranch became tempered by a vague feeling of sadness that began to creep in as I thought of all the boys who would never be making the trip home. I had an overwhelming wish to thank God for allowing me to be on a train that was fast bringing me closer and closer to home, instead of being buried in a trench grave by a bulldozer on that far away island of Okinawa as so many other boys had been.

I didn't know it then, but I would know later that we of Shackelford County lost in the war:

Edwin Dyess—a young man I admired as much as a youth of today admires a sports star, especially when he did a fly-over of Albany down Main Street in his fighter plane. After being captured on Bataan, surviving the death march, escaping from a Japanese prison camp, and returning to the U.S., he was killed in California in the crash of his P-38 fighter plane. Dyess Air Force Base in Abilene was named for him;

Evan English—we sat next to each other in the coronet section of the band and were good friends. He was a quiet boy, kind and gentle;

Norman Hatcher—we went to the same Sunday school and church and were close friends, a tall and gangly boy with a wry sense of humor; he was killed when the plane he was piloting was shot down over Mindoro in the Philippine Islands;

Richard Klinger—we were close friends; he was a little fellow in my grade, quick of movement with a happy nature. He was a marine killed at Saipan;

Gene and Glen Mauldin—brothers, they were both my close friends and both were killed in Asia;

Boyce Ray Nichols—he was handsome, olive-skinned, well-built, calm and unassuming. He was killed when a torpedo crashed into his ship in the Mediterranean Sea;

Carroll Reese—he was in my sister's class; he was a bright, blond-headed, self-confident, handsome, somewhat debonair lad who was a B-26 pilot, shot down over Holland on his sixth mission in a B-26;

Martin Lee Riley—former Sheriff Ben Jack Riley's older brother and as good a young cowboy as ever rode a horse in Shackelford County; he was a marine killed at Saipan;

Curtis Shepperd—he was the Methodist preacher's son and perhaps my brother Tom's closest friend; Tom still occasionally visits his grave in Lubbock, where he died as a flight instructor in a plane crash.

Once again I shook my head in wonder at how lucky I had been and once again my mind wrestled with the problem many surviving combat veterans encounter—trying to understand or make sense of what kind of unknown lottery it was that determined who got to live and who didn't in the maelstrom of the just-finished war. The question bothered me very much back then and even today, so many years later, occasionally it still creeps into my mind, and I still become bothered by this unanswered question, for I never have come up with a very satisfactory answer.

I know now that the ancient Greeks believed that three old women were responsible for determining how long a man got to live. They thought the first old woman spun the thread of life while the second old woman casually measured out different lengths of the thread, some being of short length, some medium, and some lengthy. The third old woman snipped it in two with her scissors. I have decided that is probably about as good an explanation as any.

Thinking about it almost gave me a headache back then on the train home as the wheels clicked-clicked-clicked over the rail joints. Why was I getting to ride the train home while so many others lay buried on that beat up island? I tried to figure out if our lives are actually ordained by some kind of force or if there is someone or something far beyond our comprehension away out there somewhere in the cosmos that determines when we die and how long we get to live. If so, does that make a fatalistic belief or validate a belief in predestination?

I always cringed on Okinawa when I heard someone who had just escaped being killed say, "The Lord really looked after me," while another person standing right next to him was done away with. Did the Lord deliberately not look after the dead man? The one killed may have possessed many more laudable attributes than the one who was allowed to live on, so what in the hell does it mean? I had seen too much death in too short a time, and it had knocked askew my perception of whether there was an orderliness to life. I gave up trying to figure it out and decided to just go with and accept the fact that for whatever reason, I had just been one of the lucky ones. As the long years have passed, this unanswered question of why him and not me still creeps into my mind. It doesn't come nearly as often as it used to, but occasionally, in the witching hours of a long night, my soul is once again filled with longing for an answer. Perhaps on down at the end of the road, I'll finally find out the answer to that question. It would be funny if it were three old hags cackling and spinning in a rocky cave.

When I reached Fort Bliss, the actual discharging didn't take long, only about three days. I went downtown the first evening and walked into the old Paso Del Norte Hotel. The first person I saw sitting in the lobby was smoking a big, black Mexican cigar—an old rancher friend of my dad named John Honeycutt. He had come from Albany, but now ranched near Sierra Blanca. He insisted on taking me over to Juarez to celebrate my coming home from the war, so he gathered up three or four old cronies and off we went.

It was a hilarious evening, as all those old codgers proceeded to get carried away at my return, although no one but John Honeycutt knew me. Before long, they were all roaring drunk from tequila toasts raised to the returning soldier— me. The band entered in with gusto, playing loud and rousing Mexican songs, many of which John and his cronies had requested, and they sang along in Spanish with great feeling when they weren't whirling around the dance floor with dark-eyed señoritas.

Just before midnight, U.S. MPs appeared and anyone in a U.S. uniform was advised to go across the Rio Grande into U.S. territory before 12:00. John and his bunch were still going strong with no sign of weakening and didn't even know it when I left with the MPs who had offered me a ride back to Fort Bliss, where they were going anyway.

The next morning, in the midst of yet another, but final, physical by army doctors, a sergeant came in and hollered if anyone named "Green" was present. If so, there was someone to see him out in the hall. I wrapped a towel about me and went outside to see John Honeycutt standing there. Although he must have never gone to bed, he looked pretty good and alert. His old eyes were twinkling when he said, "Well, you sneaked out on us last night, and I just wanted to make sure you wasn't in the Juarez jusgatho. I'm on my way to the ranch now that I know you're all right. Have a good trip home and tell your dad hello. He's the best friend I ever had."

With that, he lit up a fresh Mexican cigar with a kitchen match and, flipping the match away, clonked rapidly away down the hall on his high-heeled cowboy boots. I shook my head in wonder at John's stamina and went back inside to finish my physical.

I caught a plane to Abilene the next day where I was met by Mother, Dad, Bill and Tom. Mary Anna's husband was still in the navy, and she was in California with him, but everybody else was there to greet me. It was a grand reunion, and now I was really excited as we drove down One-Mile Hill into the familiar Main Street of Albany and headed on out to the ranch.

When we turned off the pavement onto the dirt road that led into the ranch, I realized that all the time I was fighting the Japanese, I had it in my mind that somehow I was fighting not only for my country, but also for this ranch that I loved and that I never, ever wanted to leave again. Now, nearly sixty years, later, I still feel the same way.

Photograph by Michael O'Brien

Here I am today, taking a break from work on the Green Ranch with my dog, Maggie.

EPILOGUE

Why do old soldiers want to return to old battlefields? I don't know for sure, but I wanted to do so for some time, and on a trip with my wife, Nancy, I got to fulfill this wish in 1978. It took about two hours for our Nippon Airlines plane to go from Osaka, Japan, to the island of Okinawa.

From our plane I looked down on the inland Sea of Japan and then the scattered islands that dotted the sea occasionally in the 350 miles between the Japan home islands and Okinawa. I thought of the hundreds of young Japanese kamikaze pilots who had flown this same route on their one-way trip to attack American warships around Okinawa. I wondered what they thought about as they looked down on such a beautiful sight and knew they were droning along closer every minute to a flaming death. I decided it would have been much easier not to know beforehand what was going to happen at the end of their trip.

Upon arrival on Okinawa, we rented a car and driver, and I took my traveling companions on a tour of the Okinawan battlefields. The hills looked smaller to me this time. There was also something changed in the islands' appearance that I couldn't quite put my finger on, but in time it came to me. The last time I was there, during the battle, the hills were blasted clean, clear down to the white coral rock by shells, bombs, flame-throwers and rockets. Now, with an annual rainfall of over sixty inches, the hills had as emerald a covering as Ireland. It's a very pretty island.

We started our battlefield tour at the Hagushi beaches where we Americans landed that Easter Sunday. On that day, we came ashore in three eight-mile-long lines of assault boats and Amtracs. Our young Okinawan driver had no idea where the landings had been, but I did. The beaches were pictures of serenity now. There was a new concrete seawall. A noisy flat-wheel roller was busy smoothing the paving for a new seaside housing development. It could have been Galveston, Texas.

Yontan airstrip was just inland from the beaches. Our American forces quickly overran it on the first day of the invasion. They had just captured it when a Jap zero flew the pattern and made a perfect landing. The young pilot, unaware of the change in ownership, got out, saw he wasn't among friends, and drew his pistol. He never got to use it.

It was also at Kadena Airstrip, sometime later, that I watched a wing of our Marine Corsair fighter planes whistle over, peel off and land. I peered intently as the pilots climbed down, until I picked out the stocky form of my old Albany buddy, Gene Mauldin. I'll never forget how, when he recognized me, we ran together whooping, hollering and beating on each other.

Good old curly-headed, grinning Gene. He made it through that war, but was fated to die in the next. Communist gunfire brought his Corsair fighter smashing down into a Korean mountainside while he was giving his hard-pressed marine buddies on the ground close-in fire support.

Why do old soldiers go back? To remember, I guess, when life was exciting and full of lofty ideas about being involved in something really important.

Kadena airstrip is now a huge American airbase that sprawls out over much of central Okinawa. Kakazu Ridge, where twenty-six American tanks were lost in one afternoon of ferocious fighting, is now covered with apartment high rises and a golf course. I remembered how desperate the voices had sounded over our tank radios as the surviving crew members of the knocked-out tanks, many of them burned and wounded, pleaded for assistance that couldn't and didn't reach them.

Now an electric golf cart carrying two bored-looking American officers whirred smoothly by the place where long ago, the burned-out hulks of M-4 tanks had been scattered about like a stricken elephant herd. This time, as we drove away from Kakazu Ridge, I watched a blond-headed guy in shorts hit a nice, high-arcing shot to the green. I'll bet he didn't know that golf course he was playing on was fertilized with American blood, but not many people do know that now. Even fewer would care. What a difference timing makes, in golf or life.

We now drove south to where the second main Japanese defensive line had been skillfully dug in along the Maeda Escarpment. Why on earth had this little old insignificant-looking ridge seemed so important? We Americans suffered hundreds of casualties in savage fighting for possession of this seemingly unimpressive piece of real estate. It took many days to finally wrest it away from the deeply dug-in and tenacious Japanese youths who were instructed to hold it for their Emperor.

I'm sure the bones of many of those defenders are still moldering there today inside the closed-over honeycomb tunnels deep in that coral rock ridge.

They are spending eternity with honor intact, as they died with weapons in hand in obedience to their Samurai warrior code of fighting to the death. Does that really matter when you are dead? I hope so. It should.

Our last stop was Mabuni Point, on the very south end of the island. It was also the end of the Japanese resistance as there was no place for them to go from here. The rocky cliffs of Mabuni dropped straight off to the sea far below. So did hundreds of Japanese soldiers, who chose suicide in this fashion rather than disgrace by surrender. We were horrified that they would do such a thing, but they did and in droves.

Today, these suicide cliffs are the sites of many granite monuments in a beautifully landscaped area. Our guide read the Japanese inscriptions on several of the monuments. They were erected by the Japanese people in memory of the many different detachments that had served and died in the defense of Okinawa. Fresh bunches of flowers were mounded up on the monuments, gifts of honor and respect from the many Japanese tourists who throng the island today. We saw no American monuments on the island.

We returned from our odyssey at dusk to the city of Naha and our modern hotel. I dreamed wildly all night. Over 200,000 people lost their lives in this obscure little facet of World War II. That's lots of ghosts for a little island with less land area than Shackelford County and lots of lives to lose in just three months of fighting. Today I wondered what for? It sure seemed important at the time—important enough for 200,000 people to die, but I guess that's timing again and we don't have much to do with that.

I've now fulfilled that vague, persuasive urge to return, and I know this time that I'll never see Okinawa Island again. That's okay. It's just another out of the way place where for a brief moment of history something happened, and by chance, I happened to be there when it did. Again, timing was involved. Not much is going on there now. It probably won't ever again.

In retrospect, I would have to say that the three months I spent as a youth participating in that deadly contest were the most vivid three months of my life. I guess maybe that is why I wanted to return once more to the old forgotten battlefields—to remember how it was then when youthful blood ran hot in a hell of a fight, and victory was sweet, for in those long ago days we believed in winning wars.

[Editor's note: On his return trip to Okinawa, Bob found the following paper during a foray into the caves:

OLD JAPANESE NAVY UNDERGROUND HEADQUARTERS

This is a spot where approximately 4,000 officers and enlisted men of the Japanese Navy, led by Rr. Adm. Minoru Ota committed suicide, on June 13th of 1945. This mass suicide was committed in an underground cave to live up to faithfully the firm belief that the Japanese fighting man would prefer death to dishonor by capture. In those days, Okinawa was witnessing, as the last battlefield of the World War II, one of the most fierce battles fought in the war.

In more than 80 days of savage struggle against overwhelming U.S. forces, the Japanese detachment had suffered severe losses. Still worse, it had lost, through transfer, a company of 2,500 men strong to the command of the Japanese Army. Thus, some 4,000 fighting men, minus sufficient arms to defend themselves, sheltered themselves in a cave and desperately fought to the finish, some using handmade spears.

Commanding General Ushijima of the Japanese 32nd Army, who had retreated to Mabuni, ordered the detachment to evacuate their present position and withdraw their forces to the southern part of Shimajiri. However, on the 5th of June, the General received a message from Rr. Adm. Ota's station, 'Detachment under attack … cannot retreat … will fight to the last.' General Ushijima again issued for an immediate evacuation, following it with a personal letter sincerely urging Admiral Ota to withdraw his troops to the southern part of Shimajiri. Admiral Ota, however, remained firm in his determination to fight to the finish. General Ushijima had no other alternative but to let the situation ride.

On the evening of June 6th, Admiral Ota dispatched a message to General Ushijima stating 'situation critical … request permission to sign off …' The message also contained his death poem, which reads, 'Even if my body perishes in Okinawa, the noble Japanese spirit within my soul shall defend Japan forever.' With this report of June 6th on the development of the battle, Admiral Ota also sent to the Vice-Minister of the Navy, a lengthy telegram commending the self-sacrifice and co-operation displayed by the prefectural people during the military operations.

In the message, he gave a detailed account of how Okinawan prefectural people, both young and old, women as well as men, devoted themselves whole-heartedly in aiding the military operations. His message ended with this statement: 'thus, the prefectural people fought the battle … request special consideration for the future posterity of the Okinawan people.' This last telegram dispatched from the cave amply shows his deep concern over the future of the Okinawan people.

On the night of June 11th, realizing that the battle was nearing its decisive stage, he sent this final message, 'Headquarters under heavy enemy tank attack … those at our position will all die in honor … thank you for kindness in the past … wish you a victory.'

At 1 A.M. on June 13th, Admiral Ota and more than 4,000 of his officers and enlisted men died an honorable death inside the cave. The cave still retains traces of what had been the last Japanese fort, constructed with hoes and picks. On the wall of the Commanding Officer's room you can see a poem written by Admiral Ota just prior to his death. His death poem reads, 'How could we rejoice over our birth but to die an honorable death under the Emperor's flag.' We earnestly urge you to kindly express your sympathy for those Japanese comrades who died heroically for their homeland, and also to pray for a just and lasting peace for a world that will see no such further tragedy."]

Mounted on horseback I am ready for a busy day of cattle working on the ranch.

ACKNOWLEDGMENTS

This book is the response to years of urging by my wife, Nancy, and my three children to write of my experiences in World War II. My thanks to veteran editor Fran Vick, who encouraged me in this endeavor and worked diligently with me to get it organized and birthed. Copy editor/writer Karen Smith carefully edited the book and wrote the book jacket copy. Charles Shaw added the striking cover illustrations, map, and tank diagram, while Isabel Lasater Hernandez contributed a beautiful, dramatic design for the project. Raymond Smith provided exceptional service in researching and organizing photographs from various Washington, D.C., archives. Bright Sky Press, thank you for believing in this book and seeing it through to publication.

Three museums have lent their support, advice and encouragement:

John Ferguson at the 12th Armored Division Museum in Abilene, Texas; the Admiral Nimitz State Historic Site and National Museum of the Pacific War in Fredericksburg, Texas; and The National D-Day Museum in New Orleans, Louisiana.

To all, I give thanks.

Bob Green

BIBLIOGRAPHY

Appleman, Roy. The War in the Pacific—Okinawa: The Last Battle. Washington, D.C.: Historical Division, Department of the Army, 1948.

Astor, Gerald. Operation Iceberg. New York: Dell Publishing Co., 1996.

Bolote, James & William Bolote. Typhoon of Steel: the Battle for Okinawa. New York: Harper & Row, 1970.

Davidson, Orlando. The Deadeyes—The Story of the 96th Infantry Division. Washington, D.C.: Infantry Journal Press. 1947.

Daws, Gavan. Prisoner of the Japanese. New York: Morrow & Co., 1994.

Feifer, George. The Battle of Okinawa: The Blood and the Bomb. Guilford, Connecticut: Lyons Press, 1992.

Feifer, George. Tennozan. New York: Ticknor & Fields, 1992.

Foster, Simon. Okinawa: Final Assault on the Empire. Westport, Connecticut: Arms & Armor Press, 1994.

Frank, Elsevier. Okinawa: The Great Island Battle. New York: Dutton, 1978.

Frank, Benis. Okinawa: Touchstone to Victory. New York: Ballentine, 1970.

Fussell, Paul. Thank God for the Atom Bomb. New York: Summit Books, 1988.

Gow, Ian. Okinawa 1945: Gateway to Japan. New York: Doubleday & Co., 1985.

Hallas, James H. Killing Ground on Okinawa: The Battle for Sugar Loaf Hill. Westport, Connecticut: Praeger, 1996.

Harrier, Maison and Susie. Soldier of the Sun: Rise & Fall of the Imperial Japanese Army. New York: Random House, 1991.

Leckie, Robert. Okinawa: The Last Battle of WW II. New York: Viking, 1995.

Philips, Craig. Last Stands. London: Grange Books, 1994.

Sledge, E. B. With the Old Breed at Peleliu & Okinawa. Novato, CA: Presidio Press, 1980.

Spiller, Robert J. "My Guns: A Memoir of the Second World War." American Heritage. Dec. 1991, Vol. 42, No. 8, 45.

Spurr, Russell. A Glorious Way to Die. New York: Bantam Books, 1983.

Tanaka, Yuki. <u>Hidden Horror: Japanese War Crimes in WW II.</u> Boulder: Westview Press, 1996.

Kolb, Richard K., Ed. <u>Faces of Victory: The Fall of the Rising Sun.</u> Kansas City, Missouri: Addax Publishing, 1995.

Werstein, Irving. <u>Okinawa: The Last Ordeal.</u> New York: Thomas Crowell, Co., 1968.

Yahara, Colonel Hiromichi. <u>The Battle of Okinawa.</u> New York: John Wiley & Sons, Inc., 1995.